A MULTIMEDIA APPROACH TO CHILDREN'S LITERATURE

A MULTIMEDIA APPROACH TO CHILDREN'S LITERATURE

A Selective List of Films (and Videocassettes), Filmstrips, and Recordings Based on Children's Books

THIRD EDITION

Edited by
Mary Alice Hunt

With a Foreword by
Ellin Greene

Chicago
AMERICAN LIBRARY ASSOCIATION
1983

Composed by Superior Type in Times Roman
on an Alphatype CRS typesetting system

Printed on 50-pound Glatfelter,
a pH-neutral stock, and
bound in 10-point Carolina cover stock
by The University of Chicago
Printing Department

Library of Congress Cataloging in Publication Data
Main entry under title:

A Multimedia approach to children's literature.

Rev. ed. of: A multimedia approach to children's literature / compiled and edited by Ellin Greene. 2nd ed. 1977.
"Materials selected by a committee of the Association for Library Service to Children."
Includes indexes.
1. Children's literature—Bibliography—Catalogs. 2. Children's literature—Study and teaching—Audio-visual aids—Catalogs. 3. Teaching—Aids and devices—Catalogs. 4. Libraries, Children's—Activity programs—Audio-visual aids—Catalogs. I. Hunt, Mary Alice. II. Greene, Ellin, 1927- . A multimedia approach to children's literature. III. Association for Library Service to Children.
Z1037.M94 1983 [PN1009.A1] 011'.37 83-15517
ISBN 0-8389-3289-4

Printed in the United States of America.

CONTENTS

FOREWORD
It's a Multimedia World
Ellin Greene

From the mid-eighteenth century, when John Newbery began publishing attractive books for children, through the mid-twentieth century, children's enjoyment of literature has been closely associated with print materials. Today, nonprint materials offer another approach to sharing literature with children. The purpose of A MULTIMEDIA APPROACH TO CHILDREN'S LITERATURE is to provide easy access to quality media adaptations—films, filmstrips, and recordings—based on children's books.

Audiovisual presentations offer variety and a change of pace. Research studies indicate that children have various styles of learning and respond differently to the same material presented in different modes, for example, to a story presented through storytelling, film, or creative drama. The child who is not interested in books or who is experiencing difficulty in mastering reading skills often responds with enthusiasm to the audiovisual presentation of a book. A television or motion picture adaptation of a book may result in hundreds of children going to the library to demand that book, but the underlying assumption that the translation of print into nonprint medium will *automatically* lead the child back to print has not been subject to research. Nonprint versions that catch a child's fancy may (1) lead the potential reader to the original work, (2) entice the reluctant reader to the book, or (3) give the nonreader a literary experience.

The audiovisual version, like the printed book, should be able to stand on its own artistically. This is especially important if we recognize that for some children the audiovisual presentation may be their only experience of the literary work. The best audiovisual versions expand the child's experience of the book and in addition offer a unique visual or aural experience. For example, the film version of *Time of Wonder* intensifies the poetic mood of Robert McCloskey's story. Film producer Morton Schindel of Weston Woods Studios comments:

> When transferred to the screen with due respect for the artistry of the original, a motion picture can give life to a book. Animation can release the motion that the artist had to freeze onto the page. Music and sensitive storytelling—direct auditory stimuli—can recreate actions and feelings that the writer had to communicate by words in print.
>
> [of filmstrips]
> Projecting the pictures onto a large screen enables a large number of children to simultaneously "get into" the book, to become involved in the story as it is being told by a teacher or librarian.
>
> None of these media duplicates the child's private pleasure in holding his own book, yet they can also transmit with integrity and fidelity what the author and illustrator have to say. The medium you choose—reading a book, showing a film or filmstrip, having children listen to records or tape, or combining the various media—should depend on the number of children you are trying to reach at any one time, the surroundings they will be in, and the talent, materials, and equipment available to you . . . Through electronic and mechanical means, given materials artfully prepared, you have at your disposal many ways to share with children more of the thoughts and feeling that you, yourself, have discovered between the covers of good books.*

One of the best ways of introducing literature to children is through storytelling and reading aloud. There are times, however, when a live storyteller is not available. Children can discover the pleasure of the spoken word by listening to fine recordings of favorite books and stories. Individual children, or two or three together, enjoy this kind of activity, but they tend to grow restless when listening to a recording in a large group situation. Recordings can be used successfully in a group situation to introduce an author reading aloud short selections from his or her own works. For children with special needs, the blind or partially sighted, for example, records have especial appeal.

A multimedia program combines two or more art forms—storytelling, film, music, dance—into a creative whole. The parts should complement each other, but each segment should be strong enough to stand on its own. This type of program offers the child an exceptionally rich sensory experience, but the adult planner should not delude him- or herself that it will take less planning than the traditional story hour. There is as much, or even more, planning involved to make this type of program a success. Preparation of a multimedia program involves careful selection of materials. The most effective programs usually are those that center around a theme,

---

*Morton Schindel, "The Picture Book Projected," *School Library Journal* 93:836–37 (February 15, 1968).

subject, or person. This bibliography and other selection aids listed in the Resources section will help you locate suitable materials.

In planning a multimedia program, ask yourself: "What do I wish to accomplish in the time available? What is the mood I wish to create?" To a great extent, your choice of materials and their placement in the program will determine the result. Like a piece of music, the multimedia program should have a form. There should be a relation between the parts and each part should lead to the next. Rhythm and balance are essential. If the first part of the program demands intense listening or viewing, the second part should offer a release from tension.

Over the years students and colleagues have shared their creative approaches to multimedia programming with me. Here are a baker's dozen to start you planning your own:

1. During the first week of April have a birthday story hour in honor of Hans Christian Andersen. Decorate the area or children's room with posters of Denmark. (These are occasionally available free from airline and travel agencies.) Display picture book editions of Andersen's stories. Show the children pictures of Andersen's birthplace and the town of Odense. Talk about his childhood and show reproductions of his paper cut work. Tell an Andersen fairy tale. Then show a film version of another of his tales, for example, "The Steadfast Tin Soldier" or "The Ugly Duckling." Tell the children that Andersen's birthday, April 2, was chosen as International Children's Book Day.
2. Start an author-book discussion group. Discuss the books of one author each week. Have an "Author of the Week" display. Write to the author's publisher(s) for promotional materials. Show a film or filmstrip about the author or use interview tapes (*see* the Authors and Illustrators section). Discuss the author's books, and if a film or filmstrip version of one of his or her books is available, show it after the discussion. Children also enjoy hearing an author read from his or her own work, such as E. B. White reading *Charlotte's Web* or Langston Hughes reading from *The Dream Keeper and Other Poems*.

   In one library in North Carolina, this program was conducted over an eight-week period. The eighth week's discussion focused on the qualities that make a book last and which of the books discussed in the preceding seven weeks the children thought would last.
3. Celebrate Midsummer. Open the program with incidental music from Mendelssohn's *A Midsummer Night's Dream*. Talk about Midsummer beliefs and customs. Tell a story from *Midsummer Magic*.

Afterwards, if appropriate, serve Midsummer Cake from the recipe in that book.

4. Present a Laura Ingalls Wilder program. Display the "Little House" books. Show pictures of the Wilder Museum and former Wilder house, Almanzo's boyhood home, and the doll collection of the Ingalls family (available from the Laura Ingalls Wilder Home/Museum). Read excerpts from Laura's diary, *On the Way Home*, or letters from *West from Home*. If the group is not too large, play an excerpt from the Julie Harris record. Tell the drawing story from *On the Banks of Plum Creek*. Serve gingerbread made from the recipe in *The Little House Cook Book*. Distribute bookmarks listing Wilder's books and her gingerbread recipe.
5. Show the filmstrip version of a wordless picture book, such as *Changes, Changes* or *The Silver Pony*. Encourage the children to write their own stories to go with the pictures.
6. Read aloud a picture book based on a song, for example, *The Foolish Frog* or *The Cool Ride in the Sky*. Show the audiovisual version and invite the children to sing along.
7. Tell a folktale, such as "Anansi the Spider," or "The Fisherman and His Wife" to a group of older children; then show the film version of the same tale. Lead the children in a discussion of the differences in the two art forms.
8. Combine body movement, music, and poetry. Nancy Larrick's article, "Poetry in the Story Hour" (*see* Resources) will suggest ideas to you.
9. Show the film "Why the Sun and Moon Live in the Sky." Have the children make masks and act out the story.
10. Plan an ethnic or regional program, featuring stories, music, and dances of a particular people or region. Serve appropriate ethnic or regional foods.
11. Design a unit on collage. Show the Weston Woods film about Ezra Jack Keats. Have several books by Keats on hand for the children to look at. Demonstrate how to make a collage, then let the children make their own.
12. Plan a multimedia program around a spring theme. A school media specialist I know read aloud *When the Root Children Wake Up* to a kindergarten class while showing the illustrations in the book by means of the opaque projector. She then showed an 8mm film of tree buds bursting and flowers opening, accompanied by a recording of "The Waltz of the Flowers" from Tchaikovsky's *Nutcracker Suite*. These young children were so entranced they went up to the screen to touch the flowers and spontaneously began dancing to the music. This same librarian planned a unit for older children to show

how an illustrator uses real scenes as inspiration for his artwork. Using three screens she projected the filmstrip version of Robert McCloskey's *Make Way for Ducklings* on the center screen and slides of scenes from Boston on the two side screens. The closing segment of the program featured McCloskey on film talking about his work.

13. Introduce a program on tall tales with Leadbelly singing "John Henry." Make brief mention of several variations of the John Henry legend, including *A Man Ain't Nothing But a Man*. Lead into a discussion of what constitutes a tall tale. End with the showing of the film, *The Legend of John Henry*.

Creative approaches like the ones described encourage children to participate in literature, and to read!

PREFACE

Purpose and Procedures

A MULTIMEDIA APPROACH TO CHILDREN'S LITERATURE: A SELECTIVE LIST OF FILMS (AND VIDEOCASSETTES), FILMSTRIPS, AND RECORDINGS BASED ON CHILDREN'S BOOKS is designed as a buying guide to a quality collection of book-related nonprint materials for use with children from preschool to grade 6. Its purpose is to assist libraries, teachers and others who wish to introduce a book or story in nonprint form to locate appropriate material quickly. Suggestions for using nonprint materials in programming may be found in Ellin Greene's Foreword and in the related readings section, Resources.

A committee of the Association for Library Service to Children was appointed to select and revise materials from the second edition and add new materials covering the period from 1977 to January 1983. Ellin Greene, one of the editors of the first and second editions, served as consultant to this committee.

Audience

This list was compiled for use by librarians, teachers, media specialists, paraprofessionals, recreational leaders, and other adults working with children, teachers of children's literature and storytelling, and producers of nonprint materials.

Scope

Within are listed 568 books, 153 16mm films (and when available, videocassettes), 365 filmstrips (sound and silent), and 348 recordings (33 rpm disc and cassette), with brief annotations and buying information. Nearly all titles were available at the cutoff date, January 31, 1983. Some out-of-print books were included in this list to accompany recently produced nonprint materials.

The list includes picture books, traditional and folk literature, literary fairy tales, fiction, the dramatic arts, poetry and song, as well as materials concerned with the background of specific books and with the people who write and illustrate books for children. The latter material, found in Authors and Illustrators (p. 131), is not indexed but will prove very useful for the user who wishes to expand his knowledge of a particular work.

Although in most instances the material listed originated as a book, in some cases the nonprint material has been the original creation and later a book has been made from it. These include: *And Now Miguel, Arrow to the Sun, The Foolish Frog*, and *Free to Be . . . You and Me*.

Books in this list are primarily hardbound editions, but paperbacks have, at times, been included. It is suggested that libraries which do extensive programming avail themselves of multiple copies in paperback editions.

All titles are in English. Spanish editions of the nonprint materials are indicated whenever available in recognition of the increased need for this type of material.

Sets have been included when the material is available only as a set and when the individual items within the set meet the stated criteria. Total price of the set also was a consideration.

Arrangement

The list is arranged alphabetically by book title. Films, filmstrips, and recordings based on the book immediately follow each book title. Videocassettes, when available, are included under the film entry. A directory of distributors and a subject index follow. In actual practice, the program planner will rely on books with a strong story line, but use those emphasizing mood and participation for variety. The uses of these types of picture books are amplified in the film *The Pleasure Is Mutual* and in the handbook *How to Conduct Effective Picture Book Programs.*

Entry

Book titles are numbered consecutively from 1 to 568.

Any information not given in an entry—date of publication, producer's numbers, etc.—was unobtainable either from the material itself or from the catalogs and other reference sources.

The exact playing time of each side of a recording is given when this information was readily available from the producer.

All filmstrips are without captions unless otherwise noted in the entry.

Book prices are given for both trade editions and reinforced library editions whenever both could be located. Prices for nonprint materials are as listed by producers and distributors at the time of the preparation of the entry. Prices quickly change, inevitably upward.

When available, producers' serial numbers are given for nonprint materials. A word of caution is necessary: since producers frequently change their serial numbers, it is suggested that title be included when ordering nonprint materials.

Approach

Selection is based on the knowledge and experience of committee members. Books upon which the nonprint materials are based vary in literary quality from acceptable to excellent, but all have brought genuine pleasure to children.

Whenever possible, the committee has matched versions of translations of print and recorded materials. For example, when the Keigwin translation of an Andersen tale has been recorded, the Keigwin edition of the book is listed. When the recorded version was not available in print, an appropriate substitute has been listed.

Because picture books lend themselves to program use and have special appeal to children with reading problems, a single title has been listed whenever possible. When the story is available only in a collection, the selector has chosen a suitable book edition which she felt would be readily available in school and public libraries throughout the country, and the individual stories on the nonprint media have been singled out in the book annotation.

Although teaching guides have been noted in the annotations, the committee hopes such material will be used with discretion. The primary satisfaction of imaginative literature is personal discovery, and this should not be diminished (or even destroyed) by follow-up questions that attempt to dissect the story or prompt a regimented response.

Criteria

The general criteria for evaluating children's books—respect for children's intelligence and imagination; storytelling quality (plot, characterization, theme, and style); and content of interest to children—also apply to nonprint materials, with special provision made for the nature of the medium. Each medium is a unique art form. The problem in film, for example, is to translate the writer's story into moving images with sound while keeping the author's style and plot. Gene Deitch's article "Filming 'Zlateh the Goat' " describes some of the problems and unexpected events that may occur in the process. In transferring a story from one medium to another, departures from the original may be necessary, but the adaptation should be sympathetic to the spirit of the original work upon which it is based and preserve its artistic and dramatic qualities. In addition to integrity of adaptation, the other criteria used in evaluating nonprint materials for this list were appropriateness of medium to the message, appropriateness of length of time or number of frames for the intended audience, and technical excellence. The latter includes picture quality (clarity, framing, color); sound quality (audibility, voice, music, effects); and artistic balance and design.

From the second edition we have dropped nonprint titles no longer available, as well as marginal material that was included because fewer titles were available to choose from at that time.

When a title is available in more than one medium and we think that one medium is more effective, we have listed that medium only—for example, when both a film and a filmstrip are available and motion adds to the presentation we have listed the film only, or where a record made to accompany the filmstrip does not stand on its own we have listed the sound filmstrip only.

The terms used in connection with audiovisual materials will be familiar to most users of this list. The novice will find the articles under Resources (p. xix) helpful. Anyone who is not familiar with the iconographic techniques, in which still pictures in a book are made to move through subtle movement of the camera, is referred to Morton Schindel's article, "The Picture Book Projected." Animation—a very different technique in which an illusion of movement is given by filming in sequence hundreds of static drawings or objects, such as puppets—is amplified in Blair Lent's article "How the Sun and the Moon Got into a Film."

Recommendation to Producers

In general, more and better films are available and more use is made of films since publication of the first and second editions of A MULTIMEDIA APPROACH TO CHILDREN'S LITERATURE. Films were rejected for any of the following reasons: poor technical production, background music that intrudes, slight story, coyness, sentimentality.

The quality of filmstrips has improved over the years. In general, the most successful filmstrips are those made from quality picture books using art work from the book itself. An additional problem with filmstrips is that the art work sometimes suffers in the enlargement process. Filmstrips with vocabulary drill or discussion questions on frames interspersed with the story have not been included.

In our culture both children and adults are continually bombarded visually. We need to rediscover the pleasure of the spoken word. Children enjoy listening to fine recordings of favorite books and stories. Also, recordings can be used to introduce an author reading his or her own work. For children with special needs, the blind or partially sighted, for instance, recordings have exceptional value. We have not included recordings in which the story is interrupted at intervals by a narrator who poses a question or explains a concept. We understand the rationale behind this format—that is, the attempt to personalize the reading or listening experience, but the recorded voice is not a substitute for a responsive human being. We feel that, at best, this format interrupts the pleasure of hearing a story as a whole, and at its worst, it is condescending.

In the past ten years, producers have recognized the problems involved in shelving multimedia and are designing packaging to facilitate use by children as well as by librarians and teachers. Hang-up bags and freestanding hang-up storage racks are convenient for libraries and popular with children.

The neglected age range in media for children seems to be the toddler and preschool age (2–5-year-olds). There is a great need for short films and filmstrips (3–6 minutes) based on children's books and nursery rhymes that are of high quality, action-packed and colorful. Children's librarians in public libraries have particularly sought this type of media for programming for this age group.

Acknowledgments

The editor gratefully acknowledges the hard-working Committee members who selected materials for this manual: Lynne Pickens, Altanta, Georgia, chairperson; Alice P. Bartz, Jenkintown, Pennsylvania; Wendy Caldiero, Bronx, New York; Bernice Cullinan, Sands Point, New York; Elizabeth Long, New York, New York; and Teresa Poston, Gallup, New Mexico. We also wish to thank Ellin Greene, Chicago, Illinois, who served as our consultant and contributed the Foreword for this third edition of MULTIMEDIA APPROACH TO CHILDREN'S LITERATURE.

We are grateful for the assistance of Ann Weeks, Executive Director, Association for Library Service to Children, and we would also like to thank Helen Cline and the staff of Publishing Services at the American Library Association for their help in preparing this publication.

Finally, the editor wishes to thank Hunter L. Barnett and Mary L. Melton, word processing systems operators at Florida State University, Tallahassee, Florida, for their patience and assistance in preparing the final manuscript.

MARY ALICE HUNT
School of Library and Information Studies
Florida State University
Tallahassee, Florida

Materials Selected by a Committee of the
Association for Library Service to Children

Alice Bartz
Wendy Caldiero
Bernice Cullinan
Elizabeth Long
Teresa Poston
Lynne Pickens, Chairperson

RESOURCES

Related Readings

Bauer, Caroline Feller. *Handbook for Storytellers.* Chicago: American Library Association, 1977. *See* pp. 181-279, "Multimedia Storytelling."

Ideas on presenting stories using a variety of media from films and filmstrips to puppets for production of a television show.

Cullinan, Bernice E. *Literature and the Child.* New York: Harcourt Brace Jovanovich, 1981. *See* pp. 459-76.

Suggestions for extending literature through use of audiovisual presentations and activities such as art, drama, and puppetry.

Deitch, Gene. "Filming 'Zlateh the Goat'." *Horn Book* 51:241-49 (June 1975).

A behind-the-scenes look at filming Isaac Bashevis Singer's story, and the close cooperation between Morton Schindel, Maurice Sendak, and the film director. Read this *after* viewing the film.

Gaffney, Maureen, ed. *Young Viewers.* Media Center for Children, Inc. (MCC), 3 West 29th Street, New York, NY 10001. Four issues a year.

Each issue focuses on a different theme. Issues of special interest to program planners include: Spring 1980, *Museum Programs*, Winter/Spring 1982, *Using Folktale Films*, and Summer 1982, *The Basics of Film Programming with a Special Emphasis on Museums.*

———— and Gerry Bond Laybourne. *What to Do When the Lights Go On: A Comprehensive Guide to 16mm Films and Related Activities for Children.* Phoenix, Ariz.: Oryx Press, 1981.

Many suggestions are given for activities to follow film programs, including crafts, creative dramatics, and games. Recommended films are annotated with a suggested age level.

Gitter, Lana L. "A Picture Window to the World." *Academic Therapy* 5:109-14 (Winter 1969).

The use of visual materials to help children with learning handicaps. Focuses on materials produced by Weston Woods Studios.

Heins, Ethel L. "Literature Bedeviled: A Searching Look at Filmstrips." *Horn Book* 50:306-13 (June 1974).

A provocative article which points out the difficulties of adapting a wholly verbal work into filmstrip format.

Huck, Charlotte S. "Extending Literature through Creative Activities" and "The Literature Program." In *Children's Literature in the Elementary School*, pp. 640-756. New York: Holt, 1979.

Creative approaches for using books and audiovisual materials to enhance the curricula.

Lembo, Diana. "A Stepchild Comes of Age." *Library Journal* 92:3122-23 (September 15, 1967).

The filmstrip's strengths and weaknesses, together with information on sources of filmstrips and criteria for selection.

Lent, Blair. "How the Sun and the Moon Got into a Film." *Horn Book* 47:589-96 (December 1971).

The author describes in detail the experience of transferring his picture book onto film.

May, Jill P., ed. "The Audio-visual Arts and Children's Literature." *Children's Literature Association Quarterly* 7:2-33 (Fall 1982).

A collection of articles dealing with media, particularly film, and its relationship to children's literature.

Movshow, Rae S. "The Reluctant Reader." *Elementary English*, 52:340-41 (March 1975).

How one reading specialist uses films and filmstrips to "turn on" reluctant readers to reading and enjoying books.

Paulin, Mary Ann. *Creative Uses of Children's Literature*. Hamden, Conn.: Library Professional Publication for the Shoe String Press, 1982. 730p.

Plot elements from over 5,800 children's books and audiovisual media, highlighting how art, music, poetry, "acting out," and riddles, magic, jokes, and folk themes can enhance interest in literature.

Robotham, John S. and Lydia LaFleur. *Library Programs: How to Select, Plan and Produce Them*. Metuchen, N.J.: Scarecrow Press, 1981. *See* pp. 118-67, "Children's Programs."

Examples of successful programs using a variety of media are given, along with general guidelines for children's programs.

Schindel, Morton. "The Picture Book Projected." *School Library Journal* 93:836-37 (February 15, 1968).

The origin of the iconographic technique behind Picture Book Parade films.

Segel, Elizabeth. "But Is It Faithful to the Book? Children's Literature on Film." *The Advocate* 2:7-14 (Fall 1982).

A discussion of the importance of fidelity to the original source when evaluating film adaptations of children's books. "Zlateh the Goat" is used as an example of a successful adaptation.

Selection Aids

Booklist. American Library Association, 50 East Huron Street, Chicago, IL 60611.
Reviews of books, 16mm films, filmstrips, and recordings in each issue.

Emmens, Carol A., ed. *Children's Media Market Place.* New York: Neal-Schuman, 1982. 353p.
A directory of names, addresses, key personnel and product lines of publishers, producers, and distributors of children's book and audiovisual materials. Includes sections on review media, allied professional associations, awards for children's media, and children's television and radio.

Gaffney, Maureen, ed. *More Films Kids Like.* Chicago: American Library Association, 1977. 168p.
A catalog of short films for children with selections based on observed feelings and responses of children themselves. Includes comments on film length and program format and a section on activities relating to films. A continuation of *Films Kids Like* (American Library Association, 1973), it does not list any of the same films as the earlier book.

The Horn Book Magazine. The Horn Book Inc., Park Square Building, 31 St. James Avenue, Boston, MA 02116.
Reviews of books, 16mm films, filmstrips, and recordings in each issue.

Media and Methods. American Society of Educators, 1511 Walnut Street, Philadelphia, PA 19102.
Contains articles on the use of audiovisual materials in the classroom and regularly reviews 16mm films, filmstrips, recordings, and other forms of media.

New York Library Association. Youth Services Section. *Films for Children: A Selected List.* New York: The Association, 1977. 28p.
Highly selective, annotated list of short noninstructional films for use in library programs.

__________ *Recordings for Children.* New York: The Association, 1980. 28p.
Selective listing by subject. Musical and nonmusical records included and annotated.

Rufsvold, Margaret I. *Guides to Educational Media.* 4th ed. Chicago: American Library Association, 1977. 168p.
A guide to catalogs and lists, services of professional organizations, and special periodicals which systematically give information on availability of films, filmstrips, recordings, slides, transparencies, and programmed instruction materials.

School Library Journal. R. R. Bowker Co., 1180 Avenue of the Americas, New York, NY 10036.
Filmstrips, 16mm films, recordings, and videocassettes are reviewed in the "Audiovisual Review" section which has replaced *Previews* magazine.

Program Aids

Gene Deitch: Animating Picture Books. Weston Woods, 1980 (SF 458C) 64fr color 13min with cassette $30. WW (I-U)
The magic of how Deitch translates picture books into animated films that enhance and expand the particular mood and character of each book is the subject of this filmstrip.

Gene Deitch: Animating Strega Nona. Weston Woods, 1979 (SF 459C) 59fr color 13min with cassette $30. WW (P-A)

This trip takes the viewer behind the scenes in Gene Deitch's making of his animated motion-picture adaptation of Tomie de Paola's Caldecott Honor Book, *Strega Nona*. Deitch shows how he designs an entire village, creates a storyboard, interprets the characters, and selects the music and singing voices. The viewer learns how an animator brings a picture book to life.

Gene Deitch: The Picture Book Animated. Morton Schindel 16mm color 25min $325, $25. WW

A visit with Deitch in his home-studio in Prague leaves the viewer with an appreciation of the process involved in animating a picture book. Deitch discusses several of the books he has animated for Weston Woods films, including *Drummer Hoff, Patrick, Changes, Changes, The Three Robbers*, and *Where the Wild Things Are*. A fascinating film for students of children's literature and for older children who are interested in filmmaking.

The Lively Art of Picture Books. Morton Schindel 16mm color 57min $500, $25. WW

This film presents the work of thirty-six outstanding picture book artists and features three of them, Robert McCloskey, Barbara Cooney, and Maurice Sendak. Narrated by John Langstaff. Produced under the auspices of the Association for Library Service to Children of the American Library Association.

The Pleasure Is Mutual: How to Conduct Effective Picture Book Programs. Westchester (New York) Library System 16mm color 24min $325, WDS; $35. PFD

Using excerpts from actual programs conducted by librarians and volunteers in libraries, schools, and playgrounds, this film illustrates the principles of effective picture book programs. A handbook, *How to Conduct Effective Picture Book Programs*, by Joanna Foster is available for use in connection with the films from the Westchester Library System (WLS).

Prelude: Mini-Seminars on Using Books Creatively. Children's Book Council 7 sets, each containing 6 cassettes, approximately 30 minutes each. Print supplement with each set. Series 1-6 $67.50 each, series 7 $75. CBC

A series of taped sessions by authors, librarians, teachers, and other children's literature specialists that gives advice and suggestions relating to using books with children. Uneven in quality, but only available in sets.

Reaching Out: The Library and the Exceptional Child. Connecticut Films 16mm color 25min $35 rental. PFD

Describes the Cincinnati Public Library and Hamilton County's program for children who are physically handicapped, mentally retarded, or socially maladjusted. Excerpts from actual programs, including story hours and book discussions.

Rohrlick, Paula. *Exploring the Arts: Films and Video Programs for Young Viewers*. New York: R. R. Bowker, 1982. $29.95.

An annotated bibliography of over 500 films and videotapes on the visual, performing, and literary arts for young people, aged 2 to 15. Includes helpful lists of resources: awards, festivals, organizations, periodicals, books, and articles.

There's Something about a Story. Connecticut Films 16mm color 27min $325, WDS; $35 rental. PFD

Ten storytellers with different styles and varying degrees of experience talk about storytelling—the values, choice of material, techniques of learning and telling stories. The film shows the telling of three complete stories and parts of seven others to groups of children.

What's So Great about Books? Orlando (Florida) Public Library 16mm color 15min $195. ORL

A parent education film which encourages parents to instill in their children a love of books and reading through sharing stories with them from infancy through preadolescence.

Realia

Realia can be used effectively in displays to call attention to books, as appropriate decoration for the children's room/media center, or in work with exceptional children. Suggestions for creating book characters, wall hangings, mobiles, and other three-dimensional artwork can be found in *Children's Literature in the Elementary School*, by Charlotte S. Huck (Holt, 1979) and in *Handbook for Storytellers*, by Caroline F. Bauer (American Library Association, 1977).

Posters. "Poster A-Plenty" (*Top of the News*, June 1976, pp. 369–72) is an annotated list of "posters representing themes from children's literature or drawn by children's book illustrators," compiled by the Print and Poster Evaluation Committee of the Association for Library Service to Children, American Library Association. To the sources listed, we would add the Green Tiger Press, Box 868, La Jolla, CA 92038. The Green Tiger Press also sells card-size reproductions of the drawings and paintings of well-known illustrators of children's books.

Figurines. Beswick pottery models of more than thirty characters from the Beatrix Potter books are available in many department stores and gift shops.

Sebastian Studio, Inc., 13 Bassett Street, Marblehead, MA 01945, sells figurines of characters from the books of Dickens, Mark Twain, Washington Irving, and others.

Stuffed animals and dolls. F.A.O. Schwarz, 745 Fifth Avenue, New York, NY 10022, has Beatrix Potter animals as well as Curious George, Babar and Celeste, and Paddington stuffed animals. These stuffed animals are also available in many department stores and toy stores.

Cornhusk dolls, including Little Red Riding Hood, Old Mother Hubbard, Bo Peep and others are available from the Southern Highland Handicraft Guild, P.O. Box 9545, Asheville, NC 28815.

The Laura Ingalls Wilder Home/Museum, Rocky Ridge Farm, Mansfield, MO 65704, has a replica of Laura's doll, nut doll, and other art objects and pictures related to the "Little House" books.

Max and the "Wild Things" from *Where the Wild Things Are*, 21-inch stuffed dolls, can be ordered from Weston Woods, Weston, CT 06883.

Miscellany. Beatrix Potter Creations (jigsaw puzzles, tiles, notelets, calendars, etc.), Kate Greenaway, and Randolph Caldecott postcards are available from Frederick Warne and Company, Inc., 2 Park Avenue, New York, NY 10016.

Directions for construction of a Penny Theatre are available free from Penny Theatre, Department of Public Libraries, Montgomery County, MD 20850.

Several sets of paperdolls based on book characters such as Curious George and Flopsy, Mopsy and Cottontail are published by Dover Publications. These can be found in many book stores.

Christmas ornaments of the Beatrix Potter characters and Paddington Bear are available in gift shops.

Calendars featuring illustrations from children's books are available from several publishers. Examples are a *Winnie-the-Pooh* calendar (Dutton), a *Narnia* calendar (Macmillan) and a *Wind in the Willows* calendar (Holt). These can be found in most book stores and can also be ordered from the publishers. The 1984 Caldecott Calendar is available to ALA members for $5.95 ($6.95 for nonmembers) from the Order Department, ALA, 50 E. Huron Street, Chicago, IL 60611.

An extensive collection of realia based on the character of Paddington Bear can be found at the Paddington and Friends Shop, 22 Crawford Place, WI, London, England.

Children's museum shops and art museum shops are usually good sources for a variety of realia related to children's books.

For free and inexpensive materials available from publishers, an excellent source of information is the Calendar of the Children's Book Council, Inc., 67 Irving Place, New York, NY 10003.

For prices of all materials listed, write directly to sources given.

KEY TO ABBREVIATIONS

arr.	arranged, arranger
av	average
bd.	bound
b/w	black and white
comp.	compiled, compiler
dist.	distributed
ed.	edited, edition, editor
F	film
fr	frame, frames
FS	filmstrip
I	intermediate level; for use by and with chidren in grades 4–6
illus.	illustrations, illustrated
in	inches
introd.	introduced, introduction
lib.	library
LP	long-playing record
min	minute, minutes
mm	millimeters
N	preschool level
n.d.	no date
OP	out-of-print
P	primary level; for use with and by children in grades K-3
p.	pages
pap.	paperbound

prod.	produced
R	record
rel.	released
rev.	revised
rpm	revolutions per minute
s	sides
sel.	selected, selector
tr.	translated, translator
U	upper level; for children in grades 6 and up
unp.	unpaged
v.	volume, volumes
yr	year

SAMPLE ENTRIES

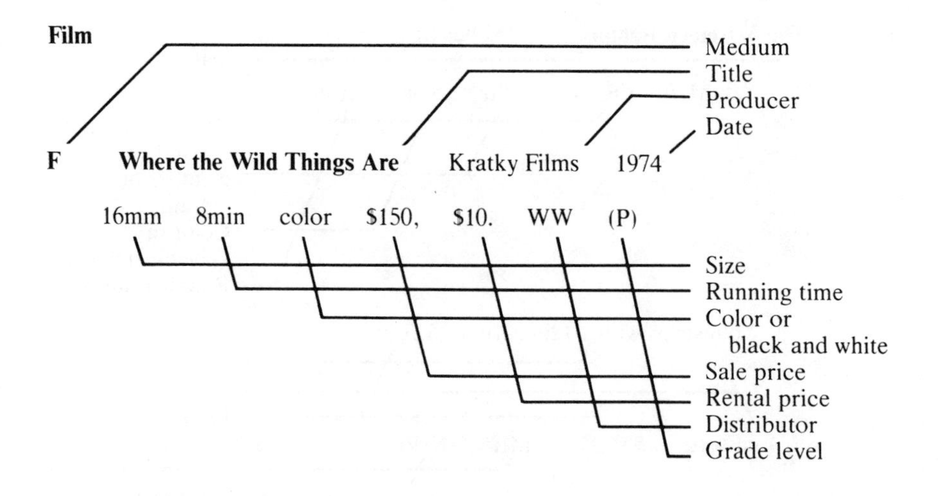

Filmstrip

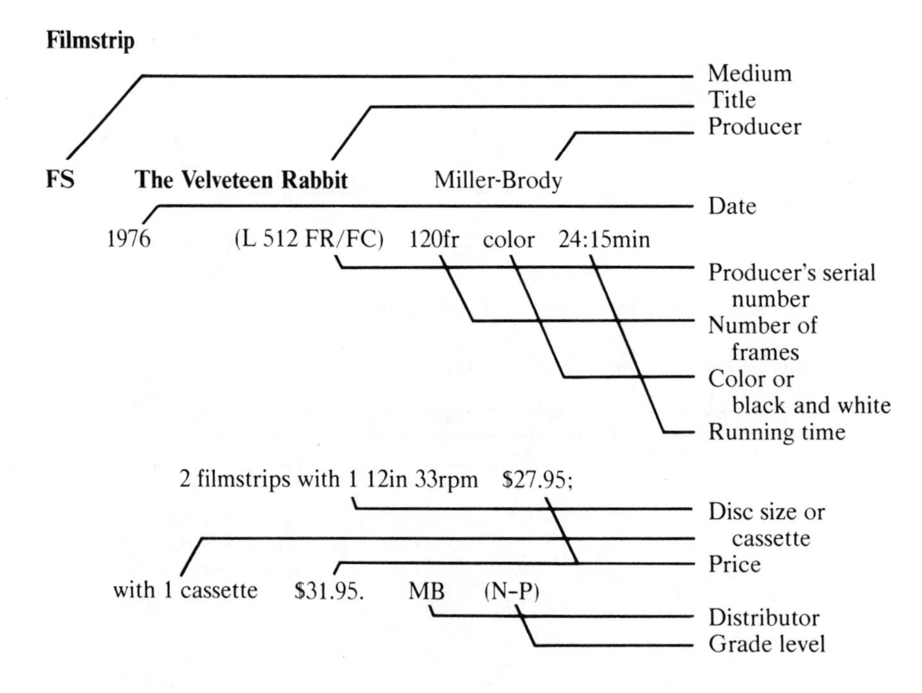
Medium
Title
Producer
FS
The Velveteen Rabbit
Miller-Brody
Date
1976
(L 512 FR/FC)
120fr
color
24:15min
Producer's serial number
Number of frames
Color or black and white
Running time
2 filmstrips with 1 12in 33rpm
$27.95;
Disc size or cassette
Price
with 1 cassette
$31.95.
MB
(N-P)
Distributor
Grade level

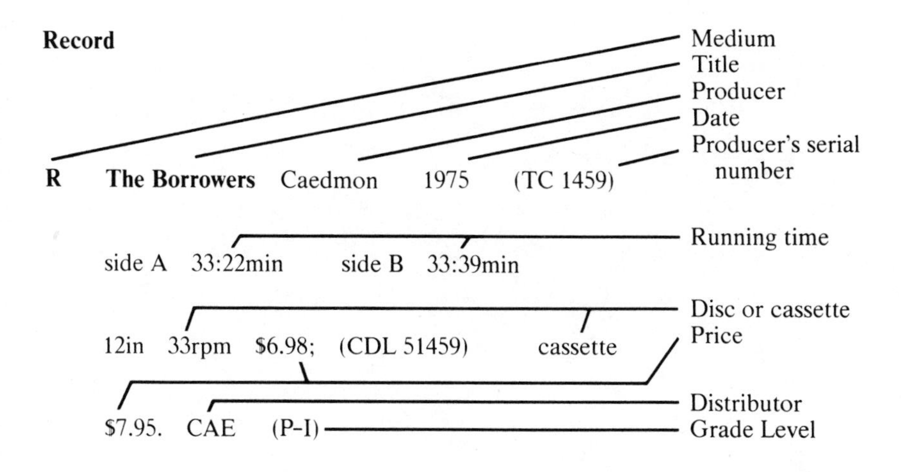
Record
Medium
Title
Producer
Date
Producer's serial number
R The Borrowers Caedmon 1975 (TC 1459)
Running time
side A 33:22min side B 33:39min
Disc or cassette
Price
12in 33rpm $6.98; (CDL 51459) cassette
Distributor
Grade Level
$7.95. CAE (P-I)

BOOKS, FILMS (AND VIDEOCASSETTES), FILMSTRIPS, AND RECORDINGS

1 **Across Five Aprils**, by Irene Hunt. Follett, 1964. $4.95; lib. ed. $4.98 (U)

The Civil War becomes a reality for a family in southern Illinois. All of the men leave with only the youngest, Jethro, to run the farm. A warm and moving story.

1R **Across Five Aprils**, Random House/Miller-Brody, 1973 (76921-X) record side 1: 20min, side 2: 17:36min 12in 33rpm $8.97; (76922-8) cassette $8.97. RH/M-B (U)

Dramatization of the book. Narrated by Peter Thomas, supported by a cast, appropriate music, and sound effects. The production brings out the horror of war.

2 **Adam of the Road**, by Elizabeth Janet Gray. Viking, 1942 (I)

In a story set in 1294, Adam must fend for himself when he is separated from his minstrel father. He travels from one English village to another meeting hardship and kindness along the way. The historical setting shows that loneliness, loyalty, independence, and friendship are always timely. 1943 Newbery Medal winner.

2R **Adam of the Road**, Live Oak Media (0-670-10438-8) record 12in $8.95; (0-670-10437-X) cassette 60:08min $8.95. LOM (I)

Dramatization which captures the exciting points of the story.

3 **The Adventures of Pinocchio**, tr. and adapted by Marianna Mayer; illus. by Gerald McDermott. Four Winds, 1981. $14.95 (I)

This edition of the story of the wooden puppet whose nose grows longer each time he tells a lie includes exceptional illustrations.

3FS **The Adventures of Pinocchio**, Educational Enrichment Materials, n.d. (51011) color 6 filmstrips 6 cassettes 1 paperback $129 (individual FS $24). EEM (P)

Adapted from the novel by C. Collodi; full dramatizations and exciting illustrations. Filmstrip titles: *Gepetto Makes a Puppet* (52047), *Pinocchio Leaves Home* (52048), *Pinocchio Meets the Blue-Haired Fairy* (52049), *The Village of Industrious Bees* (52050), *The Land of Boobies* (52051), and *Pinocchio & Gepetto Reunited* (52052).

4 **The Adventures of Robin Hood**, by Bernard Miles. illus. Rand, 1979. $8.95 (I)

The exploits of Robin Hood and his

merry men, as they strive to right the wrongs and inequities of the medieval class system, continue to appeal to young people.

4FS **The Adventures of Robin Hood**, Educational Enrichment Materials, n.d. color 4 filmstrips with cassettes 8 paperbacks 8 spirit masters $90. EEM (I)

This famous tale is recreated visually and aurally in this abridged version based on several anonymous renditions.

5 **The Adventures of Tom Sawyer**, by Samuel L. Clemens. Dodd, 1979, (Great Illus. Classics) $8.95; Bantam pap. $1.50 (I-U)

Escapades of a nineteenth-century boy in a midwestern town.

5F **The Adventures of Tom Sawyer**, David Selznick, 1938, 16mm color 77min $27.50 (rental only). BFI (I-U)

Tommy Kelley, May Robson, Victor Jory, Walter Brennan, and Ann Gillis star. Directed by Norman Taurog. Screenplay by John V. Weaver. Music by Lew Forbes. Photography by James Wong Howe.

5FS **The Adventures of Tom Sawyer**, Educational Enrichment Materials, n.d. color 8 filmstrips 8 cassettes 1 paperback $172 (individual FS $24). EEM (I-U)

Eight of Tom's adventures greatly enhanced by dramatic narration, music, sound effects, and good illustrations.

5R **Tom Sawyer**, Caedmon, 1966 (TC 1205) 2s 12in 33rpm $8.98; (CDL 51205) cassette $8.98. CAE (U)

Ed Begley reads "The Glorious Whitewasher" and other episodes from Mark Twain's classic.

6 **Aesop's Fables**. illus. Viking, 1981. $12 (P-I)

Selections from the various fables. Includes such titles as "The Fox and the Grapes," "The Hare and the Tortoise," and "The Cock and the Jewel."

6FS **An Aesop Anthology**, Educational Enrichment Materials, 1978, color 6 filmstrips 6 cassettes $119 (individual FS $22). EEM (P-I)

Illustrations are upbeat, bright, and visually pleasing presentations of old favorites as well as of some not as well known.

#52109: The Country Mouse and The City Mouse; The Frog and the Ox; The Dog and His Shadow
#52110: The Grasshopper and the Ant; The Oak and the Reed; The Gardener and His Dog
#52085: The Lion and the Mouse; The Wind and the Sun; The Crow and the Pitcher
#52086: The Milkmaid and Her Pail; The Fox and the Grapes; Belling the Cat
#52087: The Hare and the Tortoise; The Two Frogs; The Fox and the Crow
#52088: The Boy Who Cried Wolf; The Lion and the Goat; The Fisherman and His Catch.

7 **Alexander and the Wind-up Mouse**, by Leo Lionni. Pantheon, 1969. unp. $6.99 (P)

Alexander wishes that he were a toy mouse rather than a real one, but he changes his mind when he sees that toys, though once loved, can be discarded for new ones.

7FS **Alexander and the Wind-up Mouse**, prod. by Westport Communications Group, rel. by Random House, 1978 (394-05306-0) 36fr color 7min with 7in 33-1/3rpm $21; (394-05305-2) with cassette $21. RH/M-B (P)

Filmstrip utilizes Lionni's bold collages from the book. Guide.

7R **Frederick and Ten Other Stories of Mice, Snails, Fish and Other**

Beings. Caedmon (TC 1674) 12in LP $8.98; (CP 1674) cassette $8.98. CAE (P)

The ten stories are read by Carol Channing, whose voice adapts well to Lionni's creatures. Includes *Frederick, Fish Is Fish, In the Rabbitgarden, Tico and the Golden Wings, Alexander and the Wind-up Mouse, The Biggest House in the World, The Alphabet Tree, The Greentail Mouse, Swimmy, Pezzettino, Theodore and the Talking Mushroom.*

7R **Alexander and the Wind-up Mouse**, by Leo Lionni. Random House/ Miller-Brody (394-05307-9) read-along cassette with hardcover book $15; (394-05308-7) read-along cassette with paperback book $10.98. RH/M-B (P)

A read-along version of the story.

8 **Alfred's Alphabet Walk**, by Virginia Chess. illus. Greenwillow, 1979. $7.95; lib. ed. $7.63 (N-P)

When given a book and instructed to stay in the yard and learn the alphabet, Alfred takes off on an adventurous journey and learns the alphabet the best way, through experience.

8FS **Alfred's Alphabet Walk**, Listening Library, n.d. (ATFS178) color 1 filmstrip 1 cassette $21. LL (N-P)

Victoria Chess tells what happens when Alfred's mother tells him to stay in the front yard and learn the alphabet. His encounters (outside the yard) with zany animals and other adventures come across well in a filmstrip presentation.

9 **Alice's Adventures in Wonderland** with **Through the Looking Glass**, by Lewis Carroll; illus. by John Tenniel. St. Martin's, 1977. $7.95 (I-U)

A much-quoted classic with pictures by its best-known illustrator.

9FS **Alice's Adventures in Wonderland**, Educational Enrichment Materials, n.d. color 6 filmstrips 6 cassettes or records 1 guide 1 paperback $129 (individual FS with sound $24). EEM (P-I)

Brightly colored illustrations, dramatic narration with precise enunciation by each character. Each filmstrip can be used separately.

9R **Alice in Wonderland**, Caedmon, 1966 (TC 1097) 2s 12in 33rpm $8.98; (CP 51097) cassette $8.98. CAE (I)

Well-chosen excerpts from the Lewis Carroll story are interpreted by a group of talented English actors, including Stanley Holloway and Joan Greenwood. Companion record to *Through the Looking Glass*, Caedmon, TC 1098.

9R **Through the Looking Glass**, Caedmon, 1966 (TC 1098) 2s 12in 33rpm $4.98; (CDL 51098) cassette $8.98. CAE (I)

Joan Greenwood as Alice, Stanley Holloway as the narrator and a cast of eight. Companion record to *Alice in Wonderland*. Caedmon, TC 1097.

10 **All in the Morning Early**, by Sorche Nic Leodhas; illus. by Evaline Ness. Holt, 1963. unp. lib. ed. $3.27 net; pap. $1.65 (P-I). OP

Traditional Scottish counting rhyme about a miller on his way to the mill, and the many amiable companions he meets. Repetitive verse invites participation.

10F **All in the Morning Early**, BFA Educational Media, 1969, 16mm color 10min $190, $27. BFA (P-I)

A Stephen Bosustow Production, with artwork adapted from the book. Narration by male voice with pleasant Scottish accent is enhanced by a background of bagpipe music.

11 **Alligators All Around: An Alphabet**, by Maurice Sendak. Harper, 1962. unp. lib. ed. $7.89 (P)

Rhymed nonsense tale with amusing illustrations.

11FS **Alligators All Around**, Weston Woods, 1976 (FS 222) 30fr color 4:20min $12; (SF222C) with cassette $18. WW (P)

Read by Maurice Sendak. Original music by H. D. Buch. Sound filmstrip adapted by C. B. Wismar; artwork adapted by Stephanie Adam.

12 **Amahl and the Night Visitors**, by Gian-Carlo Menotti, adapted by Frances Frost; illus. by Roger Duvoisin. McGraw-Hill, 1952. 86p. lib. ed. $6.95 (I-U)

The story of the crippled shepherd boy who entertained the Wise Men on their way to Bethlehem. Originally written for television and later made into a book.

12R **Amahl and the Night Visitors**, RCA Victor, n.d. (LSC 2762) 2s 12in 33rpm $9.98. RCA (P-I)

Menotti's opera for children with the original cast of the 1963 NBC-TV production.

13 **The Amazing Bone**, by William Steig. Farrar, 1976. unp. $7.95 (P)

One beautiful spring day, a happy young pig named Pearl unexpectedly strikes up an acquaintance with a small magic bone which speaks in any language. They immediately like each other and the bone agrees to gome home with Pearl. But on the way home, the resourceful bone must deal with a band of highway robbers and a fox who wants to eat the young, plump, tender Pearl.

13FS **The Amazing Bone**, Random House/Miller-Brody, 1978 (394-76474-9) 111fr color 17min with cassette $21. RH/M-B (P)

Read by Tammy Grimes. The delightful illustrations of William Steig are taken directly from the book. Expressive background music adds to the suspense of the story.

13R **The Amazing Bone**, by William Steig. Random House/Miller-Brody (394-07625-7) read-along cassette with hardcover book $16.50. RH/M-B (P)

A pig named Pearl meets a small magic bone which later saves her from highway robbers.

14 **Amelia Bedelia**, by Peggy Parrish; illus. by Fritz Siebel. Harper, 1963. unp. $5.95; lib. ed. $6.89 net; Scholastic pap. $1.25 (P)

Amelia Bedelia is a maid whose talent for interpreting instructions literally results in comical situations, such as "dressing" the chicken in fine clothes.

14FS **Amelia Bedelia**, Educational Enrichment Materials, 1971 (71039) 54fr color 10min 4 filmstrips 4 cassettes or discs $80 (individual FS with sound $22). EEM (P)

Filmstrip titles: Amelia Bedelia (72152); Thank You, Amelia Bedelia (72151); Come Back, Amelia Bedelia (72153); Play Ball, Amelia Bedelia (72150). Taken directly from the series of popular children's books, the lively illustrations and narration of these filmstrips bring humourous entertainment.

15 **American Tall Tales**, by Adrien Stoutenburg; illus. by Richard M. Powers. Viking, 1966. 112p. lib. ed. $8.95 net; Penguin pap. $.95 (I-U)

An excellent collection of tales told with a regard for the oral tradition from which they stem.

15R **American Tall Tales Soundbook**, Caedmon, 1982 (SBC 110) 4 cassettes program booklet $29.95. ISBN 0-89845-044-7. CAE (I-U)

Ed Begley reads tales of John Henry, Johnny Appleseed and Paul Bunyan in a vigorous style.

16 **Anansi the Spider: Tales from an Ashanti Village**, by Peggy Appiah; illus. by Peggy Wilson. Pantheon,

1966. 152p. lib. ed. $5.99 net (I-U)

This handsome edition of thirteen well-told tales centering about Anansi includes "Why the Spider Has a Narrow Waist."

16R **Pearl Primus' Africa**, Miller-Brody, 1970 (76577-X) 3 12in 33rpm record set 15min each side $26.91; (76578-8) 3 cassette set $26.91. M-B (I-U)

Traditional legends, folktales, and proverbs of Africa in a superb recording which combines storytelling, music, and dance. Includes a version of "Why the Spider Has a Narrow Waist."

17 **Anansi the Spider: A Tale from the Ashanti**, retold and illus. by Gerald McDermott. Holt, 1972. unp. lib. ed. $6.95 net; Penguin pap. $1.95 (P)

Anansi's six sons save their father's life with their special abilities. When Anansi finds the moon he wishes to give it to one of his sons, but since he can never decide which son is most deserving the moon remains in the sky. Illustrated with vibrant geometric drawings derived from African folk art. Based on the award-winning film.

17F **Anansi the Spider**, Gerald McDermott Films, 1969, 16mm color 10min $140, $15. LEM (P-U)

First in African Folklore series. Animated. Designed and directed by Gerald McDermott. Mythology scholar Joseph Campbell directed the research. Music by Thomas Wagner. Narrated by Athmani Magoma, African Information Officer for United Nations Radio.

17FS **Anansi the Spider**, Weston Woods, 1973 (FS 151) 43fr color 10min $12; (SF151C) with cassette $18. WW (P-I)

Illustrations from the book, accompanied by picture-cued booklet. When showing this to a younger audience you may wish to skip the introductory frames which explain the nature of folklore and the Ghana legend of Anansi.

17R **Anansi the Spider**, Weston Woods, 1973 (LTR151C) cassette 10min $6. WW (P-I)

Narrated by John J. Akar, former ambassador to the United States from Sierra Leone, accompanied by original music played on African drums.

18 **Anatole and the Piano**, by Eve Titus; pictures by Paul Galdone. McGraw-Hill, 1966. 32p. lib. ed. $6.95 net (P)

The brave and daring little mouse helps a hundred Paris orphans and is most surprisingly rewarded.

18F **Anatole and the Piano**, McGraw-Hill, 1968 (627100) 16mm color 12min $195, $12; videocassette $150. MH (N-P)

Animated film based on the book illustrations.

19 **And I Mean It, Stanley!**, by Crosby Bonsall. Harper, 1974.

An adorable ragamuffin child tempts Stanley to join in her creative play as she builds elaborate monsters from odds and ends in the backyard. Only on the final page, when Stanley bursts onto the scene, do we discover that Stanley is a huge lovable sheepdog.

19R **And I Mean It, Stanley!**, Random House/Miller-Brody (394-69121-0) cassette with hardcover book 2:46min each side, listening and read-along version $13.50. RH/M-B (P)

A straightforward reading with authentic expression. The read-along version has brief instructions to the reader and unobtrusive tonal beeps for page turning.

20 **And Now Miguel**, by Joseph Krumgold; illus. by Jean Charlot. Crowell, 1953. 245p. $10.95; Apollo Editions pap. $4.95 (I-U)

Miguel, son of a New Mexican sheepherder, longs to be old enough to join the men in taking the sheep to summer pasture. Newbery Medal winner, 1954.

20F **And Now Miguel**, Universal-International, 1966 (26613) 16mm color 95min $37.50 (rental only). UEVA (I-U)

Guy Stockwell, Pat Cardi, and Clu Gulager star. Produced by Robert Radnitz. Directed by James B. Clark. Screenplay by Ted Sherdeman and Jane Klove. Photography by Clifford Stine. Music by Phillip Lambro.

20FS **And Now Miguel**, Random House/Miller-Brody, 1980 (394-78415-4) 2 filmstrips 99, 91fr color 13, 14min with 2 cassettes $45. RH/M-B (I)

Filmstrip based on the book. Narration, appropriately done with Spanish accent, is underlined with an unobtrusive, yet expressive, musical background. Realistic illustrations based on book descriptions.

20R **And Now Miguel**, by Joseph Krumgold. Random House/Miller-Brody (394-76935-X) record $8.97; (394-76936-8) cassette $8.97. RH/M-B (I)

Miguel wants to help the herders take the sheep to summer pasture.

21 **And to Think That I Saw It on Mulberry Street**, by Dr. Seuss. Vanguard, 1937. unp. $5.95 (P)

A small boy's imagination converts a plain horse and wagon into a circus parade led by an elephant and two giraffes.

21R **Happy Birthday to You and Other Stories**, Caedmon, 1970 (TC 1287) 2s 12in 33rpm $8.98; (CP 51287) cassette $8.98. CAE (P)

Five Dr. Seuss stories read with verve by Hans Conreid. The electronic sounds of the Octopus, a sound machine with eight channels, emphasize the action and give a suitably strange flavor to the nonsense. Includes: *Happy Birthday to You! Scrambled Eggs Super, And to Think That I Saw It on Mulberry Street, Gertrude McFuzz* and *The Big Brag*.

22 **Androcles and the Lion**, by Gerald and Elizabeth Rose. Faber and Faber, 1971. (Merrimack Book Service, Inc., dist., 5 South Union Street, Lawrence, MA 01843) 32p. $6.50 (P)

A favorite story of the man who befriends a lion and earns a reward for his kindness.

22FS **Androcles and the Lion**, Listening Library, 1977 (JFS 162) 1 filmstrip color 1 cassette 6:30min $18. LL (P)

Captioned cartoon-like illustrations about the man who befriends a lion and earns a reward for his kindness. Pleasing narration, with appropriate background sounds, which holds the children's interest.

23 **Andy and the Lion**, by James Daugherty. Viking, 1938. unp. lib. ed. $8.95 net; pap. $.95 (P)

A modern version of *Androcles and the Lion*, in which Andy befriends a lion, who later reciprocates.

23F **Andy and the Lion**, by Morton Schindel, 1955 (6078) 16mm color 10:25min $140, $20. WW (P-I)

Iconographic technique using illustrations from the book. Narrated by Ralph Camargo. Music by Arthur Kleiner.

Also available in Spanish.

23FS **Andy and the Lion**, Weston Woods, n.d. (FS9) 42fr color $12; (SF 9) 6:30min with cassette $18. WW (P)

Illustrations from the book, accompanied by picture-cued text booklet.

Also available in Spanish.

23R **Andy and the Lion**, Weston Woods, n.d. (LTR 009C) cassette 6:30min $6. WW (P)

Story narrated by Owen Jordan, with

original background music by Arthur Kleiner.

Also available in Spanish.

24 **Angus and the Cat**, by Marjorie Flack. Doubleday, 1971 (c. 1931). 32p. $5.95; pap. $1.49 (N-P)

Angus learns that he cannot chase the cat and have her company, too.

24FS **Angus and the Cat**, Weston Woods, 1973 (FS 146) 34fr color 6min $12; (SF 146C) with cassette $18. WW (N-P)

Illustrations from the book, accompanied by picture-cued text booklet.

24R **Angus and the Cat**, Weston Woods, 1973 (LTR 146C) cassette 6min $6. WW (N-P)

Narrated by Buffy Allen.

25 **Angus and the Ducks**, told and illus. by Marjorie Flack. Doubleday, 1930. unp. $4.95; pap. $1.95 (N-P)

Curiosity leads a little Scottie into trouble.

25FS **Angus and the Ducks**, Weston Woods, n.d. (FS 39) 35fr color 5:42min $12; (SF39C) with cassette $18. WW (N-P)

Illustrations from the book, accompanied by picture-cued text booklet.

25R **Angus and the Ducks**, Weston Woods, n.d. (LTR 039C) cassette 5:42min $6. WW (N-P)

Story narrated by Gilbert Mack, with original background music by Jay Frederick.

26 **Animal Stories**, by Walter de la Mare. Scribner, 1940. 420p. $5.95 (I-U)

Some fifty animal tales, ballads, and rhymes "chosen, arranged and in some part rewritten" by the English writer-poet. De la Mare's introduction traces the history of animal folk literature.

26R **Animal Stories**, Caedmon, 1975 (TC 1456) 12in 33rpm $6.98; (CDL 5456) cassette $8.98. CAE (I)

Five stories from de la Mare's collection are slightly adapted and told by Lynn Redgrave. Includes "The Wolf and the Fox," "The Hare and the Hedgehog," "Mrs. Fox," "The Mouse, the Bird and the Sausage," and "All Gone."

27 **Annie and the Old One**, by Miska Miles; illus. by Peter Parnall. Little, 1971. 44p. $6.95 (I)

Miles tells the story of a young Navajo girl who cannot accept the reality of the imminent death of her ailing grandmother.

27FS **Annie and the Old One**, Newbery Award Records, 1979 (394-76919-8) 2 filmstrips 57, 59fr, color 7, 6:40min with 2 12in 33rpm $45; (394-76920-1) with 2 cassettes $45. RH/M-B (I)

The original story is followed faithfully and the stark landscape of the southwestern U.S. blazes in intense colors in the silkscreen-like art of Peter Parnall. Delicate, free-form guitar melodies heighten this dramatic presentation narrated by native Navajo/Mexican Indian Rueben Ortiz.

27R **Annie and the Old One**, by Miska Miles. Random House/Miller-Brody (394-76917-1) read-along record $8.97; (394-76918-X) read-along cassette $8.97. RH/M-B (I)

Annie cannot accept the death of her grandmother.

28 **Anpao; An American Indian Odyssey**, by Jamake Highwater. Harper, 1977. 256p. $12.45 (I)

Traditional North American Indian tales are woven into one story of a boy's growth to manhood.

28R **Anpao**, Folkways Records, 1978 (FC7776) 12in 33rpm manual $9.98. FSR (I)

Jamake Highwater reads four tales from his Newbery Honor Book, *Anpao*.

29 **Apt. 3**, by Ezra Jack Keats. Macmillan, 1971. unp. $8.95 (P)

Piercing the sounds of the pouring rain that muffle the city's blare, the plaintive wails of a harmonica reach Sam and Ben's tenement apartment, prompting the two youngsters to discover the source of the sad, free-formed melodies.

29FS **Apt. 3**, Weston Woods, 1977 (FS 183) 37fr color 8min $12; (SF 183C) with cassette $18. WW (P)

Enlivening the richly colored and deeply textured illustrations of Keats's book with the sounds that play a major role in the story, this sound filmstrip adds an extra dimension to a realistic exploration of life in a city apartment.

30 **The Arabian Nights**, retold by Amabel Williams-Ellis; illus. by Pauline Diana Baynes. Criterion, 1957. 348p. $9.95 (I). OP

Beautifully illustrated edition of Scheherazade's tales of Arabia and the East.

30R **Aladdin and His Lamp**, Caedmon, 1968 (CDL 51250) cassette only $8.98. CAE (I-U)

Anthony Quayle weaves magic into his readings of "Aladdin and the Magician" and "Aladdin and the Lovely Princess" as retold by Amabel Williams-Ellis.

30R **The Arabian Nights: Ali Baba and the Forty Thieves**, Caedmon, 1968 (TC 1251) 2s 12in 33rpm $8.98; (CDL 51251) cassette $8.98. CAE (I-U)

Superb storytelling by Anthony Quayle. Amabel Williams-Ellis's version, which is divided into four parts, is used. Included are "Ali Baba and Kassim," "Ali Baba and Morgiana," and "Ali Baba and the Invited Guest."

31 **Arrow to the Sun; A Pueblo Indian Tale**, adapted and illus. by Gerald McDermott. Viking, 1974. unp. lib. ed. $8.95; Penguin pap. $2.50 (P-I)

The legend of the Sun god's son. To prove his true identity a young Indian boy must endure four trials involving lions, serpents, bees, and lightning. 1975 winner of the Caldecott Medal.

31F **Arrow to the Sun**, Gerald McDermott and Texture Films, 1973, 16mm color 12min $210, $28. TEX (I-U)

Animation adapted from book. Very little dialogue. Music, based on Southwest Indian chants, by Thomas Wagner.

31FS **Arrow to the Sun**, Weston Woods, 1975 (FS 184) 36fr color $12; (SF 184C) with cassette only 8:40min $18. WW (P-I)

Illustrations from the book, accompanied by picture-cued text booklet. Narrated by the author-illustrator and accompanied by a musical score employing flutes, rattles, bells, and drums. McDermott's illustrations projected on the screen are even more strikingly brilliant than they appear in the book.

32 **Arthur Rackham Fairy Book**, by Arthur Rackman. Lippincott, 1950. 286p. $10 (I)

Twenty-three favorites gathered from Andersen, Grimm, Perrault, and others. Includes "Toads and Diamonds."

32R **Fairy Tale Favorites** v.2, CMS Records, 1970 (CMS 595) 2s 12in 33rpm $7.98; (CMS X-4595) cassette. CMS (I)

"The Nightingale," "The Steadfast Tin Soldier," "The Princess on the Pea," and "The Fairies" ("Toads and Diamonds"), beautifully told by Mary Strang.

33 **As I Was Crossing Boston Common**, by Norma Farber; illus. by Arnold Lobel. Creative Arts Book Co., 1982. 32p. $3.95 (P)

An enjoyable nonsense tale; an ALA Notable Children's Book, 1976.

33FS **As I Was Crossing Boston Common**, Listening Library (Look, Listen and Read) n.d. (JFS 157) 36fr color 11min 1 filmstrip 1 cassette $21. LL (P)

Norma Farber's engagingly informative nonsense tale of a pedestrian who encounters strange and exotic animals. The unusual names of these animals are great fun for the viewer.

34 **Ashanti to Zulu: African Traditions**, by Margaret Musgrove; illus. by Leo and Diane Dillon. Dial, 1976. 32p. $9.95 (P-I)

Caldecott Medal winner, 1977. Musgrove presents, in alphabetical order, twenty-six African peoples and depicts a custom important to each. Her anecdotes reflect the values and philosophies of each tribe.

34FS **Ashanti to Zulu: African Traditions**, Weston Woods, 1977 (FS 195) 32fr color 17min $12; (SF 195C) with cassette $18. WW (P-I)

Centered on black backgrounds, the Dillons' exquisite interpretations of African traditions and ways of life comprise the visuals for the sound filmstrip adaptation of Musgrove's book.

34R **Ashanti to Zulu: African Traditions**, Weston Woods, 1977 (LTR 195C) 17min cassette $6. WW (P-I)

Narrated by Spencer G. Shaw.

35 **The Awful Mess**, by Anne Rockwell. illus. Four Winds/Scholastic, 1973, reprinted 1980. 40p. $7.95 (N-P)

In Olly's room, there is a tunnel, plus two tall towers, a traffic jam and a clutter of animals and other toys that his family thinks is an awful mess but his friend David thinks is "neat."

35FS **The Awful Mess**, Listening Library, 1977 (JFS 169) color 4:45min 1 filmstrip 1 cassette $21. LL (N-P)

A messy room is a magic place for two small boys in this filmstrip reproduced from the book page by page with captions.

36 **Babar the King**, by Jean de Brunhoff. Random House, 1937. $5.99 (P)

King Babar turns his attention to building a beautiful new city for all the elephants. He selects a lovely site on the banks of a large lake, and after much hard work, the city of Celesteville is completed.

36FS **Babar the King**, Random House, prod. by Spectra Films, 1977 (394-07536-6) 2 filmstrips 131, 102fr color 9:59, 8:34min with 2 cassettes. $45. RH (P)

ALA Notable Filmstrip. Captivating blend of visuals and sound that reveals the details of de Brunhoff's vibrant illustrations while giving vivacity to the King, his subjects, and the happenings in Celesteville.

36R **Babar the King** and **Babar and Zephir**, Caedmon (TC 1487) 1 12in LP $8.98; (CDL5 1487) 1 cassette $8.98. CAE (P)

Translated by Merle S. Haas. Performance by Louis Jourdan. Music by Jean de Brunhoff and Don Heckman. Louis Jourdan provides superb narration and singing.

37 **Bartholomew and the Oobleck**, by Dr. Seuss. Random House, 1949. $5.99 (P)

The King of Didd got tired of the same four things falling down from his sky, so he ordered his magicians to make something new. And so they made oobleck—a green, sticky substance—which got into everything and made a mess of the kingdom. To stop the oobleck, the King must say the words "I'm sorry."

37FS **Bartholomew and the Oobleck**, Random House/Miller-Brody, 1981 (394-62559-5) 126fr 25min with cassette $21. RH/M-B (P)

Dr. Seuss's original illustrations—in

black and white, and asparagus-soup green— were made three-dimensional for the filmstrip. Lionel Wilson, actor and writer of children's books, performs all the characters in the story.

37R **Bartholomew and the Oobleck**, by Dr. Seuss. Random House/Miller-Brody (394-07673-7) read-along cassette with hardcover book $15. RH/M-B (P)

The king's magicians create a new substance to fall from the sky—oobleck.

38 **Bear Hunt**, by Anthony Browne. Atheneum, 1980. $7.95 (P)

A fanciful jungle planted with matchsticks, eyes, and lightbulbs in vivid primary colors is the setting for this make-believe trip into Bear's world. Bear, armed with only a pencil to draw himself out of any emergencies, ambles along undisturbed by the hunters' attempts to capture him.

38FS **Bear Hunt**, Weston Woods, 1981 (FS 268) 25fr color 3:50min $12; (SF 268C) with cassette $18. WW (P)

Adapted from Browne's picture book. Low-key, big-band sound music and squawking "jungly" sound effects provide appropriate accompaniment to the lively narration. Picture-cued text booklet.

39 **The Bear's Bicycle**, by Emilie Warren McLeod; illus. by David McPhail. Little, 1975. 32p. $6.95 (P)

The basic rules of bicycle safety are demonstrated by a small boy as he sets off on a pleasant ride. Contrasting his sensible and responsible actions are the careless feats (and their consequences) of an imaginary, and very reckless, bicycle-riding bear.

39FS **The Bear's Bicycle**, Viking, dist. by Live Oak Media, 1977 (0-670-90540-2) 37fr color 4:15min with cassette $19.95. LOM (P)

Straightforward adaptation of McLeod's story allows the book's charm to shine through. Utilizes the colorful drawings of David McPhail from the book. The addition of appropriate sound effects enhances the presentation.

Accompanied by picture-cued text booklet.

40 **The Beast of Monsieur Racine**, by Tomi Ungerer. Farrar, 1971. unp. $8.95 (P-I)

Monsieur Racine befriends a strange-looking beast who has been stealing his prize pears. When the Academy of Science invites them to Paris, the results are unexpectedly hilarious. Sophisticated cartoon-style drawings crammed with humorous detail.

40F **The Beast of Monsieur Racine**, Morton Schindel, 1975, 16mm color 9min $175, $20; #160 video-cassette $175. WW (P)

Skilled animation and lilting, French country music. Good color and excellent narration by Charles Duval. Adapted and directed by Gene Deitch. Notable Children's Film, 1974.

40FS **The Beast of Monsieur Racine**, Weston Woods, 1975 (FS 160) 52fr color 14:07min $12; (SF 160C) with cassette $18. WW (P-I)

Illustrations from the book, accompanied by picture-cued text booklet.

40R **The Beast of Monsieur Racine**, Weston Woods, 1975 (LTR 160C) cassette $6. WW (P)

A musical score composed of variations from French country music introduces the story which is charmingly narrated by Charles Duvall.

41 **Beat the Turtle Drum**, by Constance C. Greene; illus. by Donna Diamond. Viking, 1976. $7.95; Dell pap. $1.75 (I-U)

Thirteen-year-old Kate must learn to cope with her feelings after her sister's accidental death.

41F **Very Good Friends**, Martin Tahse, 1977, 16mm color 29min $450, $40. LCA (I-U)

Melissa Gilbert stars as Kate in this touching, well-acted film.

42 **The Best Horse**, by Elizabeth Van Steenwyk. Scholastic, 1977. pap. $1.25 (I)

Wendy, a young teenager, wants to perform in a rodeo but her mother forbids her to ride.

42F **The Best Horse**, Scholastic, 1979, 16mm color 28min $245. LCA (I)

Live-action television film with good acting and likable people.

43 **Best Stories of O. Henry**, by O. Henry. Doubleday, 1965. $10.95 (I-U)

Collection of the best short stories by this famous author.

43F **Ransom of Red Chief**, Marion Rosenberg, 1978, 16mm color 27min $395, $35. LCA (I-U)

Funny, live-action adaptation of the O. Henry short story which depicts rural life in the early 1900s. Stars Harry Dean Stanton as Sam, Joe Spinell as Bill and Johnny Robbie Rist as Red Chief. Scott Joplin background music enhances the fun.

44 **Beezus and Ramona**, by Beverly Cleary; illus. by Louis Darling. Morrow, 1955. 159p. $7.25 (P-I)

Ramona Quimby, a strong-willed, mischievious four-year-old, tries the patience of her well-behaved big sister, Beezus. Beezus experiences feelings of guilt when she doesn't love, or even like, her little sister.

44FS **Beezus and Ramona**, Random House/Miller-Brody, 1980 (394-64527-8) 141fr color 18:25min with cassette $21. RH/M-B (P-I)

Illustrations patterned after those in Cleary's beloved book. Choice episodes from the book are read by enthusiastic performers.

44R **Beezus and Ramona**, by Beverly Cleary. Random House/Miller-Brody (394-64514-6) cassette $8.95. RH/M-B (P-I)

Dramatized version.

45 **Behind the Back of the Mountain: Black Folktales from Southern Africa**, retold by Verna Aardema; illus. by Leo and Diane Dillon. Dial, 1973. 85p. $5.95; lib. ed. $5.47 (P-I)

These stories from various African tribes are especially good for storytelling.

45R **Zulu and Other African Folktales**, Caedmon, 1975, $8.98; (CDL 1474) cassette $8.98. CAE (P-I-U)

Ruby Dee and Ossie Davis tell stories from *Behind the Back of the Mountain*. The storytellers' contrasting styles heighten the listener's pleasure.

46 **Ben and Me**, by Robert Lawson. Little, 1939. 113p. $6.95 (P-I)

A new and astonishing life of Benjamin Franklin as told by the good mouse, Amos, who moves into Ben's hat and serves as his advisor and mentor.

46F **Ben and Me**, Walt Disney Educational Media Company, 1962, 16mm color 21min $395. DISN (P-I)

A mouse's-eye view of the life of Benjamin Franklin told with humor. Animated.

47 **Benjamin and Tulip**, by Rosemary Wells. Dial, 1973. unp. $6.95; lib. ed. $6.46; pap. $1.50 (N-P)

Every time poor Benjamin passed Tulip's house she would beat him. Finally Benjamin takes the situation in hand. An amusing story about two raccoons.

47FS **Benjamin and Tulip**, Weston Woods, 1975 (FS 176) 38fr color

$12; (SF 176C) with cassette only min $18. WW (N-P)

Illustrations from the book, accompanied by picture-cued text booklet.

48 **Ben's Trumpet**, by Rachel Isadora. Greenwillow, 1979. unp. $7.50 (P)

Ben lives across the street from the Zig Zag Jazz Club. He likes the sounds of each of the musicians, but his favorite player is the trumpeter. So Ben blows on an imaginary trumpet until the neighborhood kids taunt him. Then the trumpeter from the club takes an interest in Ben.

48FS **Ben's Trumpet**, Random House/Miller-Brody, 1980 (394-66059-5) 120fr color 11min with cassette $21. RH/M-B (P)

The visuals for the filmstrip were created by adding color and special effects to Isadora's book illustrations. The accompanying music is an original jazz composition by Arthur Custer, featuring the trumpet playing of Clark Terry and a six-piece band of jazz musicians. ALA Notable Filmstrip.

49 **The Berenstain Bears and the Spooky Old Tree**, by Stan and Jan Berenstain. Random House, 1978. unp. $4.99 (P)

Three brave little bears, armed with a light, a stick, and a rope investigate the mysteries in a spooky old tree. However, the three develop a case of the shivers and have second thoughts about their adventure.

49FS **The Berenstain Bears and the Spooky Old Tree**, Random House, 1978 (394-00933-9) 50fr color 5min with cassette $21. RH (P)

Delightfully scary story with just the right amount of eerie background music, dramatic narration, and spooky pictures taken directly from the book. ALA Notable Filmstrip.

49R **The Berenstain Bears and the Spooky Old Tree**, Random House/Miller-Brody (394-00940-1) read-along cassette with hardcover book $13.50. RH/M-B (P)

Read-along version.

50 **Big Red**, by Jim Kjelgaard; illus. by Bob Kuhn. New ed. Holiday, 1956. 254p. $8.95 (I-U)

The story of a champion Irish setter and a trapper's son who grew up together, roaming the Wintapi wilderness, and sharing the rugged life of the forest.

50F **Big Red**, Buena Vista, 1962, 16mm color 89min $55 (rental only). DISN (I-U)

Walter Pidgeon, Gilles Payant, and Emile Genest star.

51 **The Big Snow**, by Berta and Elmer Hader. Macmillan, 1948. unp. $6.95; pap. $2.50 (P)

A kindly old couple put out food for the birds and animals after a winter snowstorm. Caldecott Medal winner, 1949.

51FS **The Big Snow**, Weston Woods, n.d. (FS 25) 53fr color $12; (SF 25C) with cassette 11:10min $18. WW (P)

Illustrations from the book, accompanied by picture-cued text booklet.

51R **The Big Snow**, Weston Woods, n.d. (LTR 025C) cassette 11:10min $6. WW (P)

Story narrated by Owen Jordan, with original background music by Arthur Kleiner.

52 **The Biggest Bear**, by Lynd Ward. Houghton, 1952. 84p. lib. ed. $7.95 (P)

Johnny hunts for the biggest bear in the forest—and comes home with a very little bear that grows and grows and grows. Caldecott Medal winner, 1953.

52FS **The Biggest Bear**, Weston Woods, n.d. (FS 10) 48fr color $12; (SF 10C) with cassette 7min $18. WW (P)

Illustrations from the book, accompanied by picture-cued text booklet.

52R **The Biggest Bear**, Weston Woods, n.d. (LTR 010C) cassette 7min $6. WW (P)

Story narrated by Owen Jordan, with original background music by Arthur Kleiner.

53 **The Biggest House in the World**, by Leo Lionni. Pantheon, 1968. unp. $6.99 (P)

A little snail tells his father that he would like to have the biggest house in the world. His father tells him about another little snail who had the same wish.

53FS **The Biggest House in the World**, Westport Communications Group, rel. by Random House, 1978 (394-05315-X) 33fr color 5min with cassette $21. RH/M-B (P)

Filmstrip version utilizes Lionni's illustrations along with an expressive musical background. Guide.

54 **A Birthday for Frances**, by Russell Hoban; pictures by Lillian Hoban. Harper, 1968. 31p. $6.95; lib. ed. $7.89; pap. $1.95 (N-P)

Frances buys her sister Gloria a Chompo Bar for her birthday present but has trouble parting with it.

54FS **Frances Series**, Educational Enrichment Materials, 1971 (200781) av 57fr color 10min 6 filmstrips 6 cassettes $130 (individual FS $18, individual cassettes $12). EEM (N-P)

Filmstrip titles: *Bedtime for Frances, A Baby Sister for Frances, A Birthday for Frances, Bread and Jam for Frances, A Bargain for Frances, Best Friends for Frances.*

The narratives follow the books but color and illustrations have been added to these engaging stories about Frances the Badger.

55 **The Birthday of the Infanta and Other Tales**, by Oscar Wilde; illus. by Beni Montresor. Atheneum, 1982. 80p. $14.95 (I)

A beautiful and well-edited version of five of Wilde's best known stories for children.

55R **The Happy Prince and The Devoted Friend**, Folkways Records, 1963 (FC 7731) 12in 33rpm manual $9.98. FSR (P-I)

Claire Luce reads these two Oscar Wilde stories.

56 **Black Beauty**, by Anna Sewell. illus. Deluxe ed. Grosset, 1981, $8.95; pap. $4.95 (P-I)

Autobiography of a nineteenth-century horse who is sold from one owner to another with his treatment deteriorating each time.

56FS **Black Beauty**, Educational Enrichment Materials, 1976, color 2 filmstrips 2 cassettes or records 1 paperback $48. EEM (P-I)

Adapted from the novel by Anna Sewell. Illustrations by John Worsley who illustrated the Gold Classics Series edition of *Black Beauty*.

57 **Black Fairy Tales**, ed. by Terry Berger; illus. by David O. White. Atheneum, 1969. 137p. lib. ed. $5.95 net; pap. $1.25 (I-U)

Stories told by the Swazi, the Shangani, and the 'Msuto people of South Africa.

57R **Black Fairy Tales**, Caedmon, 1972 $8.98; (CDL 51425) cassette only $8.95. CAE (I-U)

Claudia McNeil reads three tales of beautiful black princesses, "The Moss-Green Princess," "The Serpent's Bride," and "The Fairy Frog."

58 **Blue Fairy Book**, ed. by Brian Alderson; illus. by John Lawrence. New ed. Viking, 1978. 373p. $14.95 (P-I)

This well-loved collection of fairy tale favorites includes "Beauty and the Beast" and "Toads and Diamonds."

58R **Snow-White and Rose-Red and Other Andrew Lang Fairy Tales**, Caedmon, 1973 (TC 1414) 2s 12in 33rpm $8.98; (CDL 51414) cassette $8.98. CAE (P-I)

Side 1: the title story (16:31min) and "The True History of Little Goldenhood" (8:29min). Side 2: "East of the Sun and West of the Moon" (27:32min). In her musical speaking voice, Glynis Johns reads two favorites from Lang's *Blue Fairy Book* and Lang's version of "Little Red Riding-Hood" from his *Red Fairy Book*.

58R **Fairy Tale Favorites** v.3, CMS Records, 1971 (CMS 632) 2s 12in 33rpm $7.98; (CMS-X-4632) cassette $7.98. CMS (P-I)

Mary Strang tells Laurence Housman's "Rocking-Horse Land," and three traditional tales, "Beauty and the Beast," "The Top and the Ball," and "The Frog Prince."

59 **Blue Moose**, by Manus Pinkwater. Dodd, 1975. Dell pap. 1976 (P-I)

Mr. Breton's fine restaurant located at the edge of the forest did not keep him from being lonely. One day, a blue moose clumped into the restaurant to warm himself and everything changed. The blue moose spoke French and stayed to help serve bowls of soup balanced on his antlers.

59R **Blue Moose**, Listening Library (AFTR 50) cassette with 4 books and teacher's guide 27min $16.95. LL (P-I)

A read-along version of the text.

60 **Blue Willow**, by Doris Gates; illus. by Paul Lantz. Viking, 1940. 172p. $8.95; Penguin pap. $1.50 (I)

Janey Larkin, daughter of migrant farm workers, cherishes her only possession, a blue-willow plate and dreams of the day it will sit on the mantel of a "permanent" home.

60R **Blue Willow**, Viking, 1972, 2s 12in 33rpm $8.98; cassette $8.95. LOM (I)

Dramatized version of the book.

61 **Blueberries for Sal**, by Robert McCloskey. Viking, 1948. 54p. lib. ed. $7.95 net; Penguin pap. $2.25 (N-P)

Sal and a baby bear find themselves with the wrong mothers as they pick blueberries on a Maine hillside.

61F **Blueberries for Sal**, Morton Schindel, 1967 (17995) 16mm color 9min $140, $20; videocassette $140; Super 8 $140. WW (N-P)

Iconographic technique using illustrations from the book. Narrated by Owen Jordan. Music by Daniel Sable.

61FS **Blueberries for Sal**, Weston Woods, n.d. (FS 41) 47fr color 8:40min $12; (SF41C) with cassette $18. WW (N-P)

Illustrations from the book, accompanied by picture-cued text booklet.

61R **Blueberries for Sal**, Weston Woods, n.d. (LTR 041C) cassette 8:40min $6. WW (N-P)

Story narrated by Owen Jordan, with original background music by Daniel Sable.

62 **A Book of Myths: Selections from Bulfinch's *Age of Fable***; illus. by Helen Sewell. Macmillan, 1964. 126p. $5.50 (I-U)

Beautiful illustrations suggesting classical sculpture and vase paintings illuminate thirty slightly adapted Greek myths.

62R **Heroes, Gods and Monsters of the Greek Myths**, Spoken Arts, 1968, 2s 12in 33rpm $8.98 each; cassette $9.95 each. SA (U)

#8001 (SA 989) v.1: Zeus, Hera, Hades, Demeter, Birth of the Twins, Athene,

Poseidon, Hephaestus, Aphrodite
#8002 (SA 1000) v.2: Apollo, Sons of Apollo, Artemis, and Aphrodite, The Story of Phaethon
#8003 (SA 1001) v.3: The stories of Perseus; Narcissus and Echo
#7101 (SA 1002) v.4: The stories of Theseus and Pandora
#7102 (SA 1003) v.5: The stories of Arion, Orpheus, and Atalanta
#7103 (SA 1004) v.6: The stories of Prometheus and Daedalus; Eros and Psyche
Read by Julie Harris and Richard Kiley.

62R **Greek Myths–A Treasury**, v.2. CMS Records, 1971 (CMS-X4616) cassette $8.98. CMS (U)

Contents: "Cupid and Psyche," "Tales of King Midas," "Myths of the Hellespont," "The Story of the Creation," and "The Gordian Knot." The myths on this record have been rewritten to permit ease of storytelling but the lyrical classic style has been retained. They are told with dignity and feeling by Brock Peters.

63 **The Borrowers**, by Mary Norton; illus. by Beth and Joe Krush. Harcourt, 1953. 180p. $5.50; pap. $1.50 (I)

In a miniature world beneath the floor of an old English country house live the Borrowers, tiny people who "borrow" what they need from "human beans."

63R **The Borrowers**, Caedmon, 1975 (TC 1459) 12in 33rpm side A: 33:22min, side B: 33:39min $8.98; (CDL 51459) cassette $8.98. CAE (P-I)

Mary Norton's story has been skillfully abridged for this narrative reading by Claire Bloom. The "Nightingale Song" by Carl Zeller from *The Story of the Music Box* is used to set the mood. The only sound effect is the ticking of a clock used between scenes. A good introduction to the book.

64 **A Boy, A Dog, and A Frog**, by Mercer Mayer; illus. by the author. Dial, 1967. $6.95; lib. ed. $6.46; pap. $1.75 (P)

A wordless picture book about the adventures of a small boy and his dog as they try to catch a frog.

64F **A Boy, A Dog, and A Frog**, Gary Templeton, 1980, 16mm color 9min $210, $20. PHX (P)

A live-action film with an adorable little boy and a very well-trained frog. A delightful film.

65 **The Boy Who Drew Cats, and Other Tales**, by Lafcadio Hearn; introd. by Pearl Buck; illus. by Manabu C. Saito. Macmillan, 1963. 40p. lib. ed. $4.50 net (I)

Tales from Japanese folklore.

65R **Asian Folk and Fairy Tales**. CMS Records, 1966 (CMS 508) LP 33 rpm, $8.98; (CMS-X4508) cassette $8.98. CMS (I).

Christine Price, storyteller, tells "The Valiant Chattee Maker"–India; "The Boy Who Drew Cats"–Japan; and "The Great Stone Fire Eater"–Korea.

66 **The Bremen Town Musicians**, by Ilse Plume. Doubleday, 1980. 32p. $8.95 (P)

Four animals, no longer wanted by their masters, set out to become musicians in Bremen Town but outwit a band of robbers and decide to stay in a forest cabin instead.

66FS **The Bremen Town Musicians**, Random House/Miller-Brody, 1981 (394-07715-6) 74fr color 10:45min with cassette $21. RH/M-B (P)

Ilse Plume's delicately textured, richly colored illustrations are utilized in the filmstrip version. Highlighting the filmstrip is the music by Arthur Custer, who has uniquely characterized each of the animal heroes using a different musical instrument.

66R **The Bremen Town Musicians**, Ilse Plume, reteller/illustrator. Random House/Miller-Brody (394-07661-3) read-along cassette with hardcover book side 1 (no signals) 11:57min, side 2 (page turn signals) 9:53min $18. RH/M-B (P)

A dramatized version with a narrator (unidentified) and symbolic voices for the characters. The listening version has background music and graphic sound effects. The read-along version is read naturally with unobstrusive page-turning signals. Original score.

67 **Brian Wildsmith's Birds**, by Brian Wildsmith. Oxford Univ. Pr., 1980. unp. pap. $3.95 (P-I)

Vibrant paintings of groups of birds with their group name, for example, "a nye of pheasants."

67FS **Brian Wildsmith's Birds**, Weston Woods, 1970 (FS 111) 18fr color 3:31min $12; (SF111C) with cassette $18. WW (P-I)

Includes "The North Wind and the Sun."

68 **Brian Wildsmith's Circus**, by Brian Wildsmith. Oxford Univ. Pr., 1970. 32p. pap. $3.95 (P-I)

An almost wordless picture book filled with brilliant watercolor paintings of clowns, animals, and acrobatic acts.

68FS **Brian Wildsmith's Circus**, Weston Woods, 1973 (FS 144) 20fr color 4:15min $12; (SF 144C) with cassette $18. WW (P-I)

Illustrations from the book, accompanied by picture-cued text booklet. Includes *Brian Wildsmith's Fishes.*

68R **Brian Wildsmith's Circus**, Weston Woods, 1973 (LTR 144C) cassette 4:15min $6. WW (P-I)

Sounds of the circus with applause after each act indicating page turns. Narrated by John Cunningham.

See also: *Bruno Munari's ABC* (WW LTR 050C) cassette $6; *Bruno Munari's Zoo* (WW LTR 097C) cassette $6.

69 **Brian Wildsmith's Fishes**, by Brian Wildsmith. Watts, 1968. 32p. lib. ed. $5.95 net (P-I)

The names given to groups of fishes by fishermen, zoologists, and poets, such as "a leap of salmon," stunningly illustrated in beautiful colors.

69FS **Brian Wildsmith's Fishes**, Weston Woods, 1973 (SF 144) 20fr color 5:23min $12; (SF 144C) with cassette $18. WW (P-I)

Illustrations from the book, accompanied by picture-cued text booklet. Narrated by Charles Cioffi. Includes *Brian Wildsmith's Circus.*

70 **Brian Wildsmith's Wild Animals**, by Brian Wildsmith. Oxford Univ. Pr., 1979. unp. pap. $3.95 (P-I)

Imaginatively designed and beautifully colored pictures of animals in groups (a pride of lions, a skulk of foxes) stimulate appreciation of color and awareness of new words.

70FS **Brian Wildsmith's Wild Animals** and **The Rich Man and the Shoemaker**, Weston Woods, 1972 (FS 134) 37fr color 10:28min $12; (SF 134C) with cassette $18. WW (P-I)

Illustrations from the book, accompanied by picture-cued text booklet. *Wild Animals* consists of spoken captions and natural animal sounds. Contemporary wind and piano ensemble accompany the reading of the fable.

71 **Bridge to Terabithia**, by Katherine Paterson; illus. by Donna Diamond. Harper, 1977. 128p. $8.95 (I)

Ten-year-old Jess Aarons loses a foot race to a "city girl" named Leslie Burke, but he gains a new friend and an invitation into the imaginary kingdom of Terabithia, a hide-away in the woods. 1978 Newbery Medal winner.

71FS **Bridge to Terabithia**, Random House/Miller-Brody, 1981 (394-65695-4) 2 filmstrips 128, 135fr color 16:30, 16:58min with 2 cassettes $45. RH/M-B (I)

This filmstrip is a fitting adaptation of Paterson's tender story. The narrator is aided by brief sections of faithfully enacted dialogue. The soft-colored illustrations echo the mood of the story and the background music, in which the guitar is prominent, enhances the tenderness of this story in which feelings, fear, ideas and dreams are the focus.

71R **Bridge to Terabithia**, Random House/Miller-Brody (394-76890-6) record $8.97; (394-76891-4) cassette $8.97. RH/M-B (I).

Dramatized version of the book.

72 **The Bronze Bow**, by Elizabeth G. Speare. Houghton, 1961. 255p. $7.95 (I)

When the Romans brutally kill Daniel bar Jamin's father, the young Palestinian is consumed with desire for revenge. To help drive the Roman legions from the country, Daniel joins a band of outlaws, and the bronze bow of the Psalm of David becomes the symbol of resistance for Daniel and his friends. 1962 Newbery Medal winner.

72FS **The Bronze Bow**, Random House/Miller-Brody, 1978 (394-76934-1) 2 filmstrips 125, 107fr color with 2 cassettes 22, 19min $45. RH/M-B (I)

Filmstrip visuals are color illustrations based on Speare's descriptions. Retains the spirit of the original.

72R **The Bronze Bow**, by Elizabeth George Speare. Random House/Miller-Brody (39476931-7) record $8.97; (394-76932-5) cassette $8.97. RH/M-B (I)

Dramatized version of the book.

73 **Bruno Munari's ABC**, by Bruno Munari. Philomel, 1960. unp. $8.95; lib. ed. $8.99 net (N-P)

From an ant to a fly going "Zzzz," Bruno Munari takes children through a stunning graphic display of an imaginative alphabet that gives freshness and new dimensions to the ABCs.

73FS **Bruno Munari's ABC**, Weston Woods, n.d. (FS 50) 30fr color $12; (SF 50C) with cassette 10min $18. WW (N-P)

Illustrations from the book, accompanied by picture-cued text booklet.

74 **Bruno Munari's Zoo**, by Bruno Munari. Philomel, 1963. unp. $8.95; lib. ed. $8.91 net (P)

Brilliantly colored animals characterized by brief, witty statements.

74FS **Bruno Munari's Zoo**, Weston Woods, n.d. (FS 97) 25fr color $12; (SF 97C) with cassette $18. WW (P)

Illustrations from the book, accompanied by picture-cued text booklet.

75 **Bubble, Bubble**, by Mercer Mayer. Four Winds/Scholastic, 1973. lib. ed. $7.95 (P)

In this wordless story a little boy buys a Magic Bubble Maker and discovers that he can blow bubbles in the shape of everything from dragons to elephants.

75FS **Bubble, Bubble**, Weston Woods, 1975 (FS 171) 30fr color $12. WW (P-I)

Illustrations from the book.

76 **Bugs in Your Ears**, by Betty Bates. Holiday, 1977. $7.95 (I-U)

Carrie has difficulty adjusting to her new family because she dislikes the man her mother has married.

76F **A Family of Strangers**, Highgate Pictures, 1980, 16mm color 47min $625, $50. LCA (I)

Well-done adaptation with fine performances. Winner of two Emmy awards including Danny Aiello for Best Performer. Also available in an edited 31-minute version ($450, $40).

77 **The Bunyip of Berkeley's Creek**, by Jenny Wagner; illus. by Ron Brooks. Bradbury, 1977 (c1973). unp. $9.95 (P)

The Bunyip is an Australian folk-monster who lives at the bottom of deep water holes. Having crawled out of Berkeley's Creek, the Bunyip wants to know what he looks like; so he asks a platypus, a wallaby, and an emu. The Bunyip gets an unsettling response from all.

77FS **The Bunyip of Berkeley's Creek**, Weston Woods, 1977 (FS 224) 31fr color 9min $12; (SF 224C) with cassette $18. WW (P)

Tension-heightening sound effects and music evoke suspense. Brooks' intricate, imaginative illustrations are adapted for the filmstrip version.

Accompanied by picture-cued text booklet.

77R **The Bunyip of Berkeley's Creek**, Weston Woods, 1977 (LTR 224C) cassette only 9min $6. WW (N-P)

Pauline Brailsford narrates this light-hearted story.

78 **Caddie Woodlawn**, by Carol Ryrie Brink; illus. by Trina S. Hyman. Macmillan, 1973. 240p. $7.95; pap. $1.95 (I-U)

A New England tomboy has many adventures when her family moves to Wisconsin in the mid-nineteenth century. 1936 Newbery Medal winner.

78R/FS **Caddie Woodlawn**, Random House/Miller-Brody, 1969 (394-76943-0) record $8.97; (394-76944-9) cassette $8.97. RH/M-B (I-U)

A recorded dramatization narrated by Peter Fernandez. Featured in the cast are Jamie Fields as Caddie, Randy Gayness as Tom, and Bryce Bond as Warren. The musical background, arranged by Herb Davidson, is based on motifs of the tom-tom, rattle, and flute to accompany the voice. Includes teacher's guide. Also available: 394-76945-7: 2 filmstrips/record, $45; 394-76946-5: 2 filmstrips/cassette $45; 394-65804-3: 10 student activity booklets, $12.30.

79 **Call It Courage**, by Armstrong Sperry; illus. by the author. Macmillan, 1940. 95p. $7.95; pap. $1.50 (I-U)

Because he fears the ocean, a Polynesian boy is scorned by his people and must redeem himself by an act of courage. His lone journey to a sacred island and the dangers he faces there earn him the name Mafatu, "Stout Heart." 1941 Newbery Medal winner.

79FS **Call It Courage**, Random House/Miller-Brody, 1972 (394-76962-7) 2 filmstrips 195fr color 20:20min, 23:20min with cassette $45. RH/M-B (I-U)

Striking full-color paintings resembling Polynesian prints accompany the full sound track of the original recording. Artwork by Maggie MacGowen. Includes teacher's guide.

79R **Call It Courage**, Random House/Miller-Brody, 1969 (394-76959-7) record $8.97; (394-76960-0) cassette $8.97. RH/M-B (I-U)

A recorded dramatization narrated by Howard Ross, with the role of Mafatu played by Martin Fenton. Original background music by Herb Davidson is based on Polynesian motifs. Includes teacher's guide. Also available: 394-76961-7: 2 filmstrips/cassette, $45; 394-65805-1: 10 student activity booklets, $12.30.

80 **Caps for Sale**, by Esphyr Slobodkina. Addison-Wesley, 1947. unp. lib. ed. $6.95 net (N-P)

While a cap peddler is napping, monkeys steal his caps. How he gets them back makes a very funny story.

80F **Caps for Sale**, Morton Schindel, 1960 (9693) 16mm color 5:15min $115, $15; videocassette $115. WW (N-P)

Iconographic technique using illustrations from the book. Narrated by Owen Jordan. Music by Arthur Kleiner.

80FS **Caps for Sale**, Weston Woods, n.d. 34fr color 5:23min; (SF12C) with cassette $18. WW (N-P)

Illustrations from the book, accompanied by picture-cued text booklet.

80R **Caps for Sale**, Weston Woods, n.d. (LTR 012C) cassette 5:23min $6. WW (N-P)

Story narrated by Owen Jordan, with original background music by Arthur Kleiner.

81 **The Case of the Elevator Duck**, by Polly Berrien Berends; illus. by James K. Washburn. Random House, 1973. 54p. lib. ed. $5.99; Dell pap. $.95 (I)

Gilbert lives in a housing project which does not permit animals. He is adopted by a duck in the elevator and tries to find the owner before they are discovered by the police.

81F **The Case of the Elevator Duck**, Learning Corporation of America, 1974, 16mm color 17min $325, $30. LCA (P-I)

Live action by talented young black boy. Jazz music in background. Notable Children's Film, 1974.

82 **Casey at the Bat**, by Ernest Lawrence Thayer; illus. by Paul Frame. Prentice-Hall, 1964. unp. $4.95; pap. $1.50 (I)

A picture-book edition of the famous baseball poem interpreted in broadly humorous pictures in harmony with the burlesque tone of the situation.

82FS **Casey at the Bat**, Weston Woods, n.d. (FS 74) 30fr color $12; (SF74C) with cassette 5:14min $18. WW (P-I)

Illustrations from the book, accompanied by picture-cued text booklet.

82R **Casey at the Bat**, Weston Woods, n.d. (LTR 074C) cassette 5:14min $6. WW (P-I)

Story narrated by Owen Jordan, with original background music by Mary Lynn Twombly.

83 **The Cat in the Hat**, by Dr. Seuss. Random House, 1957. 61p. lib. ed. $3.95 net; $4.99 (N-P-I)

Imaginative cat dispels boredom for a brother and a sister on a rainy day while mother is away.

83F **The Cat in the Hat**, DePatie-Freleng Production, CBS, 1972, 16mm color 24min $480, $67. BFA (N-P-I)

Freely adapted version, narrated by Allan Sherman. Originally produced for CBS televsion.

84 **The Cat Who Went to Heaven**, by Elizabeth Coatsworth; illus. by Lynd Ward. Macmillan, 1958. 62p. $7.95; pap. $1.95 (I)

Watched by his little cat, Good Fortune, a Japanese artist paints a picture of the Buddha receiving homage from the animals. By tradition the cat should not be among them, but the artist risks his reputation by adding Good Fortune and is vindicated by a miracle. 1931 Newbery Medal winner.

84FS **The Cat Who Went to Heaven**, Random House/Miller-Brody, 1971 (NSF-3004C) 2 filmstrips 187fr color 12in 33rpm manual/automatic side 1:22:08min, side 2: 23:10min $24; (NAC-3004) cassette $28. RH/M-B (I)

Delicate illustrations in traditional Japanese style by Sanal Moorehead with the full sound track of the original recording. Includes teacher's guide.

84R/FS The Cat Who Went to Heaven, Random House/Miller-Brody, 1969 (394-76947-3) record $8.97; (394-76948-1) cassette $8.97. RH/M-B (I-U)

A recorded dramatization. Narrated by Esther Benson. Original background music by Herb Davidson is based on authentic modes, scales and sounds of Japanese music. Includes teacher's guide. Also available: 394-76949-X: 2 filmstrips/record, $45; (394-76950-3): 2 filmstrips/cassette, $45.

85 Changes, Changes, by Pat Hutchins. Macmillan, 1971. unp. $5.95; pap. $.95 (N-P)

A wordless picture book in which the meaning of change is illustrated by two wooden dolls constructing forms with wooden building blocks. The illustrations have an old-fashioned charm.

85F Changes, Changes, Morton Schindel, 1973 (154) 16mm color 6min $175, $20; videocassette $175; Super 8 $175. WW (P-I)

Animated film based on the book.

86 Chanticleer and the Fox, by Geoffrey Chaucer; adapted and illus. by Barbara Cooney. Crowell, 1958. unp. $6.95; lib. ed. $6.79 (P-I)

A prose version of "The Nun's Priest's Tale," distinguished by richly colored pictures with a medieval flavor. Caldecott Medal winner, 1959.

86FS Chanticleer and the Fox, Weston Woods, n.d. (FS 26) 47fr color $12; (SF26C) with cassette 9:45min $18. WW (P)

Illustrations from the book, accompanied by picture-cued text booklet.

86R Chanticleer and the Fox, Weston Woods, n.d. (LTR 026C) cassette 9:14min $6. WW (P)

Story narrated by Owen Jordan, with original background music by Arthur Kleiner.

87 Charlie Needs A Cloak, by Tomie de Paola. Prentice-Hall, 1974. $6.95 (P)

De Paola presents the facts of clothmaking in this amusing picture book. Charlie, the shepherd, and a mischievous black-faced sheep take the reader through the steps of shearing, carding, dyeing, spinning, weaving, and sewing.

87F Charlie Needs a Cloak, Morton Schindel, 1977, 16mm color 8min $150, $10. WW (P)

Gene Deitch adapted and animated the tale of Charlie the shepherd. An Italian tarentella enlivens the film. 1979 Notable Film for Children.

87FS Charlie Needs A Cloak, Weston Woods, 1977 (FS 167) 32fr color 6min $12; (SF 167C) with cassette $18. WW (P)

De Paola's delightful story is read with warmth, affection, and humor by Gene Deitch. The filmstrip version also utilizes background music to enhance the expressive illustrations from the book.

Accompanied by picture-cued text booklet.

87R Charlie Needs a Cloak, Weston Woods, 1977 (LTR167C) cassette 6min $6. WW (P)

Gene Deitch narrates this charming story.

88 Charlotte's Web, by E. B. White; pictures by Garth Williams. Harper, 1952. 184p. $7.64 lib. ed.; $7.89 net; pap. $1.95 (P-I)

A little girl who talks to animals and a spider who can both talk and write save the life of Wilbur the pig.

88F Charlotte's Web, Paramount, 1972, 16mm color 90min (rental only) $90. FI (P-I)

Paul Lynde and Agnes Moorehead are among the background voices in this animated version of the book.

88FS **Charlotte's Web**, Stephen Bosustow, Barr 1978 (#55599E) 18 filmstrips 18 cassettes color guides $299.50. Six sets sold separately, 3 filmstrips 3 cassettes 1 guide $58.50. BA (P-I)

This poignant story of friendship and other important facets of life is told in a series of 6 sets of filmstrips of superior quality.

88R **Charlotte's Web**, Pathways of Sound, 1970 (POS 1043) 25min each side 4 12in 33rpm $42.50. Also available on 10 cassettes $79.50. POS (P-I)

In the accents of a born storyteller, E. B. White reads aloud his beloved classic. The cassettes (manufactured by RCA under license from Pathways of Sound, Inc.) are programmed with one chapter to one side of each cassette.

89 **Chicken Soup with Rice: A Book of Months**, by Maurice Sendak. Harper, 1962. unp. lib. ed. $7.89 net (P)

"I told you once/ I told you twice/ All seasons of the year are nice/ For eating chicken soup with rice! "

89FS **Chicken Soup with Rice**, Weston Woods, 1976 (FS 223) 26fr color 5min $12; (SF223C) with cassette $18. WW (P)

Narrated by Maurice Sendak. Original music by H. D. Buch. Sound filmstrip adapted by C. B.Wismar. Artwork adapted by Stephanie Adam.

89R **Chicken Soup with Rice**, Weston Books, 1976 (LTR223C) cassette only 5min $6. WW (N-P)

Maurice Sendak narrates his lively work.

90 **A Child's Garden of Verses**, by Robert Louis Stevenson; illus. by Jessie Wilcox Smith. Scribner, 1905. 120p. $12.50 (P)

Old-fashioned illustrations in color and black and white capture the many moods of these poems for little children.

90F **A Child's Garden of Verses**, Wil Berg, 1967, 16mm color 10min color $165; videocassette $130. STE (P-I)

Seven poems are woven into a day in the life of a small-town boy. The action is pantomimed while the poems are being read. The setting is contemporary.

90R **A Child's Garden of Verses**, Caedmon, 1957 (TC 1077) 2s 12in 33rpm $7.98; (CDL 51077) cassette $7.98. CAE (P)

Judith Anderson's voice seems just right for these favorite verses.

91 **Chinese Mother Goose Rhymes**, sel. and ed. by Robert Wyndham; pictures by Ed Young. Philomel, 1968. unp. pap. $4.95 (P)

Traditional Chinese rhymes, riddles, and games, similar to Mother Goose. Designed to be read vertically like an oriental scroll, with the original Chinese version of the verses, in correct calligraphy, following lengthwise on the pages.

91R **Chinese Folk Tales, Legends, Proverbs and Rhymes**, CMS Records, 1970 (CMS 594) $8.98; (CMS-X4594) cassette $8.98. CMS (P-U)

Anne Pellowski, storyteller. Contents: "Two of Everything," Chinese Nursery Rhymes, "Mrs. Number Three," "The Sick-Bed Elves," "The Kitchen God," "Rich and Poor," "The Friend Who Failed," and Chinese Proverbs.

92 **A Christmas Carol**, by Charles Dickens; illus. by Arthur Rackham. Lippincott, 1966. 147p. $8.95 (I-U). OP

Illustrations with genuine nineteenth-century English flavor distinguish this edition of the well-loved story.

92F **A Christmas Carol**, CBS-TV, 1956, 16mm b/w 54min $600; videocassette $450. CAR (I-U)

Frederic March, Basil Rathbone, Ray Middleton, and Bob Sweeney star. Music sung by Roger Wagner Chorale. Adaptation and lyrics by Maxwell Anderson. Music by Bernard Herrmann.

92F **A Christmas Carol**, Dickensian Society, London, 1963 (1582) 16mm b/w 25min $290. COR (I-U)

Basil Rathbone stars. Filmed against authentic backgrounds with an English cast. Produced by Desmond Davis.

92FS **Christmas Carol**, Educational Enrichment Materials, 1974 (41060) color 4 filmstrips 4 cassettes or records $87 (individual FS with sound $24). EEM (P-I)

Adapted but true-to-original text; excellent sound effects and illustrations. Filmstrip titles: *Marley's Ghost* (42249), *The Ghost of Christmas Past* (42250), *The Ghost of Christmas Present* (42251), *The Ghost of Christmas Yet to Come* (42252).

92R **A Christmas Carol**, Caedmon, 1960 (TC 1135) 2s 12in 33rpm $8.98; (CDL 51135) cassette $8.98. CAE (I-U)

A dramatization done with restraint and good taste by Sir Ralph Richardson, Paul Scofield, and others.

93 **Christmas in Noisy Village**, by Astrid Lindgren; illus. by Ilon Vikland. Viking, 1964. unp. $3.95; lib. ed. $3.77 net. OP

The children of a small Swedish village share the excitement of preparing for Christmas.

93FS **Christmas in Noisy Village**, Viking, 1972 (90526-7) 32fr color 8:38min cassette $19.95. LOM (P)

Narrated by Mary Linda Phillips in a breathy, childlike manner. Illustrations from the book, accompanied by picture-cued text book. Chimes at the beginning and end of the tape add a pleasing touch. The vibrant illustrations are a visual delight.

94 **Christmas in the Stable**, by Astrid Lindgren; illus. by Harald Wilberg. Coward, 1962. lib. ed. $5.99; pap. text ed. (1979) $3.95 (P)

A mother tells the Christmas story to her little girl, who sees the events as if they were happening in the present.

94FS **Christmas in the Stable** and **The Tomten**, Weston Woods, n.d. (FS 66) 20fr and 19fr color $12; (SF 66 and SF66C) with cassette $18. WW (P)

Illustrations from the book, accompanied by picture-cued text booklet.

94R **Christmas in the Stable** and **The Tomten**, Weston Woods, n.d. (LTR 066C) cassette 6:42min $6. WW (P)

Story narrated by Owen Jordan, with original background music by Barry Galbraith.

95 **The Chronicles of Narnia: Book 6: The Magician's Nephew**, by C. S. Lewis; illus. by Pauline Baynes. Macmillan, 1964. pap. $1.95 (I)

Narnia's early history and its beginnings are revealed as it is born from the Lion's song of creation. The hills form and the grassy plains roll out as Aslan sings his beautiful haunting song.

95R **The Chronicles of Narnia: Book 6: The Magician's Nephew**. Caedmon (CP 1660) cassette $8.98; (TC 1660) 12in LP 59:09min $8.98. CAE (I)

Claire Bloom captures the haunting beauty of the story of the origins of Narnia.

96 **The Circus Baby**, by Maud and Miska Petersham. Macmillan, 1950. unp. $4.95; pap. $.95 (N-P)

A mother elephant tries to teach her baby to eat the way the baby clown does, with disastrous results.

96F **The Circus Baby**, Morton Schindel, 1956 (6572) 16mm color 4:45min $115; videocassette $115. WW (N-P)

Iconographic technique using illustrations from the book. Narrated by Owen Jordan. Music by Arthur Kleiner.

Also available in Spanish.

96FS **The Circus Baby**, Weston Woods, n.d. (FS 13) 35fr color $12; (SF13C) with cassette $18. WW (N-P)

Illustrations from the book, accompanied by picture-cued text booklet. Also available in Spanish.

96R **The Circus Baby**, Weston Woods, n.d. (LTR 013C) cassette 6min $6. WW (N-P)

Story narrated by Owen Jordan, with original background music by Arthur Kleiner.

Also available in Spanish.

97 **Clementine**, by Robert Quackenbush. Lippincott, 1974. unp. $8.95 (I)

In this fractured version of the California Gold Rush song, the ending is happy and the villain is forgiven. The artist has illustrated the tale of the miner's poor daughter in the manner of a vaudeville melodrama being performed in the 1880s, when the song became a national favorite.

97FS **Clementine**, Weston Woods, 1975 (FS 168) 40fr color $12; (SF 168C) with cassette only 9:40min $18. WW (I)

Illustrations from the book, accompanied by picture-cued text booklet. Narrated by H. D. Buck. Singing by Devin Terreson and Peter McCormick. Rendered in the melodramatic style of the early talkies, with chorus and a player piano. The viewers are invited to sing along as the words are flashed on the screen.

97R **Clementine**, Weston Woods, 1975 (LTR168C) cassette only 10min $6. WW (I)

H. D. Buch's melodramatic narration is enhanced by Devin Terreson's and Peter McCormick's rendition of this favorite old song.

98 **Clever Cooks; A Concoction of Stories, Charms, Recipes, and Riddles**, compiled by Ellin Greene; illus. by Tina S. Hyman. Lothrop, 1973. 160p. $7.92 lib. ed. net (I)

A collection of folktales about cooks. It includes "Clever Oonagh," an old Irish tale that tells how Fin MacCoul's wife outwitted the giant Cucullin.

98R **Irish Fairy Tales**, Caedmon, 1971 (TC 1349) 2s 12in 33rpm $8.98; (CDL 51349) cassette $7.95. CAE (I-U)

Includes "Cucullin and the Legend of Knockmany" (Clever Oonagh) 21:32min and "Guleesh" 29:04min. Read with vitality by Cyril Cusack.

99 **The Clown of God**, by Tomie de Paola. Harcourt, 1978. unp. $9.95 (P)

Tomie de Paola retells the legend about the poor and homeless juggler—Giovanni—who, in old age, returns to the city of his birth and takes refuge in a church on Christmas Eve. When the juggler offers the only gift that he has to the Holy Child, a miracle occurs.

99F **The Clown of God**, Morton Schindel, 1982, 16mm color 10min $175, $20. WW (P-I)

Lovely animated film using a voice-over narration. Sounds of flute, recorder, and strings provide an authentic Renaissance setting. A beautiful Christmas story.

99FS **The Clown of God**, Weston Woods, 1980 (FS 260) 53fr color 15min $12; (SF 260 C) with cassette $18. WW (P-I)

The filmstrip combines de Paola's magnificent, vibrant illustrations with so-

norous narration and a background of captivating Renaissance music.
ALA Notable Filmstrip.

99R **Clown of God**, Weston Woods, 1982 (LTR 260C) cassette only 15min $6. WW (P)

Appropriate period music and well-done narration help set the tone for this moving story.

100 **Come Back, Amelia Bedelia**, by Peggy Parish; illus. by Wallace Tripp. Harper, 1970. unp. $6.95; lib. ed. $7.89 net (P)

Another story about the literal-minded and popular heroine.

100FS **Come Back, Amelia Bedelia**, Educational Enrichment Materials, 1971 (72153) 54fr color 10min with 12in 33rpm or cassette $22. EEM (P)

Original illustrations accompanied by word-for-word reading of the text.

101 **The Complete Book of Dragons**, by E. Nesbit; illus. by Erik Blegvad. Macmillan, 1973. 198p. $5.95 (I)

Nine stories about dragons and the resourceful boys and girls who tame them.

101R **The Book of Dragons**, Caedmon, 1973 (TC 1427) 12in 33rpm side 1: 27:36min, side 2: 26:48min $8.98; (CDL 51427) cassette $8.98. CAE (I)

Dame Judith Anderson lends her rich, expressive voice to a word-for-word reading of "The Dragon Tamers" and "The Fiery Dragon."

102 **The Complete Fairy Tales of Oscar Wilde**, by Oscar Wilde; illus. by Charles Mozley. Bodley Head, 1960. 189p. $7.95 (I-U)

Stories from *The Happy Prince and Other Tales* and *A House of Pomegranates*.

102F **The Happy Prince**, Murray Shostak and Michael Mills, 1974, 16mm color 25min $395, $35; videocassette $275. PYR (P-U)

Animated, award-winning film. Vocal roles of the prince and the swallow by Christopher Plummer and Glynis Johns.

102FS **The Selfish Giant**, Society of Visual Education, 1965 (BB840-R or T) 43fr color 10min with 12in 33rpm manual/automatic $21; with cassette $21. SVE (P-I)

Adapted from the story of Oscar Wilde. Narrated by Donald Gallagher. Artwork by Gordon Laite.

102R **The Happy Prince and Other Oscar Wilde Fairy Tales**, Caedmon, 1956 (TC 1044) 2s 12in 33rpm $8.98; (CDL 51044) cassette $8.98. CAE (I-U)

Basil Rathbone reads three fairy tales by Oscar Wilde: "The Happy Prince," "The Selfish Giant," and "The Nightingale and the Rose."

102R **The Happy Prince and the Devoted Friend**, Folkways/Scholastic Records, 1963 (7731) 2s 12in 33rpm $7.95. FSR (U)

Claire Luce reads two stories by Oscar Wilde.

103 **Complete Nonsense of Edward Lear**, by Edward Lear; ed. by Lady Straebey. Dodd, 1962. 430p. $8.95 (P-I)

Contains all the original pictures and verses, together with new material.

103R **Edward Lear's Nonsense Stories and Poems**, Caedmon, 1970 (LP 1279) 2s 12in 33rpm $8.98; (CS 51279) cassette $8.98. CAE (P-I)

Read by Claire Bloom. Side 1: "The History of the Seven Families of the Lake Pipple-Popple" and "Incidents in the Life of My Uncle Arly." Side 2: "The Story of the Four Little Children Who Went around the World" and "The Quangle Wangle's

Hat." Includes a portfolio containing the complete text in large, easy-to-read type.

103R **Nonsense Verse**, Caedmon, 1957 (LP 1078) 2s 12in 33rpm $8.98; (CSS 1078) cassette $8.98. CAE (P-I)

Nonsense verse by Lewis Carroll and Edward Lear read by Beatrice Lillie, Cyril Ritchard and Stanley Holloway. Includes "Jabberwocky," "The Walrus and the Carpenter," "Father William," "Will You Walk A Little Faster," "The Jumblies," "The Owl and the Pussycat," and others.

104 **Complete Version of Ye Three Blind Mice**, by John W. Ivimey; illus. by Walton Corbould. Warne, 1979. $6.95 (P)

The original version of the popular round, complete with authentic old drawings that faithfully dramatize the adventures of the mice, their narrow escape, and the happy ending to it all.

104FS **Complete Version of Ye Three Blind Mice**, Weston Woods, n.d. (FS 60) 51fr color $12; (SF 60) with cassette 5:47min $18. WW (P)

Illustrations from the book, accompanied by picture-cued text booklet.

104R **Complete Version of Ye Three Blind Mice**, Weston Woods, n.d. (LTR 060C) cassette 5:47min $6. WW (P)

The old song, sung by a group of children.

105 **The Contest Kid and the Big Prize**, by Barbara B. Wallace; illus. by Gloria Kamen. Scholastic, 1978. pap. $1.50 (I-U)

When eleven-year-old Harvey wins a gentleman's gentleman for a month in a magazine promotion, he finds his life turned upside down.

105F **The Contest Kid**, Tom Armistead, 1978, 16mm color 24min $375. ABC (I-U)

Live action after school television special based on Barbara Wallace's *The Contest Kid and the Big Prize*. Slapstick and funny.

106 **The Cool Ride in the Sky**, by Diane Wolkstein; illus. by Paul Galdone. Knopf, 1973. unp. $6.99 (P-I)

Southern folktale in which a monkey forces a scheming buzzard to "straighten up and fly right." Includes words and music to song.

106FS **The Cool Ride in the Sky**, Miller-Brody, 1975, 53fr color 11:20min with cassette $18. RH/M-B (P-I)

Told by Diane Wolkstein. Based on the book. At the end of the story, the words to Nat King Cole's song are flashed on the screen and the children are invited to sing along.

107 **Corduroy**, by Don Freeman. Viking, 1968. 32p. lib. ed. $6.95 net; pap. $2.25 (N-P)

The loss of a button from his overalls proves to be just what is needed for a department-store teddy bear to realize his greatest wish—a real home.

107FS **Corduroy**, Live Oak Media, 1970 (90004-4) 34fr color 7in 33rpm manual/automatic 4:45min $19.95; cassette $19.95. LOM (N-P)

Illustrations from the book, accompanied by picture-cued text booklet. Narrated by Andrea Duda.

108 **Could Anything Be Worse?** by Marilyn Hirsh. Holiday, 1974. unp. lib. ed. $7.95 net (P-I)

An unhappy man complains about his family to the rabbi. His daughter is lazy, his wife scolds, the baby cries, the twins fight like a cat and dog, and the cat and dog fight too. Could anything be worse? Yes, as the poor man finds out when he follows the wise rabbi's advice. A Yiddish folktale.

108FS Could Anything Be Worse? Weston Woods, 1975 (FS 181) 33fr color 9:04min $12; (SF 181) with cassette only $18. WW (P-I)

Illustrations from the book, accompanied by picture-cued text booklet. Award-winning filmstrip.

108R Could Anything Be Worse? Weston Woods, 1975 (LTR 181C) cassette only 9:04min $6. WW (P-I)

Well-paced narration by Allen Swift using a Jewish dialect. Animal sound effects extend the hilarity of the telling.

109 The Courage of Sarah Noble, by Alice Dalgliesh; illus. by Leonard Weisgard. Scribner, 1954. 52p. $6.95 (P-I)

During the pioneer days of Connecticut, eight-year-old Sarah Noble and her father journey into the wilds to build a home.

109FS The Courage of Sarah Noble, Random House/Miller-Brody, 1980 (394-65701-2) 2 filmstrips 117, 93fr color 17, 16min with 2 cassettes. $45. RH/M-B (P-I)

Filmstrip version based on book. Utilizes an expressive musical background and appropriate, effective sound effects to enhance the presentation.

109R The Courage of Sarah Noble, by Alice Dalgliesh. Random House/Miller-Brody (394-76909-0) record $8.97; (394-76910-4) cassette $8.97. RH/M-B (P-I)

Simply told for beginning readers.

110 The Cow Who Fell in the Canal, by Phyllis Krasilovsky; illus. by Peter Spier. Doubleday, 1957. Available from Weston Woods (Hardback 62) $7.90 (P)

Hendrika, a cow who lived in Holland, sometimes got bored with just giving milk; but after she fell into the canal and floated down the river on a raft, she was never bored again.

110F The Cow Who Fell in the Canal, Morton Schindel, 1970, 16mm color 9min $140, $20; video cassette $140. WW (P-I)

Directed by Cynthia Freitag. Narrated by Owen Jordan. Photographed and edited by Cordelia Head. Music by Howard Rovics.

110FS The Cow Who Fell in the Canal, Weston Woods, n.d. (FS 62) 44fr color $12; (SF 62) with cassette 6:24min $18. WW (P)

Illustrations from the book, accompanied by picture-cued text booklet.

110R The Cow Who Fell in the Canal, Weston Woods, n.d. (LTR 062C) cassette 6:24min $6. WW (P)

Story narrated by Owen Jordan, with original background music by Barry Galbraith.

111 The Cow-tail Switch, and Other West African Stories, by Harold Courlander and George Herzog; drawings by Madye Lee Chastain. Holt, 1947. 143p. lib. ed. $3.27 net (I). OP

Folktales of the Ashanti people and other West African tribes, rich in humor and native wisdom.

111FS African Legends and Folktales, CCM Films, 1969 (95520) 6 filmstrips av 40fr color 10-20min each story with 2 12in 33rpm $54. CCM (P-U)

Narrated by Moses Gunn. Stories include: "The Tortoise's Secret," "The Fox Fools Anansi," "Why the Ashanti Raise Yams," "Anansi Fools the Elephant," "Why the Turtle Has a Hard Shell," and "The Talking Yam." Full-color artwork by Jason Studios. Includes teacher's guide.

111R Folk Tales from West Africa, Folkways/Scholastic Records, 1959 (7103) 2s 10in 33rpm $4.15. FSR (I-U)

Five stories read by Harold Courlander

from his book, *The Cow-tail Switch.* Includes: "The Cow-tail Switch," "Younde Goes to Town," "Talk," "Throw Mountains," and "Don't Shake Hands with Everyone."

112 **Crictor**, by Tomi Ungerer. Harper, 1958. 32p. $8.79 (P)

Madame Bodot's son sent her a boa constrictor for her birthday. She named the snake Crictor, and he became a great pet—learned, debonair and brave. Crictor also won the esteem and affection of the townspeople after a daring act of bravery.

112FS **Crictor**, Weston Woods, 1981 (FS 263) 30fr color 5min $12; (SF 263C) with cassette $18. WW (P)

Utilizes the engaging line drawings by Ungerer. Narration is accented by expressive music. Accompanied by picture-cued text booklet.

113 **Crimson Fairy Book**, collected and edited by Andrew Lang. illus. Dover, 1966. 371p. pap. $4 (I)

A collection of stories from all over the world. Includes "Little Wildrose."

113R **Little Wildrose and Other Andrew Lang Fairy Tales**, Caedmon, 1973 (LP 1382) 2s 12in 33rpm $8.98; (CSS 1382) cassette $8.98. CAE (P-I)

Elegantly read by Cathleen Nesbitt. Side 1: "Little Wildrose" (21:52min). Side 2: "Hairy Man" (9:40min) and "Trittle, Litill, and the Birds" (16.52min).

114 **Curious George Learns the Alphabet**, by H. A. Rey. Houghton, 1963. 72p. $7.95; pap. $2.45 (N-P)

When the man in the yellow hat decides to teach his little monkey the alphabet, everyone has fun. The author's ingenious device of drawing the letters right into the pictures makes a game of the lesson.

114FS **Curious George Learns the Alphabet**, Educational Enrichment Materials, 1977 (#51039C) 2 sound filmstrips 63, 51fr color 2 cassettes 10, 9min, full-color wall chart spirit masters $55. EEM (P)

Lively musical background to match the pictures illustrating each letter of the alphabet. Illustrations from the book.

114R **Curious George Learns the Alphabet**, Caedmon, 1972 (LP 1421) 2s 12in 33rpm $8.98; (CSS 1421) cassette $8.98. CAE (N-P)

Julie Harris reads the title story, *Curious George Flies a Kite* and *Curious George Goes to the Hospital.* With music and sound effects.

115 **Curious George Rides a Bike**, by H. A. Rey. Houghton, 1952. 45p. $6.95; pap. $1.95 (P)

George starts out on his bike to deliver papers and ends up as a circus performer.

115F **Curious George Rides a Bike**, Morton Schindel, 1958 (8044) 16mm color 10:20min $140, $20; videocassette $140; Super 8 $140. WW (P-I)

Narrated by Owen Jordan. Music by Arthur Kleiner. Iconographic technique using illustrations from the book.

Also available in Spanish.

115FS **Curious George Rides a Bike**, Weston Woods, n.d. (FS 17) 59fr color $12; with LTR cassette $18. WW (P)

Illustrations from the book, accompanied by picture-cued text booklet.

Also available in Spanish.

115FS **Curious George Series**, Educational Enrichment Materials, 1971 (71027) av 60fr color 7min 6 filmstrips 6 cassettes or discs $119 (individual FS with sound $22). EEM (P)

Filmstrip titles:
Curious George (72101)
Curious George Takes a Job (72102)
Curious George Gets a Medal (72103)

Curious George Goes to the Hospital (72104)
Curious George Flies a Kite, Part I (72105); Part II (72106)

Original illustrations accompanied by word-for-word reading of the text. Also available in bilingual (Spanish/English) version (40013 $209).

115R Curious George Rides a Bike, Weston Woods, n.d. (LTR 017C) cassette 10min $6. WW (P)

Story narrated by Owen Jordan, with background music by Arthur Kleiner.

Also available in Spanish.

116 Dandelion, by Don Freeman. Viking, 1964. 48p. lib. ed. $7.95; pap. $1.95 (N-P)

Vanity overcomes a lovable lion who reacts to an invitation to a "come-as-you-are" party by securing an outlandish wardrobe and turning himself into an unrecognizable fop.

116FS Dandelion, Live Oak Media, 1970 (90008-7) 46fr color 7in 33rpm manual/automatic 5:25min $19.95; cassette $19.95. LOM (N-P)

Illustrations from the book, accompanied by picture-cued text booklet. Narrated by Jim Campbell.

117 Danny and the Dinosaur, by Syd Hoff. Harper, 1958. 64p. $6.95; lib. ed. $7.89; pap. $1.95 (P)

A tall tale about a dinosaur who goes on a tour of the city with his young friend Danny.

117FS Danny and the Dinosaur, Weston Woods, n.d. (FS 67) 61fr color $12, 8:12min with cassette $18. WW (P)

Illustrations from the book, accompanied by picture-cued text booklet.

117R Danny and the Dinosaur, Weston Woods, n.d. (067C) cassette 8:12min $6. WW (P)

Story narrated by Owen Jordan, with original background music by Barry Galbraith.

118 A Dark, Dark Tale, by Ruth Brown. Dial, 1981. 32p. $9.95; lib. ed. $9.89 (N-P)

A series of dark, dark things cumulate in this ghostly picture book with a humorous surprise ending.

118R A Dark, Dark Tale, Weston Woods, 1981 (LTR 275C) cassette only 5min $6. WW (N-P)

Eerie music and spooky sound effects combine with a suspenseful narration to build the story to a dramatic climax. Narrated by Jan Thomson. Music composed by Ernest V. Troost.

119 The Dark Is Rising, by Susan Cooper; illus. by Alan Cober. McElderry/Atheneum, 1973. $9.95 (I)

Will Stanton is destined to become one of the Old Ones, immortal Keepers of the Light who struggle against the forces of evil. As Will journeys through time to fulfill his quest, the Dark strikes against those he loves through a relentless blizzard.

119R The Dark Is Rising, by Susan Cooper, Random House/Miller-Brody (394-76903-1) 2 records $17.94; (394-76904-X) 2 cassettes $17.94. RH/M-B (I)

A dramatized version of the book.

120 David and Dog, by Shirley Hughes. Prentice-Hall, 1978. unp. $8.95 (P)

A young boy is upset by the loss of his favorite stuffed dog. His sister makes a sacrifice to get his beloved toy back.

120FS David and Dog, Weston Woods, 1979 (FS 244) 43fr color 8min $12; (SF 244 C) with cassette $18. WW (P)

Clear, distinctive, contemporary illustrations from the book that reflect warmth, a light instrumental background that sets the mood, and expressive narration bring to life Hughes' tender story of young David, who misplaces his toy dog and becomes inconsolable.

Accompanied by picture-cued text booklet.

ALA Notable Filmstrip.

121 **Dinky Hocker Shoots Smack**, by M. E. Kerr. Harper, 1972. $9.95; lib. ed. $9.89 (U)

Dinky's mother is too involved with her work at a drug rehabilitation center to notice her overweight and unhappy daughter.

121F **Dinky Hocker**, Robert Guenette and Paul Asselin, 1978, 16mm color 30min $395. LCA (U)

Live-action television adaptation starring June Lockhart as the mother. Faithful, but sometimes oversimplified, script.

122 **Don't Forget the Bacon**, by Pat Hutchins. Greenwillow, 1976. 32p. $8.95; lib. ed. $7.92; 1978 Penguin pap. $1.95 (N-P)

A little boy is given a list of things to get at the store with an extra warning not to forget the bacon. On the way numerous distractions cause him to become a bit confused. A funny nonsense story with skillful word play.

122FS **Don't Forget the Bacon**, Imperial, 1980 (#X4KG 18101M) 33fr color 5min cassette $24. IER (N-P)

From the Prime Time Collection #2 (Westport Group), this sound filmstrip version brings additional dimensions to the pleasure of this fun-filled nonsense story.

123 **The Door in the Wall**, by Marguerite De Angeli. Doubleday, 1949. 120p. $6.95; lib. ed. $7.90; pap. $1.95 (I-U)

Robin, crippled son of a thirteenth-century English knight, fears he will never be able to prove his courage. How he overcomes his handicaps and wins his knighthood is an inspiring story, faithful to the period in text and beautiful illustrations. 1950 Newbery Medal winner.

123FS **The Door in the Wall**, Miller-Brody, 1972 (76979-1) 2 filmstrips 182fr color 20min each side 12in 33rpm manual $37.98; (76980-5) with cassette manual/automatic $37.98. RH/M-B (I-U)

Full-color illustrations by Mel Greifinger accompanied by the full sound track of the original recording. Includes teacher's guide.

123R **The Door in the Wall**, Miller-Brody, 1970 (76977-5) 2s 12in 33rpm approx. 20min each side $7.95; (76978-3) cassette $7.95. RH/M-B (I-U)

Dramatization by Elise Bell. Featured in this recording are Lloyd Moss as narrator, Scott Jacoby as Robin, Larry Robinson as Brother Luke, and Joseph Ragno as John-go-in-the-Wynd. For musical background, Herb Davidson has arranged "Summer Is Incumen In," a song which dates from the early fourteenth century. Includes teacher's guide.

124 **Dragonwings**, by Laurence Yep. Harper, 1975. 248p. $9.89 (I)

Yep tells the story of a talented Chinese immigrant and his son who, in the early 1900s, succeed in making their dream of building a flying machine come true.

124FS **Dragonwings**, Miller-Brody, 1977 (parts 1, 2) 1980 (parts 3, 4) (394-66217-2) 4 filmstrips 136, 125, 102, 149fr color 4 cassettes 20:39, 17:23, 15:35, 20:58min $90. RH/M-B (I)

Illustrations reflect Yep's descriptions and are accompanied by a background of Chinese music. Expressive narration.

124R **Dragonwings**, by Laurence Yep. Random House/Miller-Brody (394-76899-X) 2 records $17.94; (394-76900-7) 2 cassettes $17.94. RH/M-B (I)

125 **The Dream Keeper and Other Poems**, by Langston Hughes; illus. by Helen Sewell. Knopf, 1932. 77p. lib. ed. $5.69 (I-U)

The author's own selection of his poems.

125R **Dream Keeper**, Folkways/ Scholastic Records, 1955 (FC 7774) 2s 10in 33rpm $8.98. FSR (I-U)

The poet, Langston Hughes, reads from his book of the same name.

125R **The Poetry of Langston Hughes**, Caedmon, 1968 (LP 1272) 2s 12in 33rpm $8.98; (CSS 1272) cassette $8.98. CAE (U)

Ruby Dee and Ossie Davis read, with feeling, selected poems of Langston Hughes.

126 **Drummer Hoff**, adapted by Barbara Emberley; illus. by Ed Emberley. Prentice-Hall, 1967. lib. ed. $6.95; pap. $1.95 (P)

A cumulative folk rhyme about the hilariously rugged characters who participate in the building and firing of a cannon. Illustrated with arresting black woodcuts accented with brillant color. Caldecott Medal winner, 1968.

126F **Drummer Hoff**, Morton Schindel, 1969 (20054) 16mm color 5min $175, $20; videocassette $175; Super 8 $175. WW (P)

Adapted and directed by Gene Deitch. Narrated by John Cunningham. Animation by Bohuslav Sramek. Music by Tom Chirco.

Also available in Spanish.

126FS **Drummer Hoff**, Weston Woods, n.d. (FS 108) 34fr color $12; with cassette $18. WW (P)

Illustrations from the book, accompanied by picture-cued text booklet.

Also available in Spanish.

126R **Drummer Hoff**, Weston Woods, n.d. (LTR 108C) cassette 4min $6. WW (P)

Story narrated by John Cunningham. Also available in Spanish.

127 **Duffy and the Devil**, by Harve Zemach; pictures by Margot Zemach. Farrar, 1973. unp. $7.95 (I)

The Cornish version of Rumpelstiltskin illustrated with fanciful humor. Caldecott Medal winner, 1974.

127FS **Duffy and the Devil**, Miller-Brody, 1975 (76478-1) 78fr color part 1: 10min, part 2: 6:47min 2 cassettes $36. RH/M-B (P-I)

Based on the book. Fine narration by Tammy Grimes.

127R **Duffy and the Devil**, Miller-Brody, 1975 (76647-4) 1 cassette $7.95. RH/M-B (P-I)

Based on the book, with narration by Tammy Grimes.

128 **Early Moon**, by Carl Sandburg; illus. by James Daugherty. Harcourt, 1958. 136p. $9.95 (I-U)

This collection includes Sandburg's "Short Talk on Poetry."

128R **Poems for Children**, Caedmon, 1961 (TC 1124) 2s 12in 33rpm $6.98; (CDL 51124) cassette $7.95. CAE (I)

Carl Sandburg discusses what poetry is for children and reads his poems.

129 **East of the Sun and West of the Moon, and Other Tales**, by Peter Christen Asbjornsen and Jorgen E. Moe; illus. by Thom Vroman; afterword by Clifton Fadiman. Macmillan, 1963. 136p. lib. ed. $3.24 net (P-I). OP

Twelve of the best-loved folk and fairy tales of the Scandinavian countries. Includes "The Cat on the Dovrefell."

129R **Favorite Christmas Stories**, CMS

Records, 1971 (CMS X4629) cassette, $7.98; 2s 12in 33rpm $7.98. CMS (P-I)

Mary Strang tells five favorite Christmas stories: "The Tailor of Gloucester," "The Poor Count's Christmas," "The Cat on the Dovrefell," "The Jar of Rosemary," and "Wee Robin's Yule Song."

130 **The Easter Egg Artists**, by Adrienne Adams. Scribner, 1976. unp. $8.95 (P)

The Abbott rabbits—mother, father, and son, Orson—travel about painting designs on everything from houses to bridges to airplanes before returning home to decorate hundreds of Easter eggs.

130FS **The Easter Egg Artists**, Random House/Miller-Brody, 1979 (394-78399-9) 63fr color 9min with cassette $21. RH/M-B (P)

The filmstrip version utilizes Adams' charming watercolor illustrations.

130R **The Easter Egg Artists**, by Adrienne Adams. Random House/Miller-Brody (394-07877-2) read-along cassette with hardcover book $16.98. RH/M-B (P)

Read-along version about the Abbott rabbits.

131 **Emil and the Detectives**, by Erich Kastner; illus. by Walter Trier. Doubleday, 1930. 224p. $5.95 (I)

Emil and his friends identify and catch a thief by a very simple trick.

131F **Emil and the Detectives**, Buena Vista, 1964, 16mm color 98min $27.50 (rental only). DISN (I) No longer available through Disney.

Walter Slezak, Bryan Russell, and Roger Mobley star.

132 **The Emperor and the Kite**, by Jane Yolen; illus. by Ed Young. Collins, 1968. unp. lib. ed. $6.99 (N-P)

The retelling of an old Chinese story about the little princess ignored by her big brothers who, when the Emperor was imprisoned in a tower, rescued him by a rope tied to her kite. A Notable Children's Book and Caldecott Honor Book.

132FS **Emperor and the Kite**, Listening Library 1976 (Look, Listen and Read JFS 151) 49fr color av 8min 2 filmstrips 2 cassettes 1 guide $21. LL (N-P)

The slow pace of the telling, the appropriate music, and the outstanding art work make this a suiable purchase for story hours or individual viewing.

133 **Encyclopedia Brown, Boy Detective**, by Donald J. Sobol; illus. by Leonard Shortall. Elsevier-Nelson, 1963. 88p. $5.95 (I)

Leroy "Encyclopedia" Brown earns his nickname by applying his encyclopedic learning to solving community mysteries.

133FS **Encyclopedia Brown, Boy Detective** from **The Best of Encyclopedia Brown** filmstrip series, Random House/Miller-Brody, 1977 (39476673-3) 4 filmstrips 46, 41, 46, 54fr color 4 cassettes 7:55, 6:45, 7:35, 7:30min $84. RH/M-B (I)

Two chapters from this book—"The Case of Natty Nat" and "The Case of the Scattered Cards"—have been adapted to the filmstrip medium. Pleasingly colorful drawings, animated narration, and lighthearted original music unravel the mysteries then pause to allow time for viewers to formulate their own conclusions.

Filmstrip series also includes "The Case of the Hungry Hitchhiker" from *Encyclopedia Brown and the Case of the Secret Pitch* and "The Case of the Whistling Ghost" from *Encyclopedia Brown Gets His Man.*

134 **English Fables and Fairy Stories**, retold by James Reeves; illus. by Joan Kiddell-Monroe. Oxford Univ. Pr., 1954. 234p. $10.95 (I-U)

These lively retellings of old favorites such as "Jack and the Beanstalk" and "Dick

Whittington and His Cat" will appeal to children.

134R **Dick Whittington and His Cat, and Other English Fairy Tales**, Caedmon, 1969 (LP 1265) 12in 33rpm side 1: 30:44min, side 2: 29:10min $8.98; (CSS 1265) cassette $8.98. CAE (P-I)

Claire Bloom reads four familiar English folktales, as retold by James Reeves. The stories are "Dick Whittington and His Cat," "Tom Tit Tot," "Tattercoats," and "Simpleton Peter."

135 **English Fairy Tales**, by Joseph Jacobs; illus. by John D. Batten. Dover, 1898. 261p. pap. $3.50 (I)

Forty-three stories retold in colloquial conversational style. Includes familiar nursery tales as well as some lesser-known ones.

135R **English Folk and Fairy Tales**, CMS Records, 1966 (CMS 504) 2s 12in 33rpm $7.98. CMS (I)

Told by Anne Pellowski from the Joseph Jacobs collections, *English Folk and Fairy Tales* and *More English Folk and Fairy Tales*. Includes "Tom Tit Tot," "Cap O'Rushes," "Jack Hannaford," "Mr. Miacca," "The Old Witch," "Molly Whuppie," and "Master of All Masters."

135R **The Three Little Pigs, and Other Fairy Tales**, Caedmon, 1962 (LP 1129) 2s 12in 33rpm $8.98; (CSS1129) cassette $8.98. CAE (P)

Read by Boris Karloff. Includes: "Jack and the Beanstalk," "The Three Sillies," "Hereafterthis," "The Old Woman and Her Pig," "Henny Penny," "The Three Little Pigs," "King of the Cats," and "The Three Bears."

136 **Evan's Corner**, by Eizabeth Starr Hill; illus. by Nancy Grossman. Holt, 1967. unp. $6.95; pap. $1.45 (P-I)

Evan, one of a family of eight living in a two-room flat, wants a place of his own. When his wise mother assigns him a corner, he at first enjoys arranging it just for himself, but eventually finds that it is more fun to help his little brother with his corner.

136F **Evan's Corner**, Stephen Bosustow, 1969 (10719) 16mm color 24min $450, $63. BFA (P-I)

Live action, warmly and delightfully performed.

137 **Fables**, by Arnold Lobel. Harper, 1980. $8.79 (P-I)

A collection of 20 twentieth-century fables richly illustrated by Lobel. Caldecott Medal winner, 1981.

137FS **Fables**, Random House/Miller-Brody, 1981 (394-07703-2) 135fr color 17min with cassette $21. RH/M-B (P-I)

Seven of Lobel's 20 fables are used in the filmstrip. Lobel's illustrations were enlarged and used as the visuals. Original music by composer Arthur Custer adds to the characterizations.

137R **Fables**, written and illustrated by Arnold Lobel. Random House/ Miller-Brody (0-394-0766-4) cassette side 1: 21:10min, side 2: 20:48min $8.97; (394-07665-6) cassette with hardcover book $18. RH/M-B (P-I)

Arnold Lobel reads his own *Fables* in a clear and understated manner. The subtle irony of each is signalled as Lobel reads the unexpected morals.

This read-along version contains instructions to the listener about the title page; a bell tinkles when it is time to turn the page. Original score.

138 **The Fairy Tale Treasury**, sel. by Virginia Haviland; illus. by Raymond Briggs. Coward, 1972. 192p. lib. ed. $8.49 (N-I)

Thirty-two well-loved tales illustrated with gusto. Sources of the stories are given. A true treasure.

138R **Goldilocks and the Three Bears and Other Stories**, Caedmon, 1972 (LP 1392) 2s 12in 33rpm $8.98; (CSS 1392) cassette $8.98. CAE (P)

Side 1: the title story (7:25min) and "Little One-Eye, Little Two-Eyes and Little Three-Eyes" (16:38min). Side 2: "The Brave Little Tailor" (15:39min) and "The Babes in the Wood" (6:56min). Read by Claire Bloom.

139 **Fairy Tales**, by Hans Christian Andersen; ed. by Svend Larsen; tr. from the original Danish text by R. P. Keigwin; illus. by Vilhelm Pedersen and Lorenz Frolich. World, 1965. 4v. $10.80 (I). OP

Eva Le Gallienne's sensitive translation of Andersen's "The Little Mermaid" has charming full-color illustrations by Edward Frascino (Harper, 1971). This is the translation preferred by the Danes.

139R **The Little Mermaid**, Caedmon, 1967 (LP 1230) 2s 12in 33rpm $8.98; (CSS 1230) cassette $8.98. CAE (I)

Cathleen Nesbitt reads the Keigwin translation. A sensitive reading which is undisturbed by extraneous sound effects.

140 **The Family under the Bridge**, by Natalie S. Carlson; illus. by Garth Williams. Harper, 1958. 99p. $9.89 (I)

Old Armand, a Parisian hobo, enjoyed his solitary, carefree life until one day he found three homeless children sheltered under the bridge he claimed.

140FS **The Family under the Bridge**, Miller-Brody, 1978 (394-76989-9) 2 filmstrips 131, 129fr color with 12in 33rpm $45; (394-76990-2) with 2 cassettes 19:35, 19:23min $45. RH/M-B (I)

Carlson's book is followed closely in the filmstrip adaptation with visuals of exceptional brightness and clarity and narration that has good fidelity and balance.

140R **The Family under the Bridge**, by Natalie Savage Carlson. Random House/Miller-Brody (394-76987-2) record $8.97; (394-76988-0) cassette $8.97. RH/M-B (I)

Old man played by Bill Griffis.

141 **Farmer Palmer's Wagon Ride**, by William Steig. Farrar, 1974. 32p. $11.95 (P)

Farmer Palmer, a pig, and his hired hand, Ebenezer, a donkey, set out for town to sell vegetables and buy gifts for the pig family. The return trip becomes a series of adventures and misadventures and the pig and donkey must call upon both brain and brawn to get home in one piece.

141FS **Farmer Palmer's Wagon Ride**, Random House/Miller-Brody, 1976 (394-76481-1) 2 filmstrips 47, 50fr color 7:51, 8:12min with 2 cassettes $42. RH/M-B (P)

ALA Notable Filmstrip. The comedy of Steig's book is intensified through the skillful reproduction of his illustrations, low-key narration, and fitting background music. Guide.

141R **Farmer Palmer's Wagon Ride**, by William Steig, Random House/Miller-Brody (394-07637-0) read-along cassette with hardcover book $16.50. RH/M-B (P)

Narrated by Jack Gilford.

142 **A Father like That**, by Charlotte Zolotow; illus. by Ben Shecter. Harper, 1971. unp. $7.95; lib. ed. $7.89 (N-P)

A small boy imagines all the things he would do during the day if he had a father. Though fatherless, he has some good and often humorous ideas about the perfect father.

142FS **A Father like That**, Listening Library, n.d. color 1 filmstrip 1 cassette $18. LL (N-P)

Charlotte Zolotow's book about the

imagined relationship between a fatherless boy and the father he never knew.

143 **Fifth Chinese Daughter**, by Jade Snow Wong; illus. by Kathryn Uhl. Harper, 1950. lib. ed. $9.87 (U)

Autobiography of the fifth daughter of a conservative Chinese family living in San Francisco's Chinatown.

143F **Jade Snow Wong**, Ron Finley, 1978, 16mm color 28min $400, $35. FI (U)

Live-action adaptation of the autobiography *Fifth Chinese Daughter* which follows Jade's life from age 7 to adulthood. An interesting study in cultural differences between generations.

144 **Finders Keepers**, by Will and Nicolas. Harcourt, 1951. unp. $6.50 (P)

Two quarrelsome dogs join forces to fight off a common enemy. Caldecott Medal winner, 1952.

144FS **Finders Keepers**, Weston Woods, n.d. (FS 27) 41fr color $12; with cassette 6:50min $18. WW (P)

Illustrations from the book, accompanied by picture-cued text booklet.

144R **Finders Keepers**, Weston Woods, n.d. (LTR 027C) cassette 6:50min $6. WW (P)

Story narrated by Owen Jordan, with original background music by Arthur Kleiner.

145 **The Fir Tree**, by Hans Christian Andersen; tr. by H. W. Dulcken; illus. by Nancy Ekholm Burkert. Harper, 1970. 36p. $8.95; lib. ed. $8.79 (P-I)

Delicate drawings and brilliantly colored paintings bring new life to the poignant story of the fir tree who longed for something greater in life than the simple forest around him.

145FS **The Fir Tree**, Live Oak Media 1978 (0-670-90574-7) 72fr color 25min 1 filmstrip 1 cassette $19.95. LOM (I)

Warmth and feeling in this Andersen fairy tale achieved through illustrations by Danish artist, Svend Otto, who paid careful attention to details in each drawing.

145R **Fairy Tales for a Winter's Night**, CMS Records, 1968 (CMS 534) 2s 12in 33rpm $7.98; (CMS-X4534) cassette, $7.98. CMS (I)

Mary Strang tells Andersen's "The Fir Tree" and "The Little Match Girl," Grimm's "The Elves and the Shoemaker," and Moore's " 'Twas the Night before Christmas."

146 **The Fire Stealer**, by William Toye; illus. by Elizabeth Cleaver. Oxford Univ. Pr., 1979. unp. $6.95 (P-I)

Nanabozho uses his magic to change shape. He is thereby able to steal fire and bring it home to make his grandmother's last years more comfortable. In this way, his people learn to use fire, while alert to its dangerous quality. The story, too, explains the bright colors of fall foliage.

146FS **The Fire Stealer**, Weston Woods, 1980 (FS 259) 33fr color 9min $12; (SF 259C) with cassette $18. WW (P-I)

Cleaver's brilliant illustrations from the book are enhanced by dramatic narration and recorders and drums that add subtle background atmosphere to this American Indian explanation of autumn's fiery burst of color.

Accompanied by picture-cued text booklet.

147 **The Fisherman and His Wife by The Brothers Grimm**; tr. by Elizabeth Shub; illus. by Monika Laingruber. Greenwillow, 1979. unp. $9.50 (I)

The greedy wife of a poor fishermen won't give him any peace until he returns time and again to make a wish of the enchanted fish he had caught and returned to the sea.

147F The Fisherman and His Wife, Minimal Produkter, Stockholm, 1970 (21379) 16mm color 20min $275; videocassette $275. WW (P-I)

Narrated by Eugene Kern. Music by Leo Rosenbluth. Striking effects have been achieved by filming hand-manipulated puppets in silhouette against transparent backgrounds taken from old copperplate engravings and architectural drawings. The treatment makes this version suitable for older children.

148 The Five Chinese Brothers, by Claire Hutchet Bishop and Kurt Wiese. Coward, 1938. unp. $5.95 (P)

Five identical-looking brothers outwit the townspeople and save themselves from a tragic end.

148F The Five Chinese Brothers, Morton Schindel, 1958 (8042) 16mm color 10:35min $140, $20; videocassette $140; Super 8 $140. WW (P)

Iconographic technique using the illustrations from the book. Narrated by Owen Jordan. Music by Arthur Kleiner.

Also available in Spanish.

148FS The Five Chinese Brothers, Weston Woods, n.d. (FS 18) 57fr color $12; with cassette 10:22min $18. WW (P)

Illustrations from the book, accompanied by picture-cued text booklet.

Also available in Spanish.

148R The Five Chinese Brothers, Weston Woods, n.d. (LTR 018C) cassette 10:22min $6. WW (P)

Story narrated by Owen Jordan, with original background music by Arthur Kleiner.

Also available in Spanish.

149 The Fool of the World and the Flying Ship, by Arthur Ransome; illus. by Uri Shulevitz. Farrar, 1968. unp. $7.95 (P-I)

The Fool of the World was the third and youngest son of parents who thought little of him. When the Czar announced that his daughter would marry the hero who could bring him a flying ship, the Fool went looking and found one. He then had to outwit the treacherous Czar, which he did with the help of eight peasants who had magical powers. Caldecott Medal winner, 1969.

149FS The Fool of the World and the Flying Ship, Weston Woods, 1979 (FS 249) 56fr color 14min $12; (SF 249C) with cassette $18. WW (P-I)

The exquisite illustrations of Uri Shulevitz are utilized in this sound filmstrip adaptation of the Caldecott Medal inning book. The delicate notes of a balalaika, appropriate sound effects, and gentle-voiced, sympathetic reader enhance the presentation of this Russian folktale.

Accompanied by picture-cued text booklet.

149R The Fool of the World and the Flying Ship, Weston Woods, 19?? (LTR 249C) cassette only 14min $6. WW (P)

Lively balalaika music accompanies this good narration of the story.

150 The Foolish Frog, by Pete Seeger and Charles Seeger; illus. by Miloslav Jagr. Macmillan, 1973. $4.95 (N-I)

Song about a frog who puffs up with pride until he bursts and nothing is left of him but the song. Book adapted and designed from the film.

150F The Foolish Frog, Firebird Films, 1971, 16mm color 8min $175, $20; videocassette $175. WW (N-U)

Brightly colored animated drawings accompanied by Pete Seeger's lively guitar and engaging singing. Award-winning film.

150FS The Foolish Frog, Weston Woods, 1974 (FS 149) 40fr color 8:50min $12; (SF 149C) with cassette $18. WW (N-I)

Illustrations from the book, accompanied by picture-cued text booklet.

150R The Foolish Frog, Weston Woods, 1974 (LTR 149C) cassette $6. WW (N-I)

Foot-stomping music sung by Pete Seeger with guitar accompaniment.

151 Forever Free, by Joy Adamson. Harcourt, 1962. 179p. $9.50 (U)

The successor to *Born Free* and *Living Free* tells the story of how the Adamsons were forced by the authorities to remove Elsa from the district and how she dies, leaving the cubs to be resettled on a game preserve in Tanganyika.

151F The Orphan Lions, Learning Corp. of America, 1973, 16mm color 17min $300, $30. LCA (I-U)

Live action combined with beautiful nature photography. Documents the Adamsons' concern with the survival of Elsa's three cubs after her early death.

152 The Four Little Children Who Went around the World, by Edward Lear; pictures by Arnold Lobel. Macmillan, 1968. 44p. $3.95 (P)

The incredible adventures of four young travelers, a cat, and a Quangle Wangle. Delicious nonsense.

152R Edward Lear's Nonsense Stories and Poems, Caedmon, 1970 (LP 1279) 2s 12in 33rpm $8.98; (CSS 1279) cassette $8.98. CAE (P-I)

Read by Claire Bloom. Side 1: "The History of the Seven Families of the Lake Pipple-Popple" and "Incidents in the Life of My Uncle Arly." Side 2: "The Story of the Four Little Children Who Went around the World" and "The Quangle Wangle's Hat." Includes a portfolio containing the complete text in large, easy-to-read type.

153 Fourteen Rats and a Rat Catcher, by James Cressey; illus. by Tamasin Cole. Prentice-Hall, 1976. unp. lib. ed. $6.95 (P)

The little old lady tried everything to get rid of the rats in her house, but to no avail until she called in the rat catcher himself. His solution pleases everyone, including the rats.

153R Fourteen Rats and a Rat Catcher, Weston Woods, 1979 (LTR 243C) cassette only 6min $6. WW (P)

Roderick Cole's English accent adds charm to his narration and H. D. Buch's piano music reminiscent of early movie music adds drama to this pleasant story.

154 The Fox Went Out on a Chilly Night: An Old Song; illus. by Peter Spier. Doubleday, 1961. unp. $6.95; lib. ed. $7.90; pap. $1.49 (P)

Myriad details of the New England countryside are included in the illustrations of this story of the fox who raided the farmer's poultry yard and escaped his wrath on the way home to Mrs. Fox and the babies. Includes music.

154F The Fox Went Out on a Chilly Night, Morton Schindel, 1968, 8min $140, $20; videocassette $140; Super 8 $140. WW (P)

Iconographic techniques using illustrations from the book. Photography and editing by Garry Sutcliffe.

154FS The Fox Went Out on a Chilly Night, Weston Woods, n.d. (FS 58) 41fr color $12; (SF58C) with cassette 8min $18. WW (P)

Illustrations from the book, accompanied by picture-cued text booklet.

154R The Fox Went Out on a Chilly Night, Weston Woods, n.d. (LTR 058C) cassette 8min $6. WW (P)

An old folk song sung by Molly Scott.

155 Freckle Juice, by Judy Blume; illus. by Sonia O. Lisker. Four Winds/Scholastic, 1971 (P-I)

Nicky's freckles cover his face, ears, and the back of his neck. Andrew has no freckles, but wants them. Know-it-all Sharon prepares a freckle juice recipe, sells it to Andrew for 50 cents, and starts a fun-packed escapade.

155R **Freckle Juice**, Listening Library (AFTR 64) cassette with 4 paperback books and teacher's guide 31min $16.95. LL (P-I)

A read-along version of the hilarious story.

156 **Free to Be . . . You and Me**, conceived by Marlo Thomas; developed and ed. by Carole Hart. McGraw-Hill, 1974. 143p. $4.95 (P-I). OP

Based on the record, with several added sections. An attempt to help children to discover equality between the sexes with humorous skits, poems, and songs.

156F **Free to Be . . . You and Me**, by Marlo Thomas and Carole Hart. McGraw-Hill, 1974, 16mm color 42min $695, $55. MH (P-I)

Live action combined with imaginative animation. Alan Alda, Harry Belafonte, and many others, in songs and skits. Divided into three sections: "Friendship and Cooperation," "Expectations," "Independence." Each available separately (16min $275, $25; 14min, $235, $25; 17min, $295, $25). Complete videocassette $525.

156R **Free to Be . . . You and Me**, by Carole Hart. Arista Records, 1972 (#4003) 2s 12in 33rpm 44:26min $7.98. ARI (N-I)

Nonsexist songs, stories, and poems performed by celebrities.

157 **Freight Train**, by Donald Crews. Greenwillow, 1978. unp. $7.95 (P)

With a minimum of descriptive words, Crews has drawn a stylized freight train passing by, slowly at first, then becoming a blur of black and bright color.

157FS **Freight Train**, Westport Communications Group, dist. by Educational Enrichment Materials, 1980 (#52289) 65fr color 5:10min with cassette $22. EEM (P)

The 1979 Caldecott Honor Book by Crews is brought vividly to life in this faithful filmstrip adaptation. As children chug along with a freight train, they learn the names and colors of the freight cars. With expressive illustrations and outstanding sound effects, this presentation is a delightful introduction to railroad transportation and to the colors in the spectrum.

158 **Frog and Toad Are Friends**, by Arnold Lobel. Harper, 1970. 65p. $7.89 (P)

Frog and Toad are best friends. They are almost always together—and some of their adventures are recounted in five funny, delightful stories. (1) "Spring": When spring comes, Frog goes to Toad's house to wake him. Tired Toad refuses to get up until "half past May," but Frog figures out a way to trick his friend out of bed. (2) "The Story": Frog is sick and asks Toad to tell him a story. But Toad has such trouble trying to think of one that finally it is Frog who tells a special tale. (3) "A Lost Button": Toad loses a button, so the two friends hunt for it. They find some interesting things, but where on earth is that button? (4) "A Swim": When Toad goes swimming, the other animals discover something very, very amusing. (5) "The Letter": Toad is sad because he never gets any mail. Frog tries to help, and together they wait for a letter that is supposed to come.

158FS **Frog and Toad Are Friends**, Random House/Miller-Brody, 1976 (394-76747-0) 5 filmstrips: *Spring* (39fr, 5:40min) *The Story* (43fr, 6:07min) *A Lost Button* (38fr, 5:32min) *A Swim* (41fr, 5:40min) *The Letter* (40fr, 5:58min) with 5 10in 33-1/3rpm records; (394-76749-7) with 5 cassettes $105. RH/M-B (P)

Filmstrip presentation is faithful to the original book. Lobel's illustrations are enhanced by a lively musical background. Lynn Ahrens performs the original song "You Are My Kind of Friend."

159 **Frog and Toad Together**, by Arnold Lobel. Harper, 1972. $7.95 (P)

Lobel presents five humorous stories about two inseparable friends—Frog and Toad. (1) "A List": Toad makes a list of things to do for the day, and he loses it. Frog keeps him company. (2) "The Garden": Frog gives some flower seeds to Toad, who plants them. Then Toad tries some unusual methods to make the seeds grow. (3) "Cookies": Toad bakes some delicious cookies. He and Frog eat until they are stuffed—and then they eat some more. (4) "Dragons and Giants": Frog and Toad decide to test their bravery and meet up with some scary adventures. (5) "The Dream": Toad dreams that he is on a big stage performing great feats of skill. Frog sits in the audience.

159FS **Frog and Toad Together**, Random House/Miller-Brody, 1976 (394-76746-2) 5 filmstrips: *A List* (54fr, 7min) *The Garden* (33fr, 5min) *Cookies* (36fr 5min) *Dragons and Giants* (36fr, 5min) *The Dream* (40fr, 6min) with 5 10in records 33-1/3rpm; (394-76748-9) with 5 cassettes $105. RH/M-B (P)

Filmstrip presentation is faithful to the original book. Lobel's illustrations are enhanced by a lively musical background. The catchy song "It's More Fun" is performed.

160 **Frog Goes to Dinner**, by Mercer Mayer. Dial, 1974. 32p. $4.58 (P)
Frog on His Own, by Mercer Mayer. Dial, 1980. 32p. Pied Piper Books, pap. $1.95 (P)
Frog, Where Are You? by Mercer Mayer. Dial, 1969. $3.95; lib. ed. $3.69; Dial, 1980. Pied Piper Books, reprint, pap. $1.75 (P)
A Boy, A Dog, and A Frog, by Mercer Mayer. Dial 1967. unp. $6.95; Dial, 1979. Pied Piper Books, pap. $1.75 (P)
A Boy, A Dog, A Frog, and A Friend, by Mercer and Marianne Mayer. Dial, 1971. $4.50; lib. ed. $4.17 (P)

Humorous illustrations, not words, tell these stories of a small boy and his pets.

160FS **Fabulous Frog Stories**, Educational Enrichment Materials, n.d. (71045) color 5 silent filmstrips guide $50 (individual FS $11). EEM (P)
Individual titles: *Frog Goes to Dinner* (72171); *Frog on His Own* (72172); *A Boy, A Dog, A Frog, and A Friend* (72173); *Frog, Where Are You?* (72108); *A Boy, A Dog, and A Frog* (72107)

These humorous adventures of a fun-loving frog delight young and old. Filmstrips from the wordless picture books by Mercer Mayer.

161 **Frog Went A-Courtin'**, retold by John Langstaff; with pictures by Feodor Rojankovsky. Harcourt, 1955. unp. $6.50; pap. $1.95 (P)

A composite version of the old Scottish ballad, illustrated with large, lively pictures. Includes music. Caldecott Medal winner, 1956.

161F **A Froggie Went A-Courtin'**, Frank Gladstone, 1978, 16mm color 4min $125. LUC (P)

Animated version of the popular folk song with catchy country music.

161F **Frog Went A-Courtin'**, Morton Schindel, 1961 (10916) 16mm color 11:55min $175, $25; videocassette $175. WW (P)

Iconographic technique using illustrations from the book. Sung by John Langstaff. Music by Arthur Kleiner.

161FS **Frog Went A-Courtin'**, Weston

Woods, n.d. (FS 28) 35fr color $12; with cassette $18. WW (P)

Illustrations from the book, accompanied by picture-cued text booklet.

161R **Frog Went A-Courtin'**, Weston Woods, n.d. (LTR 028C) cassette 13min $6. WW (P)

Sung by John Langstaff. Music by Arthur Kleiner.

162 **From the Mixed-Up Files of Mrs. Basil E. Frankweiler**, by E. L. Konigsburg. Atheneum, 1967. 168p. $7.95; pap. $1.95 (I)

Two New York children run away from home and spend a week in the Metropolitan Museum of Art, where a beautiful statue starts them on the trail of a mystery. 1968 Newbery Medal winner.

162F **From the Mixed-Up Files of Mrs. Basil E. Frankweiler**, Westfall, 1978, 16mm color 30min $590, $83. BFA (I-U)

An edited version of the feature film starring Ingrid Bergman as Mrs. Frankweiler. Authentically filmed in the Metropolitan Museum of Art.

162FS **From the Mixed-Up Files of Mrs. Basil E. Frankweiler**, Pied Piper (First Choice: Authors and Books), 1980, 2 filmstrips 72, 82fr color with 2 cassettes (interview cassette 8min; filmstrip cassette 26min) $37.50. PP (I)

The filmstrip adaptation retains the suspense, humor, and strong characterizations of the original. Electronic music is tastefully and sparingly used to heighten the mischievousness, the mystery, and the other moods developed in this story.

162R **From the Mixed-up Files of Mrs. Basil E. Frankweiler**, Miller-Brody, 1969 (394-76985-6) 12in 33rpm side 1: 24:20min, side 2: 24:30min $8.97; (394-76986-4) cassette $8.97. RH/M-B (I-U)

A recorded dramatization. Featured in this recording are Gretchin Kanne as Mrs. Frankweiler, Peter Fernandez as Saxonberg, Bryce Moss as Jamie, and Katie McMahon as Claudia. Original music by Herb Davidson. Includes teacher's guide.

163 **The Funny Little Woman**, retold by Arlene Mosel; pictures by Blair Lent. Dutton, 1972. 40p. lib. ed. $8.95; pap. $1.95 (P)

A Japanese folktale about a woman who likes to laugh and to make dumplings. When she is caught by the wicked "oni," her wits and good humor help her escape. Caldecott Medal winner, 1973.

163FS **The Funny Little Woman**, Weston Woods, 1973 (FS 162) 38fr color 9min $12; (SF 162C) with cassette $18.00. WW (P-I)

Illustrations from the book, accompanied by picture-cued text booklet.

163R **The Funny Little Woman**, Weston Woods, 1973 (LTR 162C) cassette 9min $6. WW (P-I)

Narrated by Frances Kelley.

164 **Gabrielle and Selena**, by Peter Desbarats; illus. by Nancy Grossman. Harcourt, 1968. unp. $5.50; pap. $.95 (P-I)

Two eight-year-old girls who are best friends—Selena, black, and Gabrielle, white—are tired of being themselves, and decide to change places for a day.

164F **Gabrielle and Selena**, Stephen Bosustow, 1972, 16mm color 13min $245, $13. BFA (P-I)

Live action faithfully follows book.

165 **The Gammage Cup**, by Carol Kendall; illus. by Erik Blegvad. Harcourt, 1959. 221p. $6.50 (I)

In the Land between the Mountains live a lost people, the Minnipins, who faithfully preserve their ancient customs until challenged by a few nonconformists. When they are attacked by an enemy race, it is the banished rebels who save the Minnipins from destruction.

165FS The Gammage Cup, Random House/Miller-Brody, 1976 (394-76997-X) 2 filmstrips 134, 130fr color with 12in 33-1/3rpm $45; (394-76998-8) with 2 cassettes 24:10, 20:41min $45. RH/M-B (I)

Filmstrip version utilizes color illustrations based on the original and fairy-like music to enhance the presentation.

165R The Gammage Cup, by Carol Kendall. Random House/Miller-Brody (394-76995-3) record $8.97; (394-76996-1) cassette $8.97. RH/M-B (I)

Based on the original book with lovely background music.

166 Gaucho, by Gloria Gonzalez; illus. by Wendell Minor. Knopf, 1977. $5.95; lib. ed. $6.99 (U)

A young Puerto Rican boy living in New York City becomes a hoodlum's messenger to earn money so he and his mother can return to Puerto Rico.

166F Gaucho, Martin Tahse, 1978, 16mm color 47min $600, $60. TLM (U)

Live-action television movie filmed in New York City which nicely captures the spirit of the book. Stars Panchito Gomez.

167 George and Martha Encore, by James Marshall. Houghton, 1973. 48p. lib. ed. $7.95; 1977 pap. $2.95 (N-P)

The two hippopotamus friends cavort in "a dance recital, a French lesson, an Indian diguise, a frolic on the beach and planting in the garden."

167FS George and Martha Encore, Educational Enrichment Materials, 1981 (52382) color 8min 1 filmstrip 1 cassette $22. EEM (N-P)

George and Martha celebrate their mutually supportive relationship in five heartwarming episodes based on the book by James Marshall.

168 George and Martha Rise and Shine, by James Marshall. Houghton, 1976. $6.95 (P)

These two endearing hippopotamuses demonstrate mutual understanding and misunderstanding in a give-and-take relationship.

168FS George and Martha Rise and Shine, Westport Communications Group, dist. by Educational Enrichment Materials, 1981 (52585) 53fr color 10min with cassette $22. EEM (P)

Marshall's story is endearingly adapted to the filmstrip medium. The four-color illustrations are borrowed from the original work. Playful music enhances filmstrip version.

169 Georgie, by Robert Bright. Doubleday, 1944. pap. $1.95 (N-P)

Georgie is a friendly little ghost who lives in Mr. and Mrs. Whittaker's attic and tells them when to go to bed by squeaking a step. When he gets his feelings hurt and leaves home, both he and the Whittakers are unhappy.

169F Georgie, Morton Schindel, 1956 (6522) 16mm color 7min $140, $20; videocassette $140. WW (N-I)

Iconographic technique using illustrations from the book. Narrated by Owen Jordan. Music by Arthur Kleiner.

Also available in Spanish.

169FS Georgie, Weston Woods, n.d. (FS 1) 41fr color $12; with cassette 6:15min $18. WW (P)

Illustrations from the book, accompanied by picture-cued text booklet.

Also available in Spanish.

169R Georgie, Weston Woods, n.d. (LTR 001C) cassette 6:15min $6. WW (P)

Story narrated by Owen Jordan, with original background music by Arthur Kleiner.

Available also in Spanish.

170 **The Ghost Belonged to Me**, by Richard Peck. Viking, 1975. $7.95; pap. $1.95 (I-U)

The hilarious adventures of thirteen-year-old Alexander Armsworth; his eighty-five-year-old uncle, Miles Armsworth; his schoolmate, Blossom Culp and a ghost. Set at the turn of the century.

170R **The Ghost Belonged to Me**, Live Oak Media, 1976, 2s 33rpm side 1: 27:38min, side 2: 27:29min $8.95; cassette $8.95. LOM (I-U)

Dramatized version of the book. Frank Scardino as narrator Alexander Armsworth. Authentic sound effects, including trolley car sounds recorded at the Trolley Museum, Branford, Connecticut.

171 **Gilberto and the Wind**, by Marie Hall Ets. Viking, 1963. lib. ed. $7.95; pap. $2.50 (N-P)

A little Mexican boy finds that the wind makes an unpredictable but interesting playmate.

171F **Gilberto and the Wind**, Bank Street College of Education, 1967 (655602) 16mm color 7min $100, $12.50. MH (N-P)

Read by Harry Belafonte. Reading Incentive Film series. Price includes copy of the book.

171FS **Gilberto and the Wind**, Weston Woods, n.d. (FS 104) 36fr color $12; with cassette 7:04min $18. WW (N-P)

Illustrations from the book, accompanied by picture-cued text booklet.

171R **Gilberto and the Wind**, Weston Woods, n.d. (LTR 104C) cassette 7:04min $6. WW (N-P)

Story narrated by John Cunningham, with original background music by Howard Rovics.

172 **The Girl Who Loved Wild Horses**, by Paul Goble. Bradbury Pr., 1978. unp. $9.95 (P-I)

The story of a Plains Indian girl who becomes one with the wild horses with whom she lives. Caldecott Medal winner.

172FS **The Girl Who Loved Wild Horses**, Random House/Miller-Brody, 1979 (394-78393-X) 64fr color 9min with cassette $21. RH/M-B (P-I)

The visuals are an exact reproduction of the bright, stylized paintings found in the book. The accompanying narration is well-paced and well-executed.

172R **The Girl Who Loved Wild Horses**, Random House/Miller-Brody (394-66015-3) read-along cassette with hardcover book $18. RH/M-B (P-I)

Dramatized with sound effects and background music. Single narrator (unidentified).

173 **Ginger Pye**, by Eleanor Estes. Harcourt, 1946. $8.50; pap. $1.95 (I)

The Pye family consists of diverse individuals: Mr. Pye, an authority on birds; Rachel, also interested in birds; Jerry, who collects rocks; and three-year-old Uncle Bennie, the youngest uncle in town. Mystery and adventure enter their lives when their dog, Ginger Pye, disappears. 1952 Newbery Medal winner.

173FS **Ginger Pye**, Miller-Brody, 1969 (770003-X) 2 filmstrips with record $37.98; (77004-8) with cassette $37.98. RH/M-B (I)

173R **Ginger Pye**, Miller-Brody, 1969 (76806-X) 12in 33rpm side 1: 23:28min, side 2: 23:30min $7.95; (76-816-7) cassette $7.97. RH/M-B (I)

A recorded dramatization narrated by Esther Benson. The roles of Jerry and Rachel are played by Jeff Somple and Susan Wyler. Adam Fried plays Uncle Bennie. Original background music by Herb Davidson. Includes teacher's guide.

174 **The Giving Tree**, by Shel Silverstein. Harper, 1964. unp. $5.95; lib. ed. $5.79 (P-U)

Deceptively simple story about the nature of love. Traces the relationship between a boy and a tree, from the boy's childhod to old age.

174F **The Giving Tree**, Stephen Bosustow, 1974 16mm color 10min $195. BOS (P-I)

Story, harmonica music, and narration by Shel Silverstein.

174FS **The Giving Tree**, Stephen Bosustow, 1974 (53600E) 44fr color 7min cassette guide $28. BA (P-I)

Story, harmonica music, and narration by Shel Silverstein. Wash backgrounds make the line drawings stand out.

175 **Go Away, Stay Away**, by Gail E. Haley. Scribner, 1977. $6.95 (P-I)

Troublesome, crotchety winter spirits, left behind when the ice and snow dissipate, cause problems for the villagers of a picturesque mountain community. To rid themselves of the Spinnikins, the Bunshee, the Kicklebuckets, and the Hobble Goblins, the villagers put on masks and march around every house, barn and shed ringing bells, shaking rattles, beating drums, waving branches, and chanting.

175FS **Go Away, Stay Away**, Weston Woods, 1978 (FS 239) 38fr color 10min $12; (SF 239C) with cassette $18. WW (P-I)

Filmstrip adaptation preserves the multihued beauty of Haley's active linoleum prints and captures the ethereal troublemakers in their acts. Appropriate sound effects along with accordion and flute melodies are used to bring the story to life. Picture-cued text booklet accompanies filmstrip.

175R **Go Away, Stay Away**, Weston Woods, 1978 (LTR 239C) cassette only 10min $6. WW (P)

Narrated by Jonathan Smith.

176 **God's Trombones; Seven Negro Sermons in Verse**, by James Weldon Johnson; illus. by Aaron Douglas. Viking, 1927. $9.95 (I-U)

This small book contains poetic sermons based on the Bible.

176F **The Creation**, Will Vinton, 1981, 16mm color 9min $225, $40. BUD (I-U)

Striking film done in clay animations. James Earl Jones tells the story in a rhythmic style.

177 **Golden Slippers: An Anthology of Negro Poetry for Young Readers**, compiled by Arna Bontemps; with drawings by Henrietta Bruce Sharon. Harper, 1941. 220p. $10; lib. ed. $8.97 (I-U)

A collection of lyrics and ballads, with brief biographical sketches of the poets.

177R **An Anthology of Negro Poetry for Young People**, Folkways/Scholastic Records, 1958 (7114) 2s 10in 33rpm $8.98. FSR (I-U)

Arna Bontemps reads from his anthology *Golden Slippers*.

178 **The Golem**, by Beverly Brodsky McDermott. Lippincott, 1975. 48p. $10.53 (P-I)

This is the legend of the Golem, a clay creature created and brought to life, long ago, by a Prague rabbi, to protect his people against persecution. However, the Golem grows into a giant, crushing people, leveling houses, and hurling rocks. Caldecott Honor Book.

178FS **The Golem**, Weston Woods, 1979 (FS 248) 6fr color 10min $12; (SF 248C) with cassette $18. WW (P-I)

Rich, breathtaking artwork is effectively adapted from McDermott's Caldecott Honor Book to magnify the impact of this gripping Jewish legend. An introduction

by the author/illustrator offers enlightening background information about the origin of the clay figure known as "the golem."
ALA Notable Filmstrip, 1980.

178R **The Golem**, Weston Woods, 1979 (LTR 248C) cassette only 10min $6. WW (I)
A brief lecture on the history of creatures created by man precedes the narration of Allen Swift. Somber music and a serious tone are used to present this Jewish legend.

179 **Good Work, Amelia Bedelia**, by Peggy Parish; illus. by Lynn Sweat. Greenwillow, 1976. $5.95; lib. ed. $5.71; 1980 Avon pap. $1.75 (P-I)
Irresistibly funny in her literal response to every word, Amelia delights us again as she follows her instructions from Mr. and Mrs. Rogers.

179FS **Good Work, Amelia Bedelia**, Westport Communications Group, dist. by Educational Enrichment Materials, 1981 (52383) 62fr color 10min cassette $22. EEM (P-I)
Amelia Bedelia faithfully and literally follows instructions from Mr. and Mrs. Rogers to the delight of all who follow her predicaments. A female voice convincingly takes the part of each character while catchy music enlivens the background.

180 **Grandfather Tales**, by Richard Chase. Houghton, 1948. 240p. $11.95 (I)
A collection of tales, mostly humorous, from the Appalachian mountain region. Includes "Wicked John and the Devil."

180R **The Folktellers: Tales to Grow On**, Weston Woods, 1981 (WW 711) $8; (WW 711C) cassette $8. WW (I)
The storytelling team of Barbara Freeman and Connie Regan gives solo and tandem tellings of some southern stories, including "Wicked John and the Devil" and "Sody Sallyratus", both from the *Grandfather Tales*. Notable Recording for Children, 1981.

181 **The Great Big Enormous Turnip**, by Alexei Tolstoy; illus. by Helen Oxenbury. Watts, 1969. unp. lib. ed. $3.90 net (N-P)
A cumulative folktale about a farmer who tries to pull up an enormous turnip.

181FS **The Great Big Enormous Turnip**, Weston Woods, 1973 (FS 140) 21fr color 3:45min $12; (SF 140C) with cassette $18. WW (N-P)
Illustrations from the book, accompanied by picture-cued text booklet. Includes *The Three Poor Tailors*.

181R **The Great Big Enormous Turnip**, Weston Woods, 1973 (LTR 140C) cassette only 4min $6. WW (N-P)
Narrated by Charles Cioffi with musical background. Includes *The Three Poor Tailors*.

182 **The Great Brain**, by John D. Fitzgerald, illus. by Mercer Mayer. Dial, 1967. 175p. $6.95; lib. ed. $7.45 (I)
A story about Dennis, age 7, and his brother, age 10, as they grow up together in 1896 in Adenville, Utah. The first of a series of highly imaginary exploits of swindling and swindlers in the early days of the west.

182FS **The Great Brain**, Media Basics, 1980 (MB5523) color 3 filmstrips av 150fr 3 cassettes av 12min 1 paperback $109.95. MED (I)
Jimmy Osmond stars in the still-photographed version of this story of life in Utah at the turn of the century. Quickly paced with effective musical accompaniment and lively dialogue.

183 **The Great Brain Reforms**, by John D. Fitzgerald; illus. by Mercer Mayer. Dial, 1973. 176p. $7.45 (I)
In turn-of-the-century Utah, the ingen-

ious schemes of a 12-year-old "con man" backfire.

183FS The Great Brain Reforms, Pied Piper (First Choice: Authors and Books), 1981, 1 filmstrip 97fr color with 2 cassettes (interview cassette 6min, filmstrip cassette 17min) $32. PP (I)

Filmstrip preserves the flavor of Mercer Mayer's crosshatched drawings for the book by featuring fine-lined art on textured paper seemingly washing in water colors and dappled in chalk to evoke the protagonist's episodes of mercenary mischief. Action-filled with realistic sound effects.

184 The Great Gilly Hopkins, by Katherine Paterson. Crowell, 1978. 148p. $8.79 (I)

When 11-year-old Gilly Hopkins is placed in a new foster home, she reacts in her usual brash, untamed manner—lying, stealing, running away. Newbery Honor Book.

184FS The Great Gilly Hopkins, Random House/Miller-Brody, 1980 (394-65973-2) 2 filmstrips 124, 114 fr color with 2 cassettes 17, 15min $45. RH/M-B (I)

Bold-stroked acrylic paintings faithfully transform Paterson's colorful descriptions into vivid illustrations for this sensitive adaptation of the award-winning novel. The characters are brought to life by accomplished readers.

184R The Great Gilly Hopkins, Random House/Miller-Brody (394-78370-0) record $8.97; (394-78371-9) cassette $8.97. RH/M-B (I)

Maime Trotter is played by Sloan Shelton.

185 The Green Man, by Gail Haley. Scribner, 1980. $9.95 (P-I)

Haley relates a vivid story of Claude, an arrogant young man who loses his clothes to a robber while swimming in a forest pool. He dresses in leaves, makes a life in the woods, and becomes a friend and provider to the animals as well as a protector of the village children.

185FS The Green Man, Weston Woods, 1980 (FS 257) 50fr color 14min $12; (SF 257C) with cassette $18. WW (P)

Uses lavishly detailed illustrations adapted from Gail Haley's picture book. A gentle reader warmly relates the story, while birds trill, crickets chirp, and delicate melodies enrich the idyllic ambience of the scene. 1980 Notable Recording for Children.

186 The Grey Lady and the Strawberry Snatcher, by Molly Bang. Four Winds, 1980. 48p. $10.95 (P)

In this visual narrative, an old woman is pursued by a strange man who is after her strawberries.

186FS The Grey Lady and the Strawberry Snatcher, Random House/Miller-Brody, 1981 (394-07709-1) 109fr color 10min with cassette $21. RH/M-B (P)

Molly Bang's original, richly detailed paintings were used for the filmstrip version. The accompanying musical score heightens the story's action and at the same time evokes its highly personal, yet mystically universal, beauty.

187 The Brothers Grimm: Popular Folk Tales by Jakob and Wilhelm Grimm; tr. by Brian Alderson; illus. by Michael Foreman. Doubleday, 1978. 192p. $9.95 (P-I)

A collection of thirty-one folktales, newly translated with illustrations in color and black and white.

187F The Frog King, Tom and Mimi Davenport, 1980, 16mm color 15min $260, $25. TD (I)

A live action version of the Grimm tale, "The Frog Prince," set in the Victorian period in Southern America. A rather colloquial version. Uses a live frog and a realistic frog puppet to good effect.

187F The Making of The Frog King, Tom and Mimi Davenport, 1981, 16mm color 11min $170, $20. TD (I-U)

Interesting documentary about how *The Frog King* was brought to life, narrated by Tom Davenport and Ann Clark, the 14-year-old actress from the movie. Can be used with students of acting and filmmaking.

187R Fairy Tale Favorites v.3, CMS Records, 1971 (CMS 632) 2s 12in 33rpm $7.98; (CMS-X4632) cassette $7.98. CMS (P-I)

Mary Strang tells Laurence Housman's "Rocking-Horse Land" and three traditional tales, "Beauty and the Beast," "The Top and the Ball," and "The Frog Prince."

187R Tom Thumb, Rumpelstiltskin and Other Fairy Tales, Caedmon (LP 1062) 2s 12in 33rpm side 1: 29:27min, side 2: 28:11min $8.98; (CSS 1062) cassette $8.98. CAE (P-I)

Joseph Schildkraut reads eight tales by the Brothers Grimm. Side 1: "Tom Thumb," "The Old Man and His Grandson," "The Frog Prince," and "The Elves and the Shoemaker." Side 2: "Sleeping Beauty," "Rumpelstiltskin," "The Star-Money," and "Rapunzel."

188 Gulliver's Travels, by Jonathan Swift; illus. by John N. Fago. Pendulum Pr., 1974. 64p. $5; pap. $1.95 (I) Also available in deluxe ed. Grosset $8.95; NAL (Signet Classic) pap. $1.95 (I)

Written as a satire, this tale of the Lilliputians continues to be enjoyed.

188FS Complete Gulliver's Travels, Educational Enrichment Materials, n.d. color 8 filmstrips 8 cassettes 1 paperback $172 (individual FS with sound $24). EEM (P-I)

Adapted from the novel by Jonathan Swift, this many-leveled classic will capture the imagination of every young adventurer.

189 Hangin' Out with Cici, by Francine Pascal. Viking, 1977. $9.95; Archway pap. $2.25 (U)

A teen-age girl, who is always getting into trouble and feels misunderstood by her mother, suddenly finds herself back in the 1940s and involved with a girl who turns out to be her mother.

189F My Mother Was Never a Kid, Doro Bachrach, 1980, 16mm color 46min $625, $50. LCA (I-U)

This live-action ABC After School Special was a 1982 ALA Notable Film for Children. An edited version is also available (32min, $450, $40).

190 Hansel and Gretel, by Jakob and Wilhelm Grimm; illus. by Susan Jeffers. Dial, 1975. unp. $6.95 (P-I)

The popular Grimms' fairy tale in a newly illustrated version.

190F Hansel and Gretel, an Appalachian Version, Tom Davenport Films, 1975 16mm color 16min $210, $20. TD (I)

The Grimm Brothers' tale, filmed in the Blue Ridge Mountains of Virginia. The live performance and scenery lend reality to the fairy tale, making it more suitable for showing to older children. A good lead-in to play production.

190FS Hansel and Gretel, Random House/Miller-Brody, n.d. (394-03704-9) color 1 filmstrip 1 cassette $21; (394-03700-6) disc $21. RH/M-B (N-P)

Classic, popular fairy tale, illustrated by Sheliah Beckett, follows the usual story in the longer version.

190R Hansel and Gretel, Angel, n.d. (S-3648) 4s 12in 33rpm $9.58. ANG (P-U)

The opera by Engelbert Humperdinck based on the Grimms' fairy tale. Libretto by Adelheid Wette. Sung in German by Irmgard Seefried, Anneliese Rothenberger,

Grace Hoffman, and others. Vienna Philharmonic Orchestra conducted by Andre Cluytens.

190R **Hansel and Gretel, and Other Fairy Tales**, Caedmon, 196? (LP 1274) 2s 12in 33rpm $8.98; (CSS 1274) cassette $8.98. CAE (P-I)

Four fairy tales by the Brothers Grimm, retold by Amabel Williams-Ellis, and narrated by Claire Bloom. Side 1: "Hansel and Gretel" and "The Golden Goose." Side 2: "Mrs. Owl" and "Shiver and Shake."

191 **Happy Birthday to You!**, by Dr. Seuss. Random, 1959. unp. $4.95; lib. ed. $5.99 net (P-I)

Nonsense verse in typical Seuss style of how birthdays are celebrated in the mythical land of Katroo.

191R **Happy Birthday to You! and Other Stories**, Caedmon, 1969 (LP 1287) 2s 12in 33rpm $8.98; (CSS 51287) cassette $8.98. CAE (P)

Five Dr. Seuss stories read with verve by Hans Conreid. The electronic sounds of the Octopus, a sound machine with eight channels, are used to point up the action and give a suitably strange flavor to the nonsense. Includes: *Happy Birthday to You!*, *Scrambled Eggs Super*, *And to Think That I Saw It on Mulberry Street*, *Gertrude McFuzz*, and *The Big Brag*.

192 **The Happy Day**, by Ruth Krauss; pictures by Marc Simont. New ed. Harper, 1980. $8.95 (N-P)

Slight text, beautifully illustrated, describes the animals' joy as winter comes to an end.

192FS **The Happy Day** and **Where Does the Butterfly Go When It Rains**, Weston Woods, n.d. (FS 96) 2 filmstrips 19, 20fr color $12; 2:22, 3:08min with cassette $18. WW (N-P)

Illustrations from the book, accompanied by picture-cued text booklet.

192R **The Happy Day** and **Where Does the Butterfly Go When It Rains**, Weston Woods, n.d. (LTR 096C) cassette 2:22min and 3:08min $6. WW (N-P)

Stories narrated by John Cunningham.

193 **The Happy Owls**, by Celestino Piatti. Atheneum, 1964. unp. $7.95; pap. $1.95 (P)

In simple text and glowing pictures the author-artist tells the tale of two wise owls who bring harmony to their quarrelsome neighbors.

193F **The Happy Owls**, Morton Schindel, 1969 (20055) 16mm color 6:25min $175, $20; videocassette $175; Super 8 $175. WW (P)

Adapted and directed by Gene Deitch. Narrated by Owen Jordan. Animation by Zdenka Skripkova. Music by Peter Eben.

193FS **The Happy Owls**, Weston Woods, n.d. (FS 63) 25, 22fr color $12; (SF 63) 3:42, 4:05min with 7in 33rpm $18; with cassette $18. WW (P)

Illustrations from the original book, accompanied by picture-cued text booklet.

193R **The Happy Owls** and **The Three Robbers**, Weston Woods, n.d. (LTR 063C) cassette $12. WW (P)

Stories narrated by Owen Jordan, with original background music by Barry Galbraith.

194 **Harold and the Purple Crayon**, by Crockett Johnson. Weston Woods (PB44) 1981. 64p. pap. $1.95. WW (N-P)

As Harold goes for a moonlight walk, he uses his purple crayon to draw a path and the things he sees along the way and then draws himself back home.

194R **Harold and the Purple Crayon**,

Weston Woods, n.d. (LTR 044C) cassette 6:40min $6. WW (N-P)

Story narrated by Owen Jordan, with original background music by Paul Alan Levi.

195 **Harry and the Lady Next Door**, by Gene Zion; illus. by Margaret Bloy Graham. Harper, 1960. $7.89 (P)

Harry loves all his neighbors—except the lady next door, whose singing hurts Harry's ears. He tries various ways of making her stop, but without success.

195FS **Harry and the Lady Next Door**, Random House/Miller-Brody, 1977 (394-64535-9) 93fr 14:25min with cassette $21. RH/M-B (P)

Filmstrip introduced by song "Harry and the Lady Next Door." Uses expressive illustrations from the book.

ALA Notable Filmstrip, 1979.

195R **Harry and the Lady Next Door**, Random House/Miller-Brody (394-76452-8) cassette only $8.97; (394-66016-1) cassette with paperback $10.92. RH/M-B (P)

Hilarious rendering of Harry's efforts to drown out the terrible singing of the lady next door. Word-for-word reading.

196 **Harry by the Sea**, by Gene Zion; illus. by Margaret Bloy Graham. Harper, 1965. $8.79 (P)

At the beach Harry finds the family umbrella too crowded and decides to find his own shade. When he wanders too near the water, a big wave catches him and leaves him covered with seaweed.

196FS **Harry by the Sea**, Random House/Miller-Brody, 1977 (394-64536-7) 73fr 10:14min with cassette $21. RH/M-B (P)

ALA Notable Filmstrip, 1979. Faithful adaptation of Zion's book. Filmstrip expands Graham's humorous drawings and Harry's predicaments through varied visual perspectives and animated narrative accompanied by delightful music and suitable sound effects.

196R **Harry by the Sea**, Random House/Miller-Brody (394-76450-1) cassette only $8.97; (394-07885-3) cassette with paperback $10.92. RH/M-B (P)

Harry is mistaken for a sea monster when he accidentally becomes covered with seaweed at the beach. Word-for-word reading.

197 **Harry Cat's Pet Puppy**, by George Selden; illus. by Garth Williams. Farrar, 1974. 164p. $8.95; Dell pap. $1.25 (N-I)

Harry Cat and Tucker Mouse adopt a thin stray puppy and raise it in the drainpipe in a Manhattan subway station. The puppy gets so fat he can't get through the drainpipe, but all ends well.

197FS **Harry Cat's Pet Puppy**, Random House/Miller-Brody, 1979 (77267-9) 348fr color 41:12min 2 filmstrips 2 cassettes $45. RH/M-B (N-I)

Excellent abridgement retaining important events and flavor of the story; voices are clear and convey mood and personalities of the characters; Garth Williams illustrations.

197R **Harry Cat's Pet Puppy**, Random House/Miller-Brody (394-77265-2) cassette only $9.90; (394-77274-4) record $9.90. RH/M-B (N-I)

This is an abridged, dramatized reading.

198 **Harry the Dirty Dog**, by Gene Zion; illus. by Margaret B. Graham. Harper, 1956. $7.95; lib. ed. $8.79; pap. (1976) $1.95 (N-P)

When running away from taking a bath, Harry sees many interesting urban sights and becomes so dirty his family can hardly recognize him.

198FS **Harry the Dirty Dog**. Random House/Miller-Brody, 1977 (394-

64537-5) 1 filmstrip 1 cassette $21. RH/M-B (N-P)

Taken directly from the book about a lovable dog who likes everything except taking a bath.

198R **Harry the Dirty Dog**, Random House/Miller-Brody (394-76449-8) cassette only $8.97; (394-66018-8) cassette with paperback $10.92. RH/M-B (P)

Harry runs away to avoid taking a bath. Word-for-word reading.

199 **The Hat**, by Tomi Ungerer. Scholastic/Four Winds, 1982. 32p. $11.95 (P)

A whimsical, lighthearted tale about a magical hat that falls into the life of a penniless veteran and brings him riches, but then is lost in a sweep of wind.

199F **The Hat**, Morton Schindel, 1982, 16mm color 6min $175, $20. WW (P)

Animated film using the original illustrations by Tomi Ungerer. A funny, slightly askew film.

199FS **The Hat**, Weston Woods, 1981 (FS 261) 45fr color 8:55min $12; (SF 261C) with cassette $18. WW (P)

Vivacious interpretation of Ungerer's story. Operatic choruses and organ-grinder tunes back the narrator's emotive delivery.

199R **The Hat**, Weston Woods, 1982 (LTR 261C) cassette only 9min $6. WW (P)

Lively music based on Italian melodies and a strong narration enhance this imaginative tale.

200 **The Hating Book**, by Charlotte Zolotow; illus. by Ben Schecter. Harper, 1969. 32p. $5.95; lib. ed. $6.89 (N-P)

Misunderstandings can happen to friends of any age.

200FS **The Hating Book**, Guidance Associates, 1976 (9-3004-2340) color 1 filmstrip 1 cassette, 1 guide, 4 paperback books $39. GA (N-P)

Made from the original book illustrations and accompanied by a dramatic narration complete with lively music and appropriate sound effects.

201 **Hawaiian Legends of Tricksters and Riddlers**, by Vivian L. Thompson; illus. by Sylvie Selig. Holiday, 1969. 103p. $7.95 (U)

How the people of ancient Hawaii outwitted evil chiefs and spirits.

201R **Folk Tales, Legends, Proverbs and Riddles of the Pacific Islands**, CMS Records, 1970 (CMS 596) $8.98; (CMS X4596) cassette $8.98. CMS (U)

Anne Pellowski tells stories from Malaysia, the Philippines, Hawaii, Java, and Papua and a Maori tale from New Zealand.

202 **The Headless Cupid**, by Zilpha K. Snyder; illus. by Alton Raible. Atheneum, 1971. 203p. $8.95 (I)

Conjuring a poltergeist to impress her new brothers and sisters, twelve-year-old Amanda's occult mischief stirs long-dormant mysteries of the old Westerley House.

202FS **The Headless Cupid**, Pied Piper (First Choice: Authors and Books), 1980, 1 filmstrip 110fr color with 2 cassettes (interview cassette 15min, filmstrip cassette 19min) $32. PP (I)

Retains the flavor and sense of the book through strong characterizations. Electronic music heightens the suspense of the presentation.

202R **The Headless Cupid**, by Zilpha Keatley Snyder, Random House/Miller-Brody (394-77009-9) record $8.97; (394-77010-2) cassette $8.97. RH/M-B (I)

203 **Heidi**, by Johanna Spyri; illus. by Jessie Wilcox Smith. Scribner, 1958. 380p. $7.50 (I). OP

An especially beautiful edition of the well-loved story of the little Swiss girl who brings love to her grandfather and all her friends.

203R **Heidi**, Caedmon, 1970 (TC 1292) 1 12in LP $8.98; (CDL 51292) cassette $8.98. CAE (I)

Claire Bloom recreates Johanna Spyri's well-loved story by reading passages from the original text. A living, lasting book becomes a classic. Despite its solid writing and its old-fashioned emphasis on religion and virture, *Heidi* remains after nearly a century a beloved, sought-after story.

204 **Henry and Ribsy**, by Beverly Cleary; illus. by Louis Darling. Morrow, 1954. $7.92 (P-I)

Henry must keep his dog, Ribsy, out of trouble for a whole month so his dad will take him along when he goes salmon fishing. It isn't easy, but Henry manages. Unfortunately, Ribsy causes an uproar on the fishing expedition, but, despite all, Henry manages to catch the biggest fish of the day.

204FS **Henry and Ribsy**, Random House/Miller-Brody, 1980 (394-64538-3) 106fr color 14:15min with cassette $21. RH/M-B (P-I)

Lively reconstruction of two episodes from the book. Line drawings from the book were updated in brightly painted sketches in watercolor and ink. Enhanced by playful music in the background and appropriate sound effects.

204R **Henry and Ribsy**, Random House/Miller-Brody (394-64515-4) cassette $8.97. RH/M-B (P-I)

Dramatized version.

205 **Henry Huggins**, by Beverly Cleary, illus. by Louis Darling. Morrow, 1950. 155p. $6.96 (P-I)

Henry Huggins gets himself into a series of hilariously funny situations. The first of these occurs when he picks up a hungry stray dog, puts him into a paper shopping bag, and carries him home on the bus.

205FS **Henry Huggins**, Random House/Miller-Brody, 1980 (394-64539-1) 137fr color 16:25min with cassette $21. RH/M-B (P-I)

Narrative and dramatic techniques combine to bring to life Beverly Cleary's book. Three key episodes are included in the filmstrip. Dog noises and other appropriate sound effects support the presentation. Color illustrations retain the spirit of the original.

205R **Henry Huggins**, Random House/Miller-Brody (394-64516-2) cassette $8.97. RH/M-B (P-I)

Dramatized version.

206 **Henry Reed, Inc.**, by Keith Robertson; illus. by Robert McCloskey. Viking, 1958. 239p. lib. ed. $8.95; (#362A) Follett $8.06 net (I-U)

Henry Reed, on vacation from the American School in Naples, keeps a record of his research into the American free-enterprise system, to be used as a school report on his return. With a neighbor, Midge Glass, he starts a business in pure and applied research, which results in some very free and wildly enterprising experiences, all recorded deadpan in his journal. Very funny and original escapades.

206R **Henry Reed, Inc.**, Live Oak Media, 1973, 2s 12in 33rpm side 1: 27:38min, side 2: 24:14min $8.95; cassette $8.95. LOM (I-U)

A dramatization of the book, performed by the High Tor Repertory Players. Henry Reed: Alvin Kupperman; Midge: Kathleen Gray.

207 **Henry the Explorer**, by Mark Taylor; illus. by Graham Booth. Atheneum, 1976. pap. $1.95 (N-P)

Henry and his dog, Angus, go exploring after a blizzard and get lost. One of the series of stories about Henry and Angus.

207R **Henry the Explorer**, Weston Woods, 1977 (LTR196C) cassette only 6min $6. WW (N-P)

Roderick Cook narrates this reassuring story of how Henry and Angus get lost and are found.

208 **The Hey Diddle Diddle Picture Book**, by Randolph Caldecott, Warne n.d. unp. $5.95 (N-P). OP

Nursery rhymes and verses illustrated by the nineteenth-century artist. Includes "The Milkmaid," "Hey Diddle Diddle," "Baby Bunting," "A Frog He Would A-Wooing Go," "The Fox Jumps over the Parson's Gate."

208FS **Hey Diddle Diddle, Baby Bunting**, and **The Milkmaid**, Weston Woods, n.d. (#10C) 4 filmstrips 4 booklets with record or cassette $55; (PBP #10) cassette alone $7; (PBP #10) record only (inaudible signal or audible signal) $7. WW (N-P)

Illustrations from the book accompanied by picture-cued text booklet.

208FS **Hey Diddle Diddle, Baby Bunting**, and **The Milkmaid**, Weston Woods, n.d. 9, 7, 25fr color $12; (SF 34C) with cassette 6min $18. WW (N-P)

Illustrations from the book, accompanied by picture-cued text booklet.

208R **Hey Diddle Diddle, Baby Bunting**, and **The Milkmaid**, Weston Woods, n.d. (LTE 034) 7in 33rpm 6min $1.95; (LTR034C) cassette $5.50. WW (N-P)

Stories narrated by Gilbert Mack, with original background music by Jay Frederick.

209 **The Hobbit; or There and Back Again**, by J. R. R. Tolkien. Houghton, 1938. 315p. $6.95 (I-U)

Introduction to the world of Middle Earth and some of its inhabitants.

209R **J. R. R. Tolkien Reads and Sings His *The Hobbit* and *The Fellowship of the Ring***, Caedmon, 1975 (TC 1477) $8.98; (CDL 51477) cassette $8.98. CAE (U)

This recording contains poems and prose from the first volume of Tolkien's famous *Lord of the Rings*. Also included are one of his unpublished poems and a song sung to a tune of his own invention.

209R **Poems and Songs of Middle Earth**, Caedmon, 1967 (TC 1231) $8.98; (CDL 51231) cassette $8.98. CAE (I-U)

Performance by J. R. R. Tolkien. William Elvin sings Donald Swann's "The Road Goes Ever On," a song based on Tolkien's poetry.

210 **Hole in the Dike**, retold by Norma Green; illus. by Eric Carle. Harper, 1975. unp. $9.57; lib. ed. $10.89 (P)

Vibrant and bold illustrations to this story of the boy who saves Holland by stopping up a hole in the dike give the reader the impression of actually being at the scene. The story is taken from M. M. Dodge's *Hans Brinker; or The Silver Skates.*

210R **The Hole in the Dike**, Weston Woods, 1977 (LTR 225C) cassette only 7min $6. WW (P)

Emery Battis narrates this dramatic story.

211 **A Hole Is to Dig**, by Ruth Krauss; pictures by Maurice Sendak. Harper, 1952. unp. lib. ed. $6.89; trade $5.95 (P)

A whimsical definition book.

211FS **A Hole Is to Dig**, Weston Woods, n.d. (FS 99) 46fr color $12; (SF99C) with cassette $18. WW (P)

Illustrations from the book, accompanied by picture-cued text booklet.

212 **Homer Price**, by Robert McCloskey. Viking, 1943. 149p. $8.95; pap. $1.95 (I)

An all-American boy keeps Centerburg in a state of hilarious confusion as he operates a nonstop doughnut machine, helps to catch a bank robber, and sneaks his pet skunk into his room.

212F **Case of the Cosmic Comic**, Morton Schindel, Isa Wickenhagen, 1976, 16mm color 28min $350. WW (I)

Live-action film taken from one chapter of McCloskey's *Homer Price* in which Homer and his friend meet their comic book hero, Super Duper, and discover that he is only human.

212R **Homer Price**, Live Oak Media, 1973, 12in 33rpm side 1: 25:10 min, side 2: 24:56min $8.95; cassette $8.95. LOM (I-U)

A dramatization of the book. Narrated by Mike Mearion; Homer Price played by Larry Robinson.

213 **Horton Hatches the Egg**, by Dr. Seuss. Random House, 1940. unp. $5.99 (P)

Horton, the elephant, is left in charge of a bird's egg while she flies off to rest and ends up staying away for 51 weeks. Horton guards the egg through many trials and tribulations and receives his just reward in the end.

213FS **Horton Hatches the Egg**, Random House, 1976 (R/394-07957-4 or C/394-06918-8) 2 filmstrips with 2 records or 2 cassettes. Part I-45fr color 6min; Part 2-72fr color 8min with records or cassettes $54.75. RH/M-B (P)

Dr. Seuss's popular egg-sitting elephant story is dramatized by a comic balance of voices and projected with adroitly paced colored picture sequences. (Color added to book illustrations.) Background music appropriate to the events. ALA Notable Filmstrip, 1978.

213R **Horton Hatches the Egg**, Random House/Miller-Brody (394-06943-9) cassette only $8.97; (394-07839-X) cassette with hardcover book $14.96. RH/M-B (P)

Nicely rhymed story with repetitive phrase. Word-for-word reading of the original book.

214 **Horton Hears a Who**, by Dr. Seuss. Random House, 1954. $5.95 (P)

Horton, the lovable, good-natured elephant, helps to protect the tiny inhabitants of Whoville.

214FS **Horton Hears a Who**, Random House/Miller-Brody, 1976 (394-07958-2) 2 filmstrips 67, 86fr color 8, 10min with 2 records 10in 33-1/3rpm $54.75; (394-06917-X) with 2 cassettes $54.75. RH/M-B (P)

Color is added to Dr. Seuss's illustrations. Filmstrip moves at a lively pace and retains the sense of the book.

214R **Horton Hears a Who**, Random House/Miller-Brody (394-06947-1) cassette only $8.97; (394-07843-8) cassette with hardcover book $15.96. RH/M-B (P)

This recording highlights the extravagant nonsense and rollicking verse. Word-for-word reading.

215 **The House at Pooh Corner**, by A. A. Milne; illus. by Ernest Shepard. Dutton, 1961. $7.95 (P-I)

A collection of well-loved stories about Christopher Robin and his friends. Tigger joins Christopher Robin, Winnie-the-Pooh, Eeyore, Owl, Piglet, Kanga and Little Roo and leads them on some colorful new adventures.

215R **The House at Pooh Corner**, Caedmon (TC 1670) 12in LP $8.98; (CP 1670) cassette $8.98, LC 80-74309. CAE (P-I)

Carol Channing conveys the personality and charm of Milne's characters as she tells and sings three stories: "The House at Pooh Corner," "Piglet Does a Very Grand Thing," and "Christopher Robin Gives Pooh a Party and We Say Goodbye."

216 **Houses from the Sea**, by Alice E. Goudey; illus. by Adrienne Adams. Scribner, 1959. unp. lib. ed. $8.95 net (P)

An unusually beautiful picture story of two children who gather shells on the beach and learn about the animals who inhabited them. Pictures identifying the shells are repeated at the end of the book.

216FS **Houses from the Sea**, Miller-Brody, 1974 (SMB 110FR) 49fr color 12:30min with 12in 33rpm $12.95; (SMB 110FC) with cassette $14.95. RH/M-B (P)

Illustrations from the book. Story narrated by Bill Griffis.

217 **How the Grinch Stole Christmas**, by Dr. Seuss. Random, 1957. unp. $5.95; lib. ed. $5.99 (N-P)

A mean old creature tries to find a way to eliminate Christmas but learns his lesson.

217FS **How the Grinch Stole Christmas**, Miller-Brody/Random House, 1976 (04122-4) 103fr color 18:15min 2 filmstrips 2 cassettes $57. RH (N-P)

Replete with sound effects, music, and illustrations that are more colorful than the book; dramatically narrated by Zero Mostel.

217R **How the Grinch Stole Christmas**, Random House/Miller-Brody (394-06955-2) cassette only $8.97; (394-07845-4) cassette with hardcover book $14.96. RH/M-B (N-P)

The modern Christmas story narrated by Zero Mostel.

218 **How the Hibernators Came to Bethlehem**, by Norma Farber; illus. by Barbara Cooney. Walker, 1980. 32p. $7.85 (P)

The Star of Bethlehem awakens the winter-sleeping creatures to send them to visit a newborn baby.

218FS **How the Hibernators Came to Bethlehem**, Random House/Miller-Brody, 1981 (394-07553-6) 54fr color 7:14min with cassette $21. RH/M-B (P)

A gently melodic guitar theme permeates this filmstrip adaptation of Farber's book and mingles with the peaceful, evocative narration. Cooney's delicate illustrations are adapted for the filmstrip version.

218R **How the Hibernators Came to Bethlehem**, by Norma Farber; illus. by Barbara Cooney. Random House/Miller-Brody(394-07792-X) read-along cassette with hardcover book $16.98. RH/M-B (P)

Narrated by Jane Altman.

219 **The Hundred Dresses**, by Eleanor Estes; illus. by Louis Slobodkin. Harcourt, 1944. 80p. $8.95 (P-I)

The 100 dresses are just dream dresses, pictures Wanda Petronski has drawn, but she describes them defensively as she appears daily in the same faded blue dress. Not until after Wanda moves away do the other children realize the cruelty of their taunting.

219FS **The Hundred Dresses**, Random House/Miller-Brody, 1978 (394-77021-8) 2 filmstrips 116, 106fr color with 1 record 12in 33-1/3rpm $45; (394-77022-6) with 2 cassettes each 23min $45. RH/M-B (P-I)

Illustrations reflect the descriptions given in the book. Unobtrusive musical background enhances the presentation.

219R **The Hundred Dresses**, by Eleanor Estes. Random House/Miller-Brody (394-76807-8) read-along record $8.97; (394-76817-5) read-along cassette $8.97. RH/M-B (P-I)

Narrated by Lucy Martin.

220 **The Hundred Penny Box**, by Sharon Bell Mathis; illus. by Leo and Diane Dillon. Viking, 1975. 47p. $6.95 (P-I)

Mathis portrays the conflict between Michael's 100-year-old great-great-aunt Dew and his mother, who hopes to help the old woman live in the present by disposing of reminders of the past. A Newbery Honor Book.

220F **The Hundred Penny Box**, Pieter Van Deusen and Leah Miller, 1979, 16mm color 18min $280. CHU (I)

Slow-paced live action film with good acting, but a rather melancholy mood. A special film. 1981 Notable Film for Children.

220FS **The Hundred Penny Box**, Miller-Brody, 1979 (394-76914-7) 2 filmstrips 100, 89fr color 24, 23min with 2 cassettes $45. RH/M-B (P-I)

This touching story of love and aging is portrayed in realistic, yellow- and green-tone mood photographs and sensitive narration. Unobtrusive musical background. ALA Notable Filmstrip.

220R **The Hundred Penny Box**, by Sharon Bell Mathis. Random House/Miller-Brody (394-76911-2) read-along record $8.97; (394-76912-0) read-along cassette $8.97. RH/M-B (P-I)

A sensitive, word-for-word reading of the story.

221 **Hush Little Baby: A Folk Lullaby**, illus. by Aliki. Prentice-Hall, 1968. unp. lib. ed. $5.95; pap. $1.50 (P)

A lullaby blending a child's joy and disappointment as Mama sings of gifts Papa will bring.

221F **Hush Little Baby**, Morton Schindel, 1976, 16mm color 5min $115. WW (N-P)

A beautiful film which captures the rich color and texture of the original illustrations which were painted on wood. When the words appear on the screen children spontaneously join in singing along with Buffy Allen. Also available in videocassette.

221FS **Hush Little Baby**, Weston Woods, 1970 (FS 117) 18fr color $9; (SF 117) 2:40min with 7in 33rpm disc $18; (SF 117C) with cassette $18. WW(P)

Illustrations from the book, accompanied by picture-cued text booklet.

222 **I Know an Old Lady Who Swallowed a Fly**, by Nadine Westcott. Atlantic Monthly/Little, 1980. unp. $8.95 (P-I)

The whimsical song is highlighted by imaginative color pictures.

222F **I Know an Old Lady Who Swallowed a Fly**, National Film Board of Canada, 1966 (0164103) 16mm color 6min $110, $9. IFB (P-I)

Sung by Burl Ives, accompanying himself on the guitar. Animated film.

222FS **I Know an Old Lady**, Weston Woods, n.d. (FS 59) 47fr color $12; (SF 59C) $18. WW (P)

Illustrations from the book, accompanied by picture-cued text booklet.

223 **Ida Fanfanny and the Four Seasons**, by Dick Gackenback. Harper, 1978. lib. ed. $8.89 (P)

Ida Fanfanny lives on a mountain where there is no weather and so she visits each season experiencing the good and bad of each.

223F **Ida Fanfanny and the Four**

Seasons. Persistence of Vision, 1980, dist. by Leasing Corporation of America, film or videocassette color 13min $250, $25. LCA (P)

Good humor, sprightly music, and good animation enliven this exploration of the four seasons.

224 **Invincible Louisa: The Story of the Author of Little Women**, by Cornelia Meigs. Little, 1968. 195p. $7.95 (U)

The intellectual world of nineteenth-century New England forms the background for this biography of the author of *Little Women*. 1934 Newbery Medal winner.

224R **Invincible Louisa**, Random House/Miller-Brody, 1969 (394-77023-4) record $8.97; (394-77024-2) cassette $8.97. RH/M-B (I-U)

A recorded dramatization. Narrated by Martin Bookspan. Patricia Peardon plays the role of Louisa. The cast also includes Esther Benson as Marmee and John Michael King as Bronson. Includes a teacher's guide.

225 **Ira Sleeps Over**, by Bernard Waber; illus. by the author. Houghton, 1972. $7.95; pap. $2.95 (P)

Excited by the prospect of sleeping at his friend's house, Ira doesn't know how to admit that he sleeps with a teddy bear.

225F **Ira Sleeps Over**, Andrew Sugerman, 1977, 16mm color 17min $295, $30. PHX (P)

A nice live-action adaptation of the picture book with appealing child actors.

226 **The Island of the Skog**, by Steven Kellog. Dial Pr., 1973. unp. $7.45 (P-I)

Jenny and her mouse friends become frustrated with the dangers of urban life and take to the seas in search of a more peaceful place to live. After a long, difficult voyage, they arrive at the Island of the Skog only to be confronted with one more problem— the Skog, the only inhabitant of the island.

226FS **The Island of the Skog**, Weston Woods, 1976 (FS 174) 50fr color 11min $12; (SF 174C) with cassette $18. WW (P-I)

Kellogg's intricately detailed illustrations for his book are beautifully reproduced, while a versatile narrator enhances each character's unique personality. Delicate music filters throughout this refreshing blend of suspense and human psychology.

Accompanied by a picture-cued text booklet.

227 **It Could Always Be Worse**, by Margot Zemach. Farrar, 1976. unp. $10.95 (P-I)

Zemach retells the familiar tale of the poor man whose tiny hut was so crowded and noisy that he went to the wise Rabbi for help. On advice from the Rabbi, the anguished man brought his livestock into the house, only to be told to remove them when the commotion became unbearable.

227FS **It Could Always Be Worse**, Random House/Miller-Brody, 1978 (394-76482-X) 72fr color 13min with cassette $21. RH/M-B (P-I)

Eli Wallach's richly expressive voice conveys the anguish of the poor man. Sounds of honking geese and clucking chickens accompanied by stringed instruments add an ethnic flavor to the artist's zesty, humorous paintings. Guide.

227R **It Could Always Be Worse**, Harve and Margot Zemach. Random House/Miller-Brody(394-07629-X) read-along cassette with hardcover book $16.98. RH/M-B (P-I)

A read-along version of the story.

228 **It's Like This, Cat**, by Emily Neville; pictures by Emil Weiss.

Harper, 1963. 192p. $8.95; lib. ed. $8.79 (I-U)

Dave's account of his fourteenth year gives a good picture of his parents, his New York City friends and neighbors, and his pet cat. With humor and insight he describes his growing appreciation of his father, his friendship with a troubled boy, and his awakening interest in girls. 1964 Newbery Medal winner.

228FS **It's Like This, Cat**, Miller-Brody, 1978 (394-7702-77) 2 filmstrips 132, 119fr color with 1 record 12in 33-1/3rpm $45; (394-77028-5) with 2 cassettes 17:08, 16:40min $45. RH/M-B (I)

Line drawings lavishly colored with a chalklike richness of textures and hues generously illustrate this lively adaptation of Neville's Newbery Medal book. Filmstrip moves at a quick pace with spirited readings of the roles and an original, jazz-style instrumental composition.

228R **It's Like This, Cat**, Random House/Miller-Brody, 1970 (394-77025-0) record $8.97; (394-77026-9) cassette $8.97. RH/M-B (I)

Dramatization by Margaret Albrecht. Directed by Peter Fernandez. Featured in this recording are Bryant Fraser as Dave and Amy Schachtel as Mary. Herb Davidson has composed background music with an appropriate jazz feeling. Includes teacher's guide.

229 **It's Perfectly True, and Other Stories**, by Hans Christian Andersen; tr. from the Danish by Paul Leyssac; illus. by Richard Bennett. Harcourt, 1938. 305p. $3.50 (P-I). OP

Twenty-eight Andersen tales, including many favorites.

229R **Thumbelina**, Random House/Miller-Brody, 1973 (394-07807-1) cassette with paperback $10.98. RH/M-B (I)

Actress Eva Le Gallienne brings sensitivity and zest to her reading of Andersen's fairy tale. Printed text included.

229R **The Tinderbox**, Random House/Miller-Brody, 1973 (76426-6) record $8.97; (76426-9) cassette $8.97; (64066) paperback with media $1.35. RH (I)

Actress Eva Le Gallienne brings sensitivity and zest to her reading of Andersen's fairy tale. Printed text included.

230 **It's So Nice to Have a Wolf around the House**, by Harry Allard; illus. by James Marshall. Doubleday, 1977. $7.95; pap. $2.95 (P-I)

Cuthbert Q. Devine, a wolf with a shady past, takes on the job of housekeeper to a kind old man and his pets.

230F **It's So Nice to Have a Wolf around the House**, Paul Fierlinger, 1979, 16mm color 12min $225, $25. LCA (P-I)

Excellent animation, clever story, and New York settings all combine to make a very funny film. Although much of the humor tends to be adult, this can be enjoyed by everyone. 1981 Notable Film for Children.

231 **Jack and the Beanstalk**, illus. by Agnes Molner. Knopf, 1979. $1.75 (P)

The traditional tale is retold by the artist.

231R **The Three Little Pigs and Other Fairy Tales**, Caedmon, 1962 (TC 1129) 12in 33-1/3rpm $8.98; (CDL 1129) cassette $8.98. CAE (P)

Read by Boris Karloff. Includes: "Jack and the Beanstalk," "The Three Sillies," "Hereafterthis," "The Old Woman and Her Pig," "Henny Penny," "The Three Little Pigs," "King of the Cats," and "The Three Bears."

232 **Jack Tales**, ed. by Richard Chase; illus. by Berkeley Williams, Jr. Houghton, 1943. 201p. $8.95 (I)

Authentic folktales of the Appalachian Mountains, collected from natives of the region and told with gusto and humor.

232R **Jackie Torrence: "The Story Lady,"** Weston Woods, 1982 (WW 720) 46:36min $8; (WW 720C) cassette $8. WW (P-I)

Jackie Torrence gives excellent tellings of "Jack and the Varmints" and three other Southern tales.

233 **Jake**, by Alfred Slote. Harper, 1971. 160p. $8.95; pap. $2.50 (I-U)

Eleven-year-old Jake searches for the perfect coach for his Little League team.

233F **Rag Tag Champs**, Robert Chanault, 1978, 16mm color 48min $615. ABC (I)

This television version of the book *Jake* by Alfred Slote stars Larry B. Scott and Glynn Turman. A girl is added to the Little League team. A 1980 ALA Notable Film.

234 **John Brown, Rose and the Midnight Cat**, by Jenny Wagner; illus. by Ron Brooks. Bradbury Pr., 1978. 32p. $9.95; Penguin pap. $3.25 (P)

Rose, a sweet old widow, lives with John Brown, her English sheepdog, in perfect contentment until the Midnight Cat disrupts their lives.

234F **John Brown, Rose and the Midnight Cat**, Morton Schindel, 1982, 16mm color 7min $140, $20. WW (P)

Iconographic style using natural sounds and music and a female narrator in this story of jealousy and sibling rivalry.

235 **John Henry: An American Legend**, story and pictures by Ezra Jack Keats. Pantheon, 1965. unp. lib. ed. $5.99 net (P-I)

A greatly simplified story of John Henry, the famous pile driver, embellished with large, bold pictures in color.

235FS **John Henry: An American Legend**, Guidance Associates, 1967 45fr color 14min cassette $35. GA (I)

Illustrations from the book. Accompanied by teacher's guide.

236 **Johnny Crow's Garden**, by L. Leslie Brooke. Warne, 1903. unp. $6.95 (N-P)

Nonsense rhymes about the animals who come to Johnny Crow's garden.

236FS **Johnny Crow's Garden**, Weston Woods, n.d. (FS 21) 29fr color $12; (SF 21) 4min with 7in 33rpm $9.20; (SF 21C) with cassette $18. WW (N-P)

Illustrations from the book, accompanied by picture-cued text booklet.

237 **Johnny Tremain: A Novel for Young and Old**, by Esther Forbes; illus. by Lynd Ward. Houghton, 1943. 256p. $8.95; 1969 Dell pap. $1.75 (I-U)

Johnny Tremain, courier for the Revolutionary Committee of Public Safety, loses his chance to become a silversmith when his hand is injured but plays an important part in the affairs of pre-Revolutionary Boston in spite of his handicap. 1944 Newbery Medal winner.

237R **Johnny Tremain**, Random House/Miller-Brody, 1969 (394-7641-4N) 12in 33rpm side 1: 20:47min, side 2: 20:42min $8.97; (394-7642-2N) cassette $8.97. RH (I-U)

A recorded dramatization narrated by Lloyd Moss. The cast includes Peter Fernandez, Don Barnett, Eddie Gaynes, Rick Gardner, and Corinne Orr. "Yankee Doodle" was specially scored for this recording by Herb Davidson. Includes teacher's guide.

238 **Journey Cake, Ho!**, by Ruth Sawyer; illus. by Robert

McCloskey. Viking, 1953. 45p. $3.25; lib. ed. $5.95 net; pap. $1.95 (P)

An American version of "The Johnny-Cake," in which a journey cake leads a farm boy on a merry chase.

238FS **Journey Cake, Ho!**, Weston Woods, n.d. (FS 80) 37fr color $12; (SF 80) 10:52min with 7in 33rpm $18; (SF 80C) with cassette $18. WW (P)

Illustrations from the book, accompanied by picture-cued text booklet.

239 **Journey Outside**, by Mary Q. Steele; woodcuts by Rocco Negri. Penguin, 1979. 143p. pap. $2.95 (I-U)

Dilar, one of the Raft People who drifts along an underground river in search of a Better Place, suddenly discovers light, trees, and sky.

239R **Journey Outside**, Live Oak Media, 1976, 2s 12in 33rpm side 1: 27:12min, side 2: 25:27min $8.95; cassette $8.95. LOM (I-U)

Narrated by Barrett Clark with Frank Scardino playing the role of Dilar. Excellent adaptation.

240 **The Judge**, by Harve Zemach; illus. by Margot Zemach. Farrar, 1969. unp. $7.95 (P-I)

"A horrible thing is coming this way, creeping closer day by day, its eyes are scary, its tail is hairy, I tell you, Judge, we all better pray!"

240F **The Judge**, Miller-Brody, 1976 (FAF 102) 16mm color 5min $100. M-B (P-I) OP

Excellent adaptation of book into film. Voices by William Griffis, Earl Hammond, Joan Sheppard, and Pierre Cache. Music by Herb Davidson.

240FS **The Judge**, Miller-Brody, 1975 (FA 102) 47fr color 4:57min 12in 33rpm $12.95; cassette $21. M-B (P-I)

Based on the book. Narrated by Billie Lou Watt. Also in the cast are Robert Dryden, Evelyn Juster, Gilbert Mack, Ray Owens, and Hal Studer. Delicious humor.

241 **Julie of the Wolves**, by Jean Craighead George; illus. by John Schoenherr. Harper, 1972. 180p. $7.95; lib. ed. $7.89 net (U)

A young Eskimo girl lost on the Arctic tundra is befriended by a wolf pack. 1973 Newbery Medal winner.

241FS **Julie of the Wolves**, Miller-Brody, 1975 (77035-8) 2 filmstrips 89, 106fr color with 12in 33rpm $45; (77036-6) cassette $45. M-B (I-U)

Sparsely illustrated frames done in watercolors give a feeling for the setting of the story.

241R **Julie of the Wolves**, Random House/Miller-Brody (394-77033-1) record $8.97; (394-77034-X) cassette $8.97. RH/M-B (I-U)

Dramatization of the book. Excellent narration accompanied by Eskimo music and appropriate sound effects which enrich the telling.

242 **The Jungle Book**, by Rudyard Kipling; illus. by Philip Hays. Doubleday, 1964. 213p. $4.95 (I-U)

The jungle adventures of the boy Mowgli, reared by Bagheera the panther and Baloo the bear.

242FS **The Jungle Book: Mowgli's Brothers**, Spoken Arts, 1971 (SA 2007-1) 76fr color 21:46min 12in 33rpm $28.95 record or cassette. SA (I-U)

Read by Eve Watkinson and Christopher Casson. Rousseau-like artwork by Barbara Bascove. Music by Christopher Casson. Includes teacher's guide, activity sheets, and reading script.

242FS **The Jungle Book: Rikki-Tikki-Tavi**, Spoken Arts, 1971 (SA 2007-2) 76fr color 20:47min 12in 33rpm record or cassette $28.95. SA (I)

Read by Eve Watkinson and Christopher Casson. Rousseau-like artwork by Barbara Bascove. Music by Christopher Casson. Includes teacher's guide, activity sheets, and reading script.

242FS **The Jungle Book: Tiger! Tiger!**, Spoken Arts, 1971 (SA 2007-3) 73fr color 19:29min 12in 33rpm record or cassette $28.95. SA (I-U)

Read by Eve Watkinson and Christopher Casson. Rousseau-like artwork by Barbara Bascove. Music by Christopher Casson. Includes teacher's guide, activity sheets, and reading script.

242FS **The Jungle Book: Toomai of the Elephants**, Spoken Arts, 1971 (SA 2007-4) 69fr color 20:16min 12in 33rpm $28.95; cassette $28.95. SA (I-U)

Read by Eve Watkinson and Christopher Casson. Rousseau-like artwork by Barbara Bascove. Music by Christopher Casson. Includes teacher's guide, activity sheets, and reading script.

242R **The Jungle Books**, by Rudyard Kipling, v. 1-4, Spoken Arts, 1966, $8.98 each record or cassette. v.1 (SA929) "Mowgli's Brothers" and "Rikki-Tikki-Tavi," records $8.98; (6025) "Mowgli's Brothers," (6026) "Rikki-Tikki-Tavi," individual cassettes $8.98. v.2 (SA951) "Tiger! Tiger! " and "Toomai of the Elephants," records $8.98; (6027) "Tiger! Tiger! ," (6028) "Toomai of the Elephants," individual cassettes $8.98. v.3 (SA951) "Koa's Hunting" and "The White Sea," records $8.98; (6029) "Koa's Hunting," individual cassettes $8.98. v.4 (SA952) "Letting in the Jungle" and the "Miracle of Purun Bhagat," records $8.98; (6030) "Letting in the Jungle," individual cassettes $8.98. SA (I)

These stories are read by Christopher Casson and Eve Wakinson. Indian music for introductions and backgrounds is performed by Mr. T. S. Banga of the Indian Embassy in Dublin and his two daughters.

242R **Rikki-Tikki-Tavi and Wee Willie Winkie**, Caedmon, 1969 (TC 1257) record $8.98; (CDL5 1257) cassette $8.98. CAE (I)

Anthony Quayle gives a flawless reading of two Kipling stories.

243 **Just Me**, by Marie Hall Ets. Viking, 1965. 32p. lib. ed. $6.95 net; pap. $1.50 (N-P)

Imitating the way the animals walk is fun, but it is even more fun to run just like a little boy to meet Daddy.

243FS **Just Me**, Weston Woods, n.d. (FS 106) 33fr color $7.25; (SF 106) with 7in 33rpm 7:38min $18; with cassette $18. WW (N-P)

Illustrations from the book, accompanied by picture-cued text booklet.

244 **Just So Stories**, by Rudyard Kipling; illus. by Etienne Delessert. Doubleday, 1972. 112p. $12.50 (P-I)

This well-loved collection has been embellished with strikingly modern illustrations.

244FS **How the Leopard Got His Spots**, Coronet, 1967 (MO106) 45fr color available with or without captions $12.50. COR (P)

Brilliant colors and Indian-style artwork capture the charm of this Kipling tale.

244FS **How the Rhinoceros Got His Skin**, Spoken Arts, 1974 (SA 2026-3) 26fr color 7:42min 12in 33rpm $28.95; cassette $28.95. SA (P-I)

Read by Eve Watkinson and Chris Curren. Music and sound effects by Christopher Casson. Watercolor artwork by Anne and Linda Danley. Includes teacher's guide and reading script.

244FS How the Whale Got His Throat, Spoken Arts, 1974 (SA 2026-1) 28fr color 10:08min 12in 33rpm; cassette $28.95. SA (P-I)

Read by Eve Watkinson and Chris Curren. Music and sound effcts by Christopher Casson. Watercolor artwork by Anne and Linda Danley. Includes teacher's guide and reading script.

244R Just So Stories, Caedmon, 195? (TC 1038) 1s 12in 33rpm $8.98; (CDL 51038) cassette $8.98. CAE (P-I)

Boris Karloff reads from Kipling. Contains: "How the Whale Got His Throat," "How the Camel Got his Hump," "How the Rhinoceros Got His Skin." Reverse side: an abridged version of "Mowgli's Brothers" from *The Jungle Book*.

244R The Cat That Walked by Herself and Other Just So Stories, Caedmon, 1962 (CDL 51139) cassette $8.98. CAE (I)

Boris Karloff reads the title story, "The Butterfly That Stamped," and "How the First Letter Was Written."

245 King of the Wind, by Marguerite Henry; illus. by Wesley Dennis. Rand McNally, 1948. 172p. $5.95; lib. ed. $5.97; deluxe ed. $10; pap. $2.95 (I)

The exciting story of the famous stallion Godolphin Arabian, founder of a strain of thoroughbreds and ancestor of Man o' War. 1949 Newbery Medal winner.

245R King of the Wind, Random House, 1971 (394-77041-2) 12in 33rpm 40-45min disc $8.97; (394-77042-0) cassette $8.97. RH (I)

A recorded dramatization. Narrated by Lloyd Moss. Featured in the cast are George Baxter, William Griffis, Rita Lloyd, Pat MacNamara, Larry Robinson, Fay Sappington, and Lawson Zerbe. Includes teacher's guide.

246 A Kiss for Little Bear, by Else Minarik; pictures by Maurice Sendak. Harper, 1968. 32p. $6.95; lib. ed. $7.89 (P)

Grandma Bear sends a kiss to Little Bear by Hen but the kiss gets all mixed up as Hen passes it along. An I Can Read book.

246FS A Kiss for Little Bear, Weston Woods, 1973 (FS 141) 34fr color 4:15min $12; (SF 141C) with cassette $18. WW (N-P)

Illustrations from the book, accompanied by picture-cued text booklet.

247 The Lace Snail, by Betsy Byars. Viking, 1975. 32p. $5.95 (P)

Her sudden ability to spin lace neither disturbs nor affects a snail. In fact, she accepts this gift quite naturally and generously shares it with all whom she meets on her travels.

247FS The Lace Snail, Viking, dist. by Live Oak Media, 1976 (0-670-90538-0) 33fr 9:25min with cassette $19.95. LOM (P)

Melodic guitar and flute music establish the quiet mood of Byars' book. The cool green-and-white block-print book illustrations with the delicate touches of black and the beautiful patterns of the lace trail left by the snail provide refreshing contrasts. The presentation is enlivened by the varied vocal characterizations of the bugs, frog, snake, turtle, crocodile and hippo who request lace adornments.

248 Legend of Paul Bunyan by Nanci A. Luman. New ed. Troll, 1980. 48p. lib. ed. $5.49; pap. $1.50 (P-I)

Tall tales about an enormous American lumberjack.

248FS The Legend of Paul Bunyan. Stephen Bosustow, Barr (Great American Folk Stories Set II) 1978 (#53900E) color 2 filmstrips 2 cassettes 1 guide $46. BA (P-I)

Paul Bunyan, mighty logger in the West,

earns respect by being smart and considerate.

248R Paul Bunyan in Story and Song, Caedmon (TC 1275) 12in LP $8.98; (CDL 51275) cassette $8.98. CAE (P-I)

A lively rendition of Paul Bunyan's notable deeds. The stories are read by Ed Begley and the songs are sung by Oscar Brand. Recordings include "Paul Bunyan Was a Mighty Man," "Paul's Cradle," "The Winter of the Blue Snow," "The Lumberman's Life," "Paul and the Giant Mosquitoes," "Paul Bunyan Digs the St. Lawrence River," "The Logging Life," Bunyan's Lament," "Johnnie Inkslinger and His Magic Pen," "The Wonderful Ox," "The Frozen Logger," "The Round River Drive," and "Roll on Paul."

248R Johnny Appleseed and Paul Bunyan, Caedmon (TC 1321) 12in LP $8.98; (CDL 5-1321) cassette $8.98. CAE (P-I)

Ed Begley reads the legend of the man who spread appleseeds across the country, Johnny Appleseed. Begley also reads the story of Paul Bunyan, a symbol of brawn and American ingenuity.

See also: *Davey Crockett and Pecos Bill* (Caedmon TC 1319 12in LP $8.98, CDL 5-1319 cassette $8.98), and *Mike Fink and Stormalong* (Caedmon TC 1320 12in LP $8.98). Begley narrates American tall tales.

249 The Legend of John Henry, the Steel Driving Man, by David A. Bice. illus. Jalamap, 1980. lib. ed. $6.95 (P-I)

The story of John Henry, a mighty logger, who wandered across America swinging his mighty hammer.

249FS The Legend of John Henry, Stephen Bosustow, Barr (Great American Folk Stories Set III) 1978 (#54000E) color 2 filmstrips 2 cassettes 1 guide $46. BA (P-I)

Steel driver John Henry courageously perseveres in the face of great odds.

249R John Henry and Joe Magarac, Caedmon (TC 1318) 12in LP $8.98; (CDL 5-1318) cassette $8.98. CAE (P-I)

Ed Begley reads tall tales of legendary American heroes: powerful John Henry, who blasted out the tunnels for the trains, and Joe Magarac, the greatest steel maker of all.

250 The Legend of Sleepy Hollow and Other Stories, by Washington Irving. (Classics Series) Airmont, 1964. pap. $1.25 (I)

The famous legend of schoolmaster Ichabod Crane, his rivalry with Brom Bones for the hand of Katrina Van Talles, and his encountered with the headless horseman in the Catskill Mountain area in the nineteenth century.

250FS The Legend of Sleepy Hollow, Listening Library, 1981, 66fr 20min 1 filmstrip 1 cassette 1 guide $27. LL (I-U)

A classic American short story is given a fitting retelling with lovely watercolor illustrations, notable narration, and suitable music.

250FS The Legend of Sleepy Hollow, Stephen Bosustow, Barr (Great American Folk Stories Set I) 1978, color 2 filmstrips 2 cassettes 1 guide $46. BA (P-I)

An adaptation that emphasizes the humorous vein and minimizes the frightening aspects of the story. Background guitar folk music conveys the spirit of the story and signals mood changes.

250R The Legend of Sleepy Hollow and Ichabod Crane and the Headless Horseman, Caedmon, 196? (TC 1242) 1 12in LP $8.98; (CDL5 1242) 1 cassette $8.98. CAE (U)

Ed Begley reads Irving's story.

251 Lentil, by Robert McCloskey. Viking, 1940. unp. $8.95 net; Puffin pap. $8.95 (P-I)

Scenes and activities in a small midwestern town come to life in McCloskey's humorous story and pictures of Lentil, the boy who substituted for the town band on an important occasion.

251F **Lentil**, Morton Schindel, 1956 (14) 16mm color 8:40min $140, $20; videocassette $140; also in Spanish $140. WW (P-I)

Iconographic technique using illustrations from the book. Narrated by Owen Jordan. Music by Arthur Kleiner.

Also available in Spanish.

251FS **Lentil**, Weston Woods, n.d. (FS 14) 42fr color $12; (SF 14C) 8:42min with cassette $18. WW (P-I)

Illustrations from the book, accompanied by picture-cued text booklet.

Also available in Spanish.

252 **Leopold, the See-through Crumbpicker**, by James Flora. Harcourt, 1961. unp. $6.95 (P)

Leopold felt warm and furry, sounded nice, but he was invisible. How he ate crumbs, advanced to entire lunches, and became visible, is a hilarious story.

252FS **Leopold, The See-through Crumbpicker**, Weston Woods, 1972 (FS 137) 62fr color 11:56min $12; (SF 137) with 7in 33rpm $18; (SF 137C) with cassette $18. WW (N-P)

Illustrations from the book, accompanied by picture-cued text booklet.

253 **Let's Be Enemies**, by Janice May Udry; pictures by Maurice Sendak. Harper, 1961. unp. $8.95; lib. ed. $8.79 net (P)

John, annoyed because James is entirely too bossy, decides that he no longer wants him for a friend and goes to tell him so. Instead of becoming enemies, they agree that it would be more fun to go skating.

253FS **Let's Be Enemies**, Weston Woods, n.d. 33fr color $7.25; 3:17min with cassette $18. WW (P)

Illustrations from the book, accompanied by picture-cued text booklet.

254 **Little Bear's Visit**, by Else Minarik; pictures by Maurice Sendak. Harper, 1960. unp. $6.95; lib. ed. $7.89 net (P)

On a wonderful day with his grandparents, Little Bear hears a story about his mother when she was a little girl, has lots of good things to eat, and plays games until he falls asleep.

254FS **Little Bear's Visit**, Weston Woods, n.d. 63fr color $7.25; (SF 83) 14:08min with cassette $18. WW (P)

Illustrations from the book, accompanied by picture-cued text booklet.

255 **Little Blue and Little Yellow**, by Leo Lionni. Astor-Honor, 1959. unp. $7.95 (P)

Little Blue and Little Yellow play together. One day they hug and turn green, and their families do not know them.

255F **Little Blue and Little Yellow**, David Hilberman, McGraw-Hill Films, 1962 (406873) 16mm color 9min $180, $19; (104860-X) VDC-video disc cassette $135. MH (P-U)

Animated film designed by the book's author, Leo Lionni. Directed by David Hilberman.

256 **The Little Bookroom**, by Eleanor Farjeon; illus. by Edward Ardizzone. Oxford Univ. Pr., 1979. $4.95 (I)

The author's selection of her own short stories for children, including "The Seventh Princess."

256R **The Seventh Princess and Other Fairy Tales**, CMS Records, 1968 (CMS 502) 2s 12in 33rpm $7.98; (CMSX4502) cassette $7.98. CMS (I)

Told by Anne Pellowski. Includes Eleanor Farjeon's "The Seventh Princess," Kipling's "The Potted Princess," "Cinderella," and "The Goose Girl."

257 **The Little Drummer Boy**, by Ezra Jack Keats; words and music by Katherine Davis, Henry Onorati, and Harry Simeone. Macmillan, 1968. unp. $7.95; pap. $2.50 (P-I)

The gift of a young boy, who can only offer to play his drum for the Baby, poignantly expresses the true spirit of Christmas.

257F **The Little Drummer Boy**, Morton Schindel, 1970 (124) 16mm color 7min $140, $20; videocassette $140. WW (P-I)

Iconographic technique using illustrations from the book. Words and music by Katherine Davis, Henry Onorati, and Harry Simeone. Sung by the St. Paul Choir School of Cambridge, Massachusetts, under the direction of Theodore Marier. Soloist is Anthony McLean.

257FS **The Little Drummer Boy**, Weston Woods, 1971 22fr color 6:30min; (SF 142C) with cassette $18. WW (P-I)

Illustrations from the book, accompanied by picture-cued text booklet.

Also available in Spanish.

258 **The Little Engine That Could**, by Watty Piper; illus. by Ruth Sanderson. Golden Anniversary ed. Platt and Munk, 1976. 39p. $5.99 (P)

When the little engine breaks down, it needs help to get its cargo for boys and girls over the mountain.

258F **The Little Engine That Could**, Coronet, 1963 (1510) 16mm color 11min $225. COR (N-P)

Animated film in style of book illustrations.

Also available in Spanish (*El Trencito*).

258FS **The Little Engine That Could**, Golden Anniversary edition, Society for Visual Education, 1977 (BD145-STC) 59fr color 11min with cassette. Book included. $34. SVE (P)

Each frame of the filmstrip has been copied from the original art work and reproduces an entire page of the book or several small details from a page. Appropriate sound effects enhance presentation.

259 **The Little Island**, by Golden MacDonald; illus. by Leonard Weisgard. Doubleday, 1946. unp. $3.95. OP

Richly colored pictures show a little island in changing seasons and weather as a kitten tries to discover the secret of what makes an island. Caldecott Medal winner, 1947.

259FS **The Little Island**, Weston Woods, n.d. (FS 29) 40fr color $12; (SF 29C) 6:09min with cassette $18. WW (P)

Illustrations from the book, accompanied by picture-cued text booklet.

260 **The Little Match Girl**, by Hans Christian Andersen; illus. by Blair Lent. Houghton, 1968. 43p. lib. ed. $7.95 net (P)

The poignant tale of the little match girl who lights all her matches to warm her spirit before she dies.

260R **The Little Match Girl and Other Tales**, Caedmon, 1960 (TC 1117) 1 12in LP $8.98; (CDL 51117) cassette $8.98. CAE (I)

Boris Karloff reads five Andersen tales as translated by Reginald Spink (Dutton, OP). Includes: "The Swineherd," "The Top and the Ball," "The Red Shoes," "Thumbelina," and "The Little Match Girl."

260R **Fairy Tales for a Winter's Night**, CMS Records, 1968 (CMS 534) record $8.98; (CMS X4534) cassette $8.98. CMS (I)

Mary Strang tells Andersen's "The Fir Tree" and "The Little Match Girl," Grimm's "The Elves and the Shoemaker," and "Twas the Night Before Christmas" by Clement Moore.

261 **The Little Mermaid**, by Hans C. Andersen; tr. by Eve Le Gallienne; illus. by Edward Frascino. Harper, 1971. 50p. $4.95; lib. ed. $4.79 net (P-I). OP

The poignant romance of the little mermaid who fell in love with a prince.

261R **The Little Mermaid**, Caedmon, 1967 (CDL51230) cassette 56:03min $8.98. CAE (I)

Cathleen Nesbitt reads the Keigwin translation. A sensitive reading which is undisturbed by any extraneous sound effects.

262 **The Little Prince**, by Antoine de Saint-Exupery; tr. by Katherine Woods. Harcourt, 1943. 91p. $7.95; pap. $1.95 (I-U)

A modern fairy tale about a little prince who lives on a small planet with one flower.

262F **The Little Prince**, Will Vinton, 1979, 16mm color 27min $550, $40. BUD (I)

Sophisticated claymation translates the Saint-Exupery classic into a visual delight. Narrated by Cliff Robertson. A 1981 ALA Notable Film for Children.

263 **The Little Red Hen**, by Paul Galdone. Houghton, 1973. 32p. $7.95; Scholastic pap. $1.50 (N-P)

The large colorful pictures of the domestic efforts of the little red hen while her three friends remain uncooperative delight both young and old.

263FS **The Little Red Hen**, Listening Library, n.d. color 1 filmstrip 1 cassette $22. LL (N-P)

An old favorite even more exciting with color and sound.

264 **The Little Red Lighthouse and the Great Gray Bridge**, by Hildegarde H. Swift and Lynd Ward. Harcourt, 1942. unp. $6.95; pap. $1.95 (P)

After the great beacon atop the new George Washington Bridge was installed, the little red lighthouse feared it would no longer be useful; but when an emergency arose, the little lighthouse proved that it was still important.

264F **The Little Red Lighthouse**, Morton Schindel, 1956 (15F) 16mm color 8:55min $140, $20. WW (P)

Iconographic technique using illustrations from the book. Narrated by Owen Jordan. Music by Arthur Kleiner.

Also available in Spanish.

264FS **The Little Red Lighthouse**, Weston Woods, n.d. (FS 15) 43fr color $12; (SF 15) 8:55min with 7in 33rpm $18; (SF 15C) with cassette $18. WW (P)

Illustrations from the book, accompanied by picture-cued text booklet.

Also available in Spanish.

265 **Little Red Riding Hood**, by the Brothers Grimm; retold and illustrated by Trina S. Hyman. Holiday, 1983. $13.95 (P)

Beautiful illustrations bring new life to the traditional favorite of the little girl who almost comes to grief while visiting her grandmother.

265F **Little Red Riding Hood**, Defa Film Studios, 1979, 16mm color 13min $195. LCA (P)

This animated version of a favorite tale has voice-over narration and a wolf's voice and carefully avoids any violence or scariness. The wolf is not shown eating anyone and leaps out of the window at the end.

265F **Little Red Riding Hood – A Balinese-Oregon Adaptation**, David Sonnenschein, 1979, 16mm color

17min $300. D. Sonnenschein (P.O. Box 711, Stinson Beach, CA 94970) (I)

Live-action version which was filmed in Oregon and which uses Balinese music. The actors wear wooden masks which are shown being carved in stop action sequences. A special film. 1982 Notable Film for Children.

266 **Little Sister and the Month Brothers**, retold by Beatrice de Regniers; illus. by Margot Tomas. Seabury, 1976. unp. $8 (P-I)

A retelling of a Slavic folktale about a little girl who escapes from her evil stepmother and stepsister with the help of the Twelve Month Brothers.

266R **Russian Folk and Fairy Tales**, CMS Records, 1967 (CMS515) 2s 12in 33rpm $7.98; (CMS-X4515) cassette $7.98. CMS (I)

"Kuzma Quick-Rich," "The Twelve Months," and "Two Out of the Knapsack" told by Christine Price.

267 **Little Tim and the Brave Sea Captain**, by Edward Ardizzone. Oxford Univ. Pr., 1978. unp. $8.95 (P)

Tim runs away to sea, is shipwrecked, and becomes a hero.

267F **Little Tim and the Brave Sea Captain**, Morton Schindel, 1976 (47F) 16mm color 11min $120, $25. WW (P)

The pictures come across stronger on film than in the book. Children are completely absorbed in the story which is pleasantly narrated by Michael Brew. Lively sea chanteys, accordion music, and the call of gulls accent the storytelling.

267FS **Little Tim and the Brave Sea Captain**, Weston Woods, n.d. (FS 47) 59fr color $12; (SF 47C) with cassette 9:23min $18. WW (P)

Illustrations from the books accompanied by picture-cued text booklet.

268 **Little Toot**, by Hardie Gramatky. Putnam, 1939. unp. $4.95; lib. ed. $4.49 net (P)

Playing games up and down the river, something no self-respecting tugboat would do, makes Little Toot an object of scorn, until he alone rescues an ocean liner in trouble.

268FS **Little Toot**, Weston Woods, n.d. (FS 16) 53fr color $7.25; (SF 16) with cassette 9:23min $18. WW (P)

Illustrations from the book, accompanied by picture-cued text booklet.

269 **Little Women; or, Meg, Jo, Beth, and Amy**, by Louisa M. Alcott. Centennial ed. With a new introd. by Cornelia Meigs; illus. in color by Jessie Willcox Smith. Little, 1868. 444p. $9.95 (I-U)

The story of the four March sisters, based on the life of the Alcotts of Concord, is still a favorite after a hundred years. This centennial edition has been completely reset and redesigned and is illustrated with the well-known Jessie Willcox Smith paintings.

269R **Little Women**, Caedmon, 1975 (TC 1470) 2s 12in 33rpm $6.98; (CDL5 1470) cassette $8.98. CAE (I)

Julie Harris gives a word-for-word reading of three chapters from this children's classic.

269R **Little Women**, CMS Records, 1969 (CMS 573) 2s 12in 33rpm $7.98; (CMS X4573) cassette $7.98. CMS (U)

"A Christmas Episode" read by Elinor Basescu.

270 **The Little Wooden Farmer**, by Alice Dalgliesh; illus. by Anita Lobel. Macmillan, 1968. unp. $4.95; pap. $.95 (P)

New illustrations reinterpret the old story of the little wooden farmer and his little wooden wife who acquire the animals they need to make their farm complete. A repetitive story with stiff, patterned illustrations that perfectly maintain the illusion of the little wooden world.

270FS **The Little Wooden Farmer**, Education Reading Services (Library 2) 40fr color 7min with cassette $14.95. ERS (N-P)

Illustrations from the book, accompanied by picture-cued text booklet. Excellent narration highlighted by animal sounds.

271 **London Bridge Is Falling Down!**, illus. by Peter Spier. Doubleday, 1967. unp. $6.95; pap. $1.49 (P)

Eighteenth-century London bursts with life in this gaily illustrated picture-book version of the old rhyme. Part of the Mother Goose Library.

271FS **London Bridge Is Falling Down!**, Weston Woods, 1971 (FS 122) 20fr color $12; (SF 122C) with cassette 6min $18. WW (P)

Illustrations from the book, accompanied by picture-cued text booklet.

272 **Look What I Can Do**, by Jose Aruego. Scribner, 1971. unp. $6.95 (P)

Two carabaos (water buffalos) take off in a series of follow-the-leader antics. But, trying to outdo each other, they disturb and alarm other animals—and fall into an unexpectedly dangerous adventure.

272FS **Look What I Can Do**, Random House/Miller-Brody, 1980 (394-78397-2) 72fr color 7min with cassette $21. RH/M-B (P)

Musical background appropriate to the happenings in the illustrations. Filmstrip utilizes Aruego's delightful, action-packed illustrations.

273 **The Loon's Necklace**, by William Toye; illus. by Elizabeth Cleaver. Oxford Univ. Pr., 1977. unp. $5.95 (P-I)

A Tsimshian Indian legend explaining the origin of the loon's white feather markings. An old man who cannot provide for his family because of blindness appeals to the loon, regains his sight by swimming on the loon's back under the lake, and rewards the loon with his shell necklace, which makes a permanent pattern on its feathers.

273FS **The Loon's Necklace**, Weston Woods, 1978 (FS 235) 35fr color 11min $12; (SF 235 C) with cassette $18. WW (P-I)

The filmstrip version utilizes the rich illustrations from the book. Sound effects enhance the presentation.

Accompanied by picture-cued text booklet.

274 **The Lorax**, by Dr. Seuss. Random, 1971. $5.95; lib. ed. $5.99 (P-U)

Fanciful story with serious theme: Clean up environment before it's too late. Who the Lorax is and what he does is described with typical Seussian logic.

274F **The Lorax**, DePatie-Feleng, CBS, 1972 (11083) 16mm color 24min $480, $67. BFA (P-I-U)

Animation adapted from original illustrations. Originally produced for CBS Television.

275 **Lost in the Museum**, by Lillian Hoban. Greenwillow, 1979. $7.75; lib. ed. $7.44 (N-P)

A small book with warm illustrations about Jim and his first grade classmates who become lost in the museum.

275FS **Lost in the Museum**, Educational Enrichment Materials, n.d. color 1 filmstrip 1 cassette $22. EEM (N-P)

Being lost in a museum is not much fun in this tale by Miriam Cohen illustrated by Lillian Hoban.

276 **Lovable Lyle**, by Bernard Waber. Houghton, 1969. 48p. $8.95; pap. $1.95 (N-P) OP

Lyle is upset when he begins receiving anonymous hate notes. His "enemy" turns out to be a little girl who has been forbidden to play with crocodiles. Engaging Lyle recues her from drowning and makes friends.

276FS **Lyle, the Crocodile**, Educational Enrichment Materials 1971 (Sets I & II 70003) 4 filmstrips av 75fr color 4 cassettes or discs av 15 min $87. EEM (P)

Individual titles:

Set I: *The House on 88th Street* (72115)
Lovable Lyle (72116)

Set II: *Lyle and the Birthday Party* (72117)
Lyle, Lyle Crocodile (72118)

Written and illustrated by Bernard Waber, these stories of kindness, bravery, and humor make Lyle a favorite with his neighbors and beginning readers. Also available in bilingual edition (40014) $151.

276R **Lyle, Lyle, Crocodile and Other Adventures of Lyle**, Caedmon, 1973 (TC 1350) 2s 12in 33rpm $8.98; (CDL 51350) cassette $8.98.
CAE (P)

Gwen Verdon reads the title story, "The House on East 88th Street," "Lyle and the Birthday Party," and "Lovable Lyle."

277 **Lyle and the Birthday Party**, by Bernard Waber. Houghton, 1966. 48p. $7.95; pap. $2.45 (P)

Lyle, sick with jealousy because he gets no attention on Joshua's birthday, is sent to the hospital where he recovers from his bad humor by helping others.

277FS **Lyle and the Birthday Party**, Teaching Resources Films, 1971 (721170) 71fr color 15min with 12in 33rpm $25; with cassette $27. TRF (P)

Original illustrations accompanied by word-for-word reading of the text.

278 **Lyle, Lyle, Crocodile**, by Bernard Waber. Houghton, 1965. 48p. $8.95; pap. $2.95 (N-P)

Mr. Grumps has Lyle committed to the city zoo. Lyle decides to escape to Australia but stops to say good-bye to the Primms. When he rescues Mr. Grumps and his cat from their burning house, Mr. Grumps publicly thanks Lyle and asks him to be his neighbor again.

278FS **Lyle, Lyle, Crocodile**, Teaching Resources Films, 1971 (721180) 82fr color 15min with 12in 33rpm $25; with cassette $27. TRF (P)

Original illustrations accompanied by word-for-word reading of the text.

279 **M. C. Higgins, the Great**, by Virginia Hamilton. Macmillan, 1974. 288p. $7.95 (U)

M. C. and his family live on great-great-grandmother Sarah's mountain in Appalachia where strip mining threatens to destroy their way of life. M. C. is caught trying to balance his heritage and his own emerg emerging manhood. 1975 Newbery Medal winner.

279FS **M. C. Higgins, the Great**, Random House/Miller-Brody, 1980 (394-78417-0) 2 filmstrips 138, 149fr color with 2 cassettes 20:56min $45. RH/M-B (I)

Filmstrip uses color illustrations which reflect Hamilton's descriptions. The author plays M. C.'s mother and also performs the songs.

279R **M. C. Higgins, the Great**, Random House/Miller-Brody, 1975 (394-77059-5) 2 records $17.94; (394-77060-9) 2 cassettes $17.94. RH/M-B (U)

Fine dramatization of the book with author Virginia Hamilton playing the part of the mother, Banina Higgins, and singing the songs. Narrated by Fred Morsell.

280 **McElligot's Pool**, by Dr. Seuss. Random House, 1947. $5.99 (P)

Little Marco imagines that if he waits long enough he might catch fish of all colors and sizes.

280FS **McElligot's Pool**, Random House/Miller-Brody, 1981 (394-0622565-X) 79fr color 13min with cassette $21. RH/M-B (P)

Some color added to Seuss's original illustrations. Rhyming verses read expressively by an engaging narrator.

280R **McElligot's Pool**, by Dr. Seuss Random House/Miller-Brody (394-07676-1) read-along cassette with hardcover book $15. RH/M-B (P)

Entertaining narration.

281 **Madeline**, by Ludwig Bemelmans. Viking, 1939. unp. $4.95; lib. ed. $8.95 net; pap. $2.50 (P)

Madeline, a nonconformist in the regimented world of a Parisian boarding school, makes an adventure out of having appendicitis. Authentic Paris atmosphere in text and pictures.

281F **Madeline**, Learning Corp. of America 1955 (ICP3) 16mm color 7min $100, $10. LCA (P)

Text and animated drawings from the book. Produced by Stephen Bosustow.

281R **Madeline and Other Bemelmans**, Caedmon, 1959 (TC 1113) 2s 12in 33rpm $8.98; (CDL 51113) cassette $8.98. CAE (P)

Carol Channing recounts Bemelmans' delightful tales. Includes: *Madeline*, *Madeline's Rescue*, *Madeline and the Bad Hat*, and *The Happy Place*.

282 **Madeline and the Gypsies**, by Ludwig Bemelmans. Viking, 1959. 56p. $6.95 net; pap. $1.95 (P)

Miss Clavel takes her little girls to a street fair in Paris, where Madeline and Pepito are left behind.

282R **Madeline and the Gypsies, and Other Stories by Ludwig Bemelmans,** Caedmon, 1970 (TC 1304) 2s 12in 33rpm $8.98; (CDL 51304) cassette $8.98. CAE (P)

Carol Channing reads *Madeline and the Gypsies*, *Madeline in London*, *Quito Express*, and *The Castle Number Nine*.

282R **Madeline and the Gypsies**, Live Oak Media, 1980 (0-670-44684-x) cassette 14min 8 paperbacks teacher's guide $21.95. LOM (P)

Clear narration of a delightful Ludwig Bemelman story. One side of the cassette has page turn signals, the other side does not.

283 **Madeline's Rescue**, by Ludwig Bemelmans. Viking, 1953. 56p. $8.95 net; pap. $2.50 (P)

Madeline is rescued from the Seine by a dog which becomes the school pet. When the trustees object, the dog solves the problem in a surprising way. Caldecott Medal winner, 1954.

283F **Madeline's Rescue**, William L. Snyder, 1959, 16mm color 7min $135. REMB (P-I)

Animated film based on book illustrations.

283FS **Madeline's Rescue**, Weston Woods, n.d. (SF30C) 53fr with cassette and text booklet $20; (FS30) with text booklet $14. WW (P)

Illustrations from the book, accompanied by picture-cued text booklet.

283R **Madeline's Rescue**, Weston Woods, n.d. (LTR 030) 7in 33rpm 6:14min $6; (LTR 030C) cassette $6. WW (P)

Story narrated by Owen Jordan, with original background music by Arthur Kleiner.

284 **Magic Fishbone**, by Charles Dickens; illus. by Faith Jacques. Harvey House, 1969. unp. lib. ed. $5.29 (P)

A princess, 18 brothers and sisters, a Fairy Grandmarina combine with fun and humor to produce a gem of a story.

284FS **Magic Fishbone**, Listening Library, 1977 (Look, Listen, and Read JFS 155) 66fr color 14min guide 1 captioned sound filmstrip 1 cassette $21. LL (P)

An adaptation of Dickens' delightfully nonsensical story in which Princess Alicia saves the royal family from poverty and marries the Prince.

285 **The Magic Flute**, retold by Stephen Spender; pictures by Beni Montresor. Putnam, 1966. unp. lib. ed. $4.19 net (P-I)

The enchantment of Mozart's opera is captured in his lively libretto which tells the story for children and is accompanied by handsome illustrations based on Montresor's sets for a new production of the opera.

285 **The Magic Flute**, edited by John Updike; illus. by Warren Chappell. Knopf, 1962. unp. $5.39 (P)

This picture-book version by John Updike and Warren Chappell includes some of the themes in simple piano arrangements.

285R **The Magic Flute**, London Records, n.d. (5-1397) 6s 12in 33rpm $17.95. LON (I-U)

Highlights from Mozart's opera performed by the Vienna State Opera Chorus and the Vienna Philharmonic Orchestra.

286 **The Magic Porridge Pot**, by Paul Galdone. Houghton, 1976. 32p. $7.95 (N-P)

After a strange old woman gives a poor hungry girl a magic pot, the child and her mother have all the porridge they need. All is well until the mother forgets the magic words and the entire village is flooded with porridge.

286FS **The Magic Porridge Pot**, Listening Library, n.d. color 1 filmstrip 1 cassette $21. LL (N-P)

The visual sound production of Paul Galdone's telling about the pot that wouldn't stop bubbling.

287 **The Magic Tree; a Tale from the Congo**, by Gerald McDermott. Holt, 1973. unp. $5.95; lib. ed. $5.59 net; pap. $1.95 (I-U)

Haunting story of the unloved boy, Movumgu, who leaves home to find a magic tree that gives him happiness. He returns home, betrays the tree's secret, and loses all.

287F **The Magic Tree**, Gerald McDermott and Texture Films, Inc., 1973, 16mm color 10min $155, $15. TEX (I-U)

Beautiful animation based on book illustrations. Music by Thomas Wagner. Narration by Athmani Magoma.

287FS **The Magic Tree**, Random House/ Miller-Brody, 1978 (394-76475-1) 109fr color 15min with cassette $21. RH/M-B (P)

The vibrant rust, turquoise, and blue backgrounds of McDermott's animated film pleasingly stand out in the filmstrip adaptation. Utilizes an African narrator and well-chosen stills from the film.

288 **The Magical Drawings of Mooney B. Finch**, by David McPhail. Doubleday, 1978. $6.95 (N-P)

Mooney had a special talent: when he drew anything, it became real. This led him into some peculiar situations, but fortunately he had a talent that got him out of them.

288FS **The Magical Drawings of Mooney B. Finch**, Listening Library, n.d. color 1 filmstrip 1 cassette $21. LL (N-P)

Electrical, light tones effectively accent David McPhail's charming fantasy for young readers and viewers.

289 **Make Way for Ducklings**, by

Robert McCloskey. Viking, 1941. unp. $8.95; pap. $2.50 (P)

The engaging doings of a busy mallard family living in Boston's public garden. Caldecott Medal winner, 1942.

289F **Make Way for Ducklings**, Morton Schindel, 1955 (6077) 16mm b/w 11:25min $175, $25; videocassette $175; Super 8 sound $175. WW (P)

Iconographic technique using illustrations from the book. Narration by Owen Jordan. Music by Arthur Kleiner.

Also available in Spanish.

289FS **Make Way for Ducklings**, Weston Woods, n.d. (FS 3) 47fr color $12; (SF3C) 11min with cassette $18. WW (P)

Illustrations from the book, accompanied by picture-cued text booklet.

Also available in Spanish.

289R **Make Way for Ducklings**, Weston Woods, n.d. (LTR 003C) cassette $6; hardcover book with cassette $14.95. WW (P)

Story narrated by Owen Jordan, with original background music by Arthur Kleiner.

Available also in Spanish.

290 **A Man Ain't Nothin' but a Man**, by John Oliver Killens. Little, 1975. 256p. $5.95 (U)

The adventures of John Henry told for older children.

290F **The Legend of John Henry**, Stephen Bosustow, 1974, 16mm color 11min $160, $15. PYR (I-U)

Animated film with Roberta Flack singing the legend in a blues rendition. This award-winning film has a powerful impact.

291 **The Man Who Tried to Save Time**, by Phyllis Krasilovsky; illus. by Marcia Sewall. Doubleday, 1979. unp. $5.90 (P-I)

To save time, "the man" begins eating breakfast at night and sleeping in his clothes on top of his bed, buying tons of food to save extra shopping trips, over-watering his plants so they won't need attention for a spell, etc. It's not long before everything gets out of hand.

291FS **The Man Who Tried to Save Time**, Westport Communications Group, dist. by Educational Enrichment Materials, 1981 (#52381) 63fr color 9min with cassette $22. EEM (P-I)

Utilizing Sewall's tricolor pen-and-ink art adapted from the book along with light instrumental melodies which underscore the man's capricious behavior. Realistic sound effects enhance the filmstrip presentation.

292 **Mandy's Grandmother**, by Liesel M. Skorpen; illus. by Martha Alexander. Dial, 1975. 32p. $4.95; lib. ed. $4.58. (P)

At first meeting tomboy Mandy and her genteel grandmother from England are a disappointment to each other as neither is what the other expected.

292F **Mandy's Grandmother**, Andres Sugerman, 1978, 16mm color 30min $425, $45. PHX (P)

Live-action film stars Maureen O'Sullivan as the Grandmother, Kathryn Walker as Mandy's mother, and Amy Levitan as Mandy.

293 **Many Moons**, by James Thurber; illus. by Louis Slobodkin. Harcourt, 1943. unp. $5.95; pap. $2.25 (P-I)

After the king's wise men have failed, the court jester finds a way to get the moon in order to make the little Princess Lenore well again. Caldecott Medal winner, 1944.

293F **Many Moons**, Rachel Izel, 1975, 16mm color 13min $185, $15. MH (P)

Animated. Narrated by Robert Morley

and supporting cast. Bach's Suite in G Minor for lute is the background music.

293F **Many Moons**, William L. Snyder, 1964, 16mm color 10min $135, $10. REMB (P-I)

Animated film based on book illustrations.

293R **Many Moons**, Caedmon, 1972 (CDL 51410) cassette only $8.98. CAE (P)

Peter Ustinov captures all the charm and humor of Thurber's first children's book.

294 **Mary of Mile 18**, by Ann Blades. Tundra, 1971. unp. $10.95 (P-I)

Mary Fehr finds a wolf pup which her father doesn't want her to keep until it alerts him to a chicken-thieving coyote.

294FS **Mary of Mile 18**, Weston Woods, 1978 (FS 233) 48fr color 13min $12; (SF 233C) with cassette $18. WW (P-I)

Vivid color illustrations from the book. Filmstrip version adds the old-fashioned strains of a dulcimer.

Accompanied by picture-cued text booklet.

295 **Mary Poppins**, by P. L. Travers; illus. by Mary Shepard. Harcourt, 1934. 206p. $6.95; pap. $2.25 (I)

When an astonishing nursemaid blows into the Banks family on an east wind, the children are delighted with the magical adventures she plans for them.

295R **Mary Poppins**, Caedmon, 1968 (TC 1246) 2s 12in 33rpm $8.98; (CDL 51246) cassette $8.98. CAE (P-I)

A dramatization of five episodes from the book. Narrated by Robert Stephens, featuring Maggie Smith in the title role, with supporting cast. Includes: "East Wind," "The Day Out," "Laughing Gas," "Miss Lark's Andrews," and "Bad Tuesday."

296 **Mary Poppins Comes Back**, by P. L. Travers; illus. by Mary Shepard. Harcourt, 1935. 268p. $5.95; pap. $2.45 (I)

After mysteriously disappearing from the Banks home, Mary Poppins returns on the end of a kite string, stays for a while, and then vanishes on a merry-go-round horse.

296R **Mary Poppins Comes Back**, Caedmon, 1979 (CDL 51269) cassette only $8.98. CAE (P-I)

Includes "Full Moon" and "West Wind" from *Mary Poppins* and "The Kite" from *Mary Poppins Comes Back*. Maggie Smith is Mary. Robert Stephens narrates.

297 **Mary Poppins from A to Z**, by P. L. Travers; illus. by Mary Shepard. Harcourt, 1962. unp. $4.50; lib. ed. $3.95 net (P-I)

Twenty-six short episodes about the characters in all the Mary Poppins books.

297R **Mary Poppins from A to Z**, Caedmon, 1968 (CDL 51254) cassette only $8.98. CAE (P-I)

This is Robert Stephens's word-for-word reading of the entire book, with an introduction and conclusion read by the author, Pamela Travers.

298 **Mary Poppins Opens the Door**, by P. L. Travers; illus. by Mary Shepard. Harcourt, n.d. 239p. $5.95; pap. $2.45 (I)

Mary Poppins arrives in a rocket on Guy Fawkes' Day.

298R **Mary Poppins Opens the Door**, Caedmon, 1970 (CDL 51271) cassette only $8.98. CAE (P-I)

"High Tide." "The Other Door." Maggie Smith is Mary.

298R **Mary Poppins: Balloons and Balloons**, Caedmon, 1971 (CDL 51348) cassette only $8.98. CAE (P-I)

"Balloons and Balloons" and "Mr.

Twigley's Wishes" from *Mary Poppins Opens the Door*. Narrated by Robert Stephens with Maggie Smith as Mary Poppins. This delightful dramatization perfectly captures the humor and pathos of Travers' tales.

299 **The Matchlock Gun**, by Walter D. Edmonds; illus. by Paul Lantz. Dodd, 1941. 50p. $5.95 (I)

New York State during the French and Indian War is the setting for this story of a boy's courage and resourcefulness. In his father's absence, ten-year-old Edward Alstyne helps his mother fight off an Indian attack by firing an old Spanish musket. 1942 Newbery Medal winner.

299FS **The Matchlock Gun**, Miller-Brody, 1971 (NSF-3005) 2 filmstrips 128fr color 12in 33rpm manual/ automatic side 1: 16:30min, side 2: 18:30min $24; (NAC-3005) with cassette $28. RH/M-B (P-I)

Artwork by Mel Greifinger depicting Dutch colonial times in authentic detail with the full sound track of the original recording.

299R **The Matchlock Gun**, Random House/Miller-Brody, 1969 (394-76810-8) record $8.97; (394-76819-1) cassette $8.97. RH/M-B (P-I)

A recorded dramatization. Narrated by John Hallow. The role of Teunis Van Alstyne is played by Marc Jordan, Gertrude by Jean Richards, Edward by Adam Fried, and Trudy by Leslie Silvi. The background music is based on an old Dutch lullaby and was arranged by Herb Davidson.

300 **Maurice Sendak's Really Rosie: Starring the Nutshell Kids**, by Maurice Sendak; music by Carole King. Harper, 1975. 64p. pap. $3.95 (P-I)

Scenario, lyrics, and pictures taken from the original animated television special.

300F **Really Rosie**, Sheldon Riss, 1976, 16mm color 26min $365. WW (P-I)

The critically acclaimed television program starring the Nutshell Kids from Maurice Sendak's *Nutshell Library* and *The Sign on Rosie's Door*. Animated with songs by Carole King.

300R **Maurice Sendak's Really Rosie**, Caedmon, 1981 (#TRS368) 60min $8.98; (#CP368) LC 81-740022 cassette 60min $8.98. CAE (P-I)

The original cast recording of the Broadway play starring young children who sing their hearts out. Carole King's music, Maurice Sendak's stories, and talented young singers turn out an extravaganza.

300R **The Maurice Sendak Soundbook**, Caedmon, 1981 (SBR125) 4 discs or (SBC125) 4 cassettes 49-60min $29.95. CAE (P-I)

This includes the Broadway cast of *Really Rosie*, plus Tammy Grimes performing and narrating nine of Sendak's books. A delightful performance of outstanding children's literature.

301 **May I Bring a Friend**? by Beatrice Schenk De Regniers; illus. by Beni Montresor. Atheneum, 1964. unp. lib. ed. $7.95 net; pap. $2.95 (N-P)

The king and queen tactfully accept the animal friends a little boy brings to tea, and are rewarded by being invited to tea at the zoo. Caldecott Medal winner, 1965.

301FS **May I Bring a Friend**? Weston Woods, 1973 (FS 164) with 7in 33rpm disc $9.20; (SF 164C) with cassette 6:50min $12.75. WW (N-P)

Illustrations from the book, accompanied by picture-cued text booklet. Narration is sung by Albert Hague.

302 **Mazel and Shlimazel, or Milk of a Lioness**, by Isaac B. Singer; illus. by Margot Zemach. Farrar, 1967. 42p. $8.95 (P-I)

Mazel—the spirit of good luck—and Shlimazel—the spirit of bad luck—match wits.

302FS Mazel and Shlimazel, Miller-Brody, 1976 (FA 107/108) 136fr color 34:24min with 2 10in 33rpm $25.90; cassette $29.90. M-B (P-I)

Based on the book. Fine narration by Bill Griffis. The producers chose to put this on 2 filmstrips and 2 records/cassettes and the length of the story probably justifies their decision. (Part 1: 74fr 19:12min, Part 2: 62fr 15:52min)

303 Mei Li, by Thomas Handforth. Doubleday, 1938. unp. $6.95 (P)

A little Chinese girl who lives in North China near the Great Wall goes to the New Year's fair and on her return home meets the Kitchen God at midnight. Caldecott Medal winner, 1939.

303FS Mei Li, McGraw-Hill, 1972 (105573) 49fr color 17min 12in 33rpm $18; cassette $18. MH (P)

Based on the book, but color has been added to the illustrations. Excellent background music and narration. Part of Children's Literature Series, Set 6. Includes teacher's manual.

304 Merry Ever After: The Story of Two Medieval Weddings, by Joe Lasker. Viking, 1976. unp. $7.95 (P-I)

Joe Lasker has drawn on the legacy of beauty and history left to us by artists of the medieval world by focusing on the events that bring two couples of differing backgrounds to marriage and by comparing their wedding ceremonies and feasts. The dress and customs of the people, the structure and look of their dwellings, the manner of their activity in work, play, and war—all are presented in detail.

304FS Merry Ever After: The Story of Two Medieval Weddings, Viking, 1977 (0-670-90566-6) 70fr color 18:09min with cassette $19.95. LOM (P-I)

ALA Notable Filmstrip.

The rich detail of Lasker's illustrations highlights the contrasts and similarities of the customs and people of medieval Europe. Vivid narration and contemporary music combine to create a work of aesthetic pleasure.

Accompanied by picture-cued text booklet.

305 Mice Twice, by Joseph Low. Atheneum, 1980. 32p. $9.95 (P)

Cat wants Mouse for dinner, literally. Mouse brings Dog for protection. This tale of one-upmanship goes on until Mouse brings to dinner a tiny mystery guest who packs a terrific wallop.

Caldecott Honor Book.

305FS Mice Twice, Random House/Miller-Brody, 1981 (394-07721-0) 82fr color 9min with cassette $21. RH/M-B (P)

Low's expressive ink and watercolor drawings, in shades of predominantly purple, gold-yellow, and orange, create an amusing, lively filmstrip. Backgrounds of color and sound effects heighten the dramatic narrative.

305R Mice Twice, by Joseph Low. Random House/Miller-Brody (394-07669-9) read-along cassette with hardcover book side 1 (no signals) 8min, side 2 (page turn signals) 8:15min $18.96. RH/M-B (P)

A dramatic reading of the story with authentic characterization of the animals. The read-along version uses delicate tonal sounds for page-turning that do not distract from the story.

306 The Midnight Fox, by Betsy Byars; illus. by Ann Grifalconi. Viking, 1968. 157p. $7.95; pap. $1.50 (I-U)

Tom reluctantly spends a summer on a relative's farm while his parents are abroad. There he befriends a black fox and, through the relationship, gains some understanding of himself.

306R **The Midnight Fox**, Live Oak Media, 1973 (VK 110A/B) 12in record $8.95; cassette $8.95; clothbound book $7.95; pap. $1.50. LOM (I-U)

A dramatization of the book performed by the High Tor Repertory Players.

307 **Mike Mulligan and His Steam Shovel**, by Virginia Lee Burton. Houghton, 1939. unp. $7.95; pap. $2.95 (P)

Mike and his old-fashioned steam shovel, Mary Anne, prove that they can do some things better than the new-fangled bulldozers.

307F **Mike Mulligan and His Steam Shovel**, Morton Schindel, 1956 (6507) 16mm color 10:35min $120, $5. WW (P)

Iconographic technique using illustrations from the book. Narrated by Owen Jordan. Music by Arthur Kleiner.

Also available in Spanish.

307FS **Mike Mulligan and His Steam-shovel**, Weston Woods, n.d. (FS 4) 60fr color $7.25; (SF 4) with 7in 33rpm 10:37min $9.20; with cassette $12.75. WW (P)

Illustrations from the book, accompanied by picture-cued text booklet.

Also available in Spanish.

308 **Millions of Cats**, by Wanda Gag. Coward, 1928. unp. $7.95; pap. $2.50 net (N-P)

Repetitive story and rhythmic illustrations make this tale of a little old couple who wanted a cat perfect for a story hour with young children.

308F **Millions of Cats**, Morton Schindel, 1955 (5978) 16mm b/w 10:15min $60, $4. WW (N-P)

Iconographic technique using illustrations from the book. Narrated by Owen Jordan. Music by Arthur Kleiner.

Also available in Spanish.

308FS **Millions of Cats**, Weston Woods, n.d. (FS 5) 45fr color $7.25; (SF 5) with 7in 33rpm disc 10:13min $9.20; (SF 5C) with cassette $12.75. WW (N-P)

Illustrations from the book, accompanied by picture-cued text booklet.

Also available in Spanish.

309 **Miracles on Maple Hill**, by Virginia Sorensen; illus. by Beth Krush and Joe Krush. Harcourt, 1956. 180p. $5.95 (I)

Ever since Father had returned from a prisoner-of-war camp, weary, hurt, and discouraged, home had been an unhappy place with everyone irritable and worried. But miracles began to happen when the family moved to Maple Hill farm. 1957 Newbery Medal winner.

309FS **Miracles on Maple Hill**, Random House/Miller-Brody, 1980 (394-78387-5) 2 filmstrips 128, 136fr color 17, 16min with 2 cassettes $45. RH/M-B (I)

Filmstrip based on book. Realistic illustrations. Sensitive narration.

309R **Miracles on Maple Hill**, by Virginia Sorenson. Random House/Miller-Brody (394-77061-7) record $8.97; (394-77062-5) cassette $8.97. RH/M-B (I)

A dramatic reading by Bill Griffis.

310 **Miracles: Poems by Children of the English-Speaking World**, compiled by Richard Lewis. Simon & Schuster, 1966. 215p. $8.98 (P-U)

Poems by children between the ages of four and thirteen show the power of imagination and talent for creative expression of which young people are capable.

310R **Miracles: Poems Written by Children**, Caedmon, 1967 (CDL 51227) cassette $8.98. CAE (I)

Julie Harris and Roddy McDowall read poems from Richard Lewis's collection. The poems are arranged by such themes as morning, spring, the wind and the rain, playing, etc.

311 **Miss Hickory**, by Carolyn Sherwin Bailey; illus. by Ruth Gannett. Viking, 1946. 120p. lib. ed. $7.95; pap. $1.50 (I)

The story of a doll with a hickory-nut head and an apple-twig body, left behind when a New Hampshire family moves away. 1947 Newbery Medal winner.

311R **Miss Hickory**, Live Oak Media, 1972, 12in record $8.98; cassette $8.98. LOM (I)

Dramatized version of the book, performed by the High Tor Repertory Players.

312 **Mr. Gumpy's Motor Car**, by John Burningham. Harper, 1976. lib. ed. $10.89 (N-P)

All of Mr. Gumpy's friends want to go for a ride in his motor car, but they aren't too eager to help push the car up the hill.

312R **Mr. Gumpy's Motor Car**, Weston Woods, 1982 (LTR 274C) cassette 5min $6. WW (N-P)

Ian Thomson gives an English touch to the narration, and the sound effects of the motor, the rain, etc., heighten the enjoyment of the story.

313 **Mr. Gumpy's Outing**, by John Burningham. Holt, 1971. lib. ed. $6.95 (N-P)

Mr. Gumpy takes all who ask—animals and children—for a ride in his small boat. A cumulative tale illustrated with gentle humor.

313FS **Mr. Gumpy's Outing**, Weston Woods, 1973 (FS 150) 33fr color 5min $7.25; (SF 150) with 7in 33rpm $9.20; (SF 150C) with cassette $12.75. WW (N-P)

Illustrations from the book, accompanied by picture-cued text booklet.

314 **Mr. Popper's Penguins**, by Richard and Florence Atwater; illus. by Robert Lawson. Little, 1938. 138p. $8.98 (P-I)

Mr. Popper, a mild-mannered house painter, dreams of adventure in distant lands, especially of polar expeditions. Unexpectedly, he receives an unusual gift—an Antarctic penguin. From that moment on, life was changed for the Popper family.

314FS **Mr. Popper's Penguin**, Random House/Miller-Brody, 1979 (394-77074-9) 2 filmstrips 154, 156fr color 21, 20min with 2 cassettes $45. RH/M-B (P-I)

Filmstrip based on the book. Appropriate, effective sound effects enhance the realistic illustrations.

314R **Mr. Popper's Penguins**, by Florence and Richard Atwater. Random House/Miller-Brody (394-76801-9) 2 read-along records $17.94; (394- 76802-7) 2 read-along cassettes $17.94; (394-77071-4) listening record $8.97; (394-77072-2) listening cassette $8.97. RH/M-B (P-I)

The read-along version is narrated by Jim Backus, television's Mr. Magoo. The dramatized version features Jan Miner, television and film actress. Jim Backus gives just the right touch of deadpan absurdity to all those penguins marching in and out of hotels.

315 **Mr. Rabbit and the Lovely Present**, by Charlotte Zolotow; pictures by Maurice Sendak. Harper, 1962. unp. $8.95; lib. ed. $1.95 (P)

A sympathetic rabbit helps a little girl find just the right present for her mother.

315FS **Mr. Rabbit and the Lovely Present** and **Charlotte and the White Horse**, Weston Woods, n.d. (FS 82) 27, 23fr color $7.25; (SF 82) with 7in 33rpm $9.20; (SF 82C) with cassette $12.75. WW (P)

Illustrations from the book, accompanied by picture-cued text booklet.

316 **Mrs. Beggs and the Wizard**, by Mercer Mayer. Four Winds/ Scholastic, 1980. 48p. $8.95 (N)

A wizard makes things happen—especially in Mrs. Beggs's rooming house.

316FS **Mrs. Beggs and the Wizard**, Listening Library (Look, Listen and Read series) (JFS 193) n.d. color 1 filmstrip 1 cassette guide $21. LL (N)

Strange things happen at Mrs. Beggs's rooming house when a new lodger comes to stay. Excellent sound effects, pacing, and creation of suspense through visuals.

317 **Misty of Chincoteague**, by Marguerite Henry; illus. by Wesley Dennis. Rand McNally, 1947. 172p. $6.95; pap. $2.95 (I-U)

Each year the wild ponies of Assateague, a small island in Chesapeake Bay, are driven to a neighboring island of Chincoteague to be sold as children's pets. This is the story of one pony, Misty, and the two Chincoteaguese children who owned her.

317F **Misty**, 20th Century Fox, 1961, 16mm color 92min $30 (rental only). FI (P-I)

David Ladd, Pam Smith, and Arthur O'Connell star.

318 **Mommy, Buy Me a China Doll**, adapted from an Ozark children's song by Harve Zemach; illus. by Margot Zemach. Farrar, reprint of 1966 ed. 32p. $5.95; lib. ed. $5.95 (P)

Eliza Lou's suggestion to "trade our daddy's feather bed" for a china doll sets off a shuffling of animals and people and their normal sleeping places.

318FS **Mommy, Buy Me a China Doll**, Weston Woods, 1970 (FS 120) 27fr color $7.25; (SF 120) with 7in 33rpm disc 5:20min $9.20; (SF 120C) with cassette $12.75. WW (P)

Illustrations from the book, accompanied by picture-cued text booklet.

319 **Moon Man**, by Tomi Ungerer. Harper, 1967. 40p. $12.45; lib. ed. $12.89 (N-P)

How the man in the moon came to visit the earth.

319F **Moon Man**, Morton Schindel, 1981, 16mm color 8min $175. WW (I)

Animated version with voice-over narration and Big-Band-style music. Mood is dark and bleak. Directed by Gene Deitch.

319FS **Moon Man**, Weston Woods, 1981 (FS 255) 36fr color 7:40min $12; (SF 255C) with cassette $18. WW (P)

Brassy blues notes lend a soulful air to Moon Man's adventure on Earth. Utilizes the illustrations from the book. Accompanied by picture-cued text booklet.

319R **Moon Man**, Weston Woods, 1981 (LTR 255C) cassette only 8min $6. WW (P)

A mix of jazz and science-fiction-type music by Karel Velebny provides background for Peter Hawkins' excellent narration of the story.

320 **Morris and Boris: Three Stories**, by Bernard Wiseman. Dodd, 1974. 64p. $4.95 (N-P)

Boris the Bear is exasperated when trying to teach Morris the Moose how to ask riddles, repeat tongue twisters, and play games the acceptable way. Enjoyed by youngsters who have a little trouble learning new things themselves sometimes.

320FS **Morris and Boris: Three Stories**, Listening Library, n.d. (AJFS 182) color 1 filmstrip 1 cassette $21. LL (N-P)

Know-it-all Boris tries to teach Morris some riddles and games in this amusing story by Bernard Wiseman. The slapstick humor is even more fun in the filmstrip version.

321 **Morris Has a Cold**, by Bernard Wiseman. Dodd, 1978. $6.95; 1978 Scholastic pap. $1.50 (N-P)

Even a little cold inconveniences big-nosed Morris the Moose. Boris the Bear says that since it is only a little cold, Morris's nose "walks" instead of "runs." Infantile humor at its most enjoyable.

321FS **Morris Has a Cold**, Listening Library, n.d. (AJFS 183) color 1 filmstrip 1 cassette $21. LL (N-P)

Bernard Wiseman tells about Morris getting a cold and Boris knowing just what to do to make him well. The sound effects make this tale even funnier.

322 **Morris Tells Boris Mother Goose Stories and Rhymes**, by Bernard Wiseman. Dodd, 1979. $6.95; 1980 Scholastic pap. 46p. $1.50 (N-P)

Morris's version of the Mother Goose tales and rhymes nearly drives know-it-all Boris crazy but will amuse all readers.

322FS **Morris Tells Boris Mother Goose Stories and Rhymes**, Listening Library, n.d. (AJFS 85) color 1 filmstrip 1 cassette $21. LL (N-P)

Pictures and sounds of know-it-all Boris the Bear having to listen to Morris the Moose's version of Mother Goose will surely produce giggles in every viewer.

323 **Morris's Disappearing Bag**, by Rosemary Wells. Dial, 1975. 40p. $9.95; lib. ed. $9.89; pap. $2.50 (P)

Morris, a young rabbit, isn't allowed to play with his older brothers' and sisters' Christmas toys until they find out about his disappearing bag and want to play with that.

323F **Morris's Disappearing Bag**, Morton Schindel, 1982, 16mm color 6min $175, $20. WW (P)

Animated version of the Rosemary Wells's picture book. Useful for preschool Christmas programs.

323FS **Morris's Disappearing Bag**, Weston Woods, 1978 (FS 230) 38fr color 6min $12; (SF 230C) with cassette $18. WW (P)

Illustrations are taken directly from the book. This filmstrip version of a delightful story is narrated with well-paced clarity and humor and provides a format that enables large-group enjoyment of a tiny holiday gem.

ALA Notable Filmstrip.

323R **Morris's Disappearing Bag**, Weston Woods, 1978 (LTR 230C) cassette only 6min $6. WW (N-P)

Nicole Frenchette narrates in a light style to a background of lively piano and orchestra music by H. D. Buch.

324 **Brian Wildsmith's Mother Goose**, illus. by Brian Wildsmith. Watts, 1965. 80p. lib. ed. $6.90; pap. $4.95 (N-P)

Contains 86 traditional rhymes brilliantly illustrated in a refreshing manner.

324F **Mother Goose**, Bank Street College of Education, 1968 (612219) 16mm color 11min $160, $12.50. MH (N-P)

Read by Betsy Palmer. Reading Incentive Film series. Price includes a copy of the book.

325 **The Mother Goose Treasury**; illus. by Raymond Briggs. Coward, 1966. 217p. $9.99; pap. $7.95 (N-P)

Iona and Peter Opie, eminent folklorists, selected the 408 verses in this collection. The artist's full-color illustrations are suitably robust and humorous.

325FS **The Mother Goose Treasury**, Weston Woods, 1971 (FS 109) 22fr color $7.25; (SF 109) with 7in 33rpm 12:18min $9.20; (SF 109C) with cassette $12.75. WW (N-P)

Illustrations from the book, accompanied by picture-cued text booklet.

326 **Mother, Mother, I Feel Sick, Send the Doctor Quick Quick Quick**, by Remy Charlip and Burton Supree; illus. by Remy Charlip. Scholastic, 1980. Reprint of 1966 ed. 48p. lib. ed. $8.95 (P)

An amusing story about a little boy with a most unusual stomach ache.

326FS **Mother, Mother, I Feel Sick**, Look/Listen & Learn, n.d. (51709) 43fr b/w $7.50; with 12in 33rpm manual/automatic 5:15min $12.50. HRW (P)

Presented in the form of a shadow play with different actors playing the various roles.

327 **Mothers Can Do Anything**, by Joe Lasker. Whitman, 1972. 40p. $7.50 (N-P)

A pictorial demonstration of the many roles Mothers can play, such as dentists, bus drivers, train and orchestra conductors, and many more. Lasker's illustrations are most effective.

327FS **Mothers Can Do Anything**, Imperial, 1980 (X4KG 18301) 38fr color 8min cassette $24. IER (N-P)

A timely depiction of mothers doing many types of jobs both in and outside the home. Joe Lasker's stylized, often humorous, drawings have been used. This is from the Prime Time Collection #3 (Westport Group).

328 **Mousekin's Close Call**, by Edna Miller. Prentice-Hall, 1978. $6.95 (P-I)

Informational book focuses on Mousekin's nearly fatal capture by a weasel and the beneficial distraction provided by a swamp sparrow defending her young.

328FS **Mousekin's Close Call**, Westport Communications Group, dist. by Educational Enrichment Materials, 1981 (#52586) 43fr color 7min with cassette $22. EEM (P-I)

This glimpse of wildlife survival is portrayed with realistic delicate pastel colors. Filmstrip version is enhanced by the addition of light instrumental background music suitably keyed to the mood of Miller's story.

329 **Mousekin's Woodland Sleepers**, by Edna Miller. Prentice-Hall, 1970. $5.95; pap. $2.50 (P-I)

Mousekin discovers many woodland animals in various stages of hibernation.

329FS **Mousekin's Woodland Sleepers**, Westport Communications Group (#52288), 1 filmstrip 1 cassette automatic/manual 47fr 9:50min $22. EEM (P-I)

An accurate adaptation of the cozy winter story featuring Mousekin from the appealing series.

330 **My Brother Sam Is Dead**, by James Lincoln Collier and Christopher Collier. Four Winds, 1974. 224p. $7.95; pap. $1.95 (U)

A family is torn apart by the American Revolution when sixteen-year-old Sam goes off to fight the British while the rest of the family tries to remain neutral in a Tory town in Connecticut.

330FS **My Brother Sam Is Dead**, Random House, 1981 (39466106-0) color 2 filmstrips 2 cassettes teacher's guide $45; cassettes only $8.97. RH (I)

The Revolutionary War is the setting for this 1975 Newbery Honor Book. Care has been taken to present actual historical visual details in the adaptation of this story.

330R **My Brother Sam Is Dead**, Random House/Miller-Brody, 1976 (394-77081-1) record $8.97; (394-77082-X) cassette $8.97. RH/M-B (I-U)

Dramatization of the book.

331 **My Friend Flicka**, by Mary O'Hara; illus. by Dave Blossom. New ed. Lippincott, 1973. 272p. $7.95 (I-U)

Beautiful descriptions of Wyoming mountains and plains, realistic details of ranch life, and perceptive treatment of family conflicts mark this story of a young boy's love for his colt.

331F **My Friend Flicka**, 20th Century Fox, 1943, 16mm color 90min $24 (rental only). FI (P-I)

Roddy McDowall, Preston Foster, and Rita Johnson star.

332 **My Grandson Lew**, by Charlotte Zolotow; illus. by William Pene DuBois. Harper, 1974. 32p. $7.95; lib. ed. $6.89 (P-I)

In the quiet of the night, Lewis and his mother remember Grandpa who died when Lewis was two.

332F **My Grandson Lew**, Donald MacDonald, 1976, 16mm color 13min $270. BA (P-I)

Gentle, quiet mood, well-acted. Will need some introduction for best effect as it deals with the death of the grandfather and the memories of the child. Could be used in family programs.

333 **My Mother Is the Most Beautiful Woman in the World**, by Becky Reyher; pictures by Ruth Gannett. Lothrop, 1945. unp. lib. ed. $7.44 net (P-I)

A Russian folktale about a little girl who is lost and looks for her mother.

333F **My Mother Is the Most Beautiful Woman in the World**, Stephen Bosustow, 1968 (16-246) 16mm color 9min $100. BFA (P)

Animated film based on the book illustrations.

333FS **My Mother Is the Most Beautiful Woman in the World**, McGraw-Hill, 1972 (105542) 38fr color 15min 12in 33rpm $18; cassette $18. MH (P-I)

Music, narration, and the descriptive words blend into a beautiful whole. Part of Children's Literature Series, Set 4. Includes teacher's manual.

334 **My Red Umbrella**, by Robert Bright; illus. by the author. Morrow, 1959. unp. lib. ed. $7.20 (N)

When a little girl goes for a walk in the rain she is joined by all the animals—and her red umbrella manages to cover them all. A charming little book.

334R **My Red Umbrella**, Weston Woods, 1974 (LTR 138C) cassette only $6; (LTR 138SPC) Spanish version $6. WW (N)

Buffy Allen narrates the English and John Gres the Spanish version of this gentle little picture book of a little girl sharing her bright red umbrella.

335 **My Side of the Mountain**, by Jean George; illus. by Jean George. Dutton, 1975. 178p. $7.95; pap. $2.95 (I-U)

Sam Gribley tells the story of the winter he spent alone in the Catskill Mountains. His ingenuity in improvising shelter, finding and cooking food, and devising needed implements enables him to live a comfortable and interesting Robinson Crusoe existence until the need for human companionship brings him home.

335F **My Side of the Mountain**, Paramount, 1969, 16mm color 100min $35 (rental only). FI (I-U)

Ted Eccles, Theodore Bikel, and Tudi Wiggins star. Directed by James B. Clark.

336 **The Mysterious Tadpole**, by Steven Kellogg. Dial, 1977. unp. $9.95; lib. ed. $6.46 (P)

This is a tale of a birthday tadpole delivered to Louis from his uncle in Scotland. The story centers around the problems Louis has in finding accommodations for his oversized tadpole, Alphonse.

336FS **The Mysterious Tadpole**, Weston Woods, 1980 (FS 251) 41fr color 9min $12; (SF 251 C) with cassette $18. WW (P)

Narration by Dan Diggles. Kellogg's illustrations are accompanied by a musical score that is expressive and sensitive to the story's moods.

336R **Mysterious Tadpole**, Weston Woods (LTR 251C) cassette 9min $6. WW (N-P)

The combination of the humorous musical accompaniment and sound effects with an excellent narration make this funny story come alive.

337 **Nate the Great Goes Undercover**, by Marjorie Winman Sharmat; illus. by Marc Simont. Coward, 1974. 48p. $6.59 (P-I)

Nate the Great, a ten-year-old detective who wears a Sherlock Holmes hat and trench coat, solves the smelly mystery of the overturned neighborhood garbage can.

337FS **Nate the Great Goes Undercover**, Stephen Bosustow, 1980 (#58300) 2 filmstrips 60, 59fr color 6, 5min with 2 cassettes $44. BA (P-I)

Droll line drawings dabbed with colors in cartoon style appealingly visualize the young sleuth, his dog, and the pesky neighbor created by Sharmat. The filmstrip version adheres to the story line of the book.

Accompanied by guide.

338 **New York City Too Far from Tampa Blues**, by T. Ernesto Bethancourt. Holiday, 1975. 192p. $6.95 (I-U)

Tom, a young Spanish-American boy newly arrived in Brooklyn from Florida, makes friends with Aurelio when they discover a mutual interest in rock music.

338F **New York City Too Far from Tampa Blues**, Daniel Wilson, 1979. 16mm color 47min $600. TLM (I-U)

Live-action film made for television with Alex Paez as Tom and John Femia as Aurelio. Warm-hearted film uses pop music themes for the soundtrack.

339 **The Night before Christmas**, by Clement C. Moore; illus. by Arthur Rackham. Lippincott, 1954. 32p. $5.95 (P-I)

The well-loved Christmas poem, illustrated by a great English artist.

339R **Fairy Tales for a Winter's Night**, CMS Records, 1968 (CMS 534) $8.98; (CMS-X-4534) cassette $8.98. CMS (I)

Mary Strang tells Andersen's "The Fir Tree" and "The Little Match Girl," Grimm's "The Elves and the Shoemaker," and "'Twas the Night Before Christmas" by Clement Moore.

340 **The Nightingale**, by Hans Christian Andersen; tr. by Eva Le Gallienne; designed and illus. by Nancy Ekholm Burkert. Harper, 1965. 34p. $10.95; lib. ed. $10.89 net (I)

Andersen's moving story, illustrated with exquisite paintings.

340FS **The Emperor and the Nightingale**, Educational Reading Services, 1970, 40fr color with captions $6. ERS (P-I)

Based on the fairy tale by Hans Christian Andersen. Artwork by Judith Fringuello.

340FS **The Nightingale**, Random House/ Miller-Brody (394-07903-5N) color 1 filmstrip 1 cassette $19.95. RH/M-B (P)

The relationship between fantasy and reality that exists in all Andersen's tales is heightened by illustrations that appear three-dimensional done by Swedish illustrator Kay Beckman.

340R **Hans Christian Andersen in Central Park**, Weston Woods, 1982 (713) 53min 33rpm $8. WW (I)

Diane Walkstein, New York's official storyteller, presents several of Andersen's enchanting tales including "The Nightingale," "Dance, Dance Dolly Mine," "Hans Clodhopper," "The Goblin and the Grocer," "The Ugly Duckling," and "The Emperor's New Clothes."

341 **Nightmares: Poems to Trouble Your Sleep**, by Jack Prelutsky; illus. by Arnold Lobel. Greenwillow, 1976. 40p. lib. ed. $9.95 (P-I)

Spooky poems filled with tongue-in-cheek humor.

341R **Nightmares and Other Poems to Trouble Your Sleep**, Caedmon (TC 1705) record $8.98; (CP 1705) cassette $8.98. CAE (P-I)

Prelutsky reads his own scary verses with a touch of humor. Sound effects by Don Heckman add to the eerie midnight mood of the verses.

342 **No Roses for Harry**, by Gene Zion; illus. by Margaret Bloy Graham. Harper, 1958. $8.79 (P)

As a birthday present, Grandma sends Harry a sweater decorated with roses. Harry hates the sweater as soon as he sees it and decides to lose it.

342FS **No Roses for Harry**, Random House/Miller-Brody, 1977 (394-64542-1) 69fr 9min with cassette $21. RH/M-B (P)

Faithful adaptation of Gene Zion's book. Filmstrip expands Graham's humorous drawings and Harry's predicaments through varied visual perspectives and animated narrative accompanied by delightful music and suitable sound effects.

ALA Notable Filmstrip.

342R **No Roses for Harry**, Random House/Miller-Brody (394-76451-X) cassette only $8.97; (394-07887-X) cassette with paperback $10.92. RH/M-B (P)

Harry receives a sweater covered with roses, but he is too embarrassed to wear it. Word-for-word reading.

343 **Noah's Ark**, illus. by Peter Spier. Doubleday, 1977. unp. $8.90 (P)

A pictorial retelling of the story of Noah and the flood. Spier's intricate drawings detail the flooded world outside and Noah's attempts at domesticity inside the ark.

Caldecott Medal winner 1978.

343FS **Noah's Ark**, Weston Woods, 1978 (FS 237) 67fr color 11min $12; (SF 237C) with cassette $18. WW (P)

Peter Spier's visual account of Noah's Ark is enriched by a dulcimer's delicate chiming of strains from Beethoven's Sixth Symphony and the the addition of realistic background sounds and animal noises that might have accompanied the guests aboard this ship.

ALA Notable Filmstrip.

344 **Nobody's Family Is Going to Change**, by Louise Fitzhugh. Farrar, 1974. 256p. $9.95; Dell pap. $1.50 (U)

In a middle-class black family living in New York City, 11-year-old Emma wants to be a lawyer and her 7-year-old brother wants to be a tap dancer, but their parents disapprove of their career choices.

344F **The Tap Dance Kid**, Evelyn Barron, 1978, 16mm color 48min $595. LCA (U)

Live-action film starring Honi Coles as Uncle Dipsey, James Pelham as Willie Sheridan, and Danielle Spencer as Emma. Well-acted and thoughtful adaptation. Also available in an edited version (33min, $450, $40). 1980 Notable Film for Children.

345 **Noisy Nancy Norris**, by Lou Ann Gaeddert; illus. by Gioia Flammenghi. Doubleday, 1965. 63p. lib. ed. $6.95 (P)

Nancy was loud and noisy until she wailed and clumped once too often.

345FS **Noisy Nancy Norris**, Guidance Associates, 1967 (301703) 71fr color 13min with 12in 33rpm manual/automatic $18. GA (P)

Illustrations from the book. Appropriate sound effects add to the humor. Accompanied by a teacher's guide.

346 **Noisy Nora**, by Rosemary Wells. Dial, 1973. 40p. $4.95; lib. ed. $4.58 net; pap. $.95 (N-P)

Nora, a mouse, tries to get attention from her family by making lots of noise. When this fails she leaves home. The silence makes her family aware of their loss.

346FS **Noisy Nora**, Weston Woods, 1975 (LTR 175) 28fr color $7.25; (SF 175) with cassette only 10:20min $12.75. WW (N-P)

Illustrations from the book, accompanied by picture-cued text booklet.

347 **The Noonday Friends**, by Mary Stolz; illus. by Louis S. Glanzman. Harper, 1965. 182p. $8.79 (I)

Franny hated qualifying for a free school lunch ticket, never having enough to wear, and having to hurry home to care for her little brother. Her father could not keep a job, her mother had to work, and Franny's home duties meant that the desired friendship with a classmate became largely a noonday affair shared over lunch.

347FS **The Noonday Friends**, Random House/Miller-Brody, 1977 (394-77089-7) 2 filmstrips 136, 108fr color with 1 12in 33-1/3rpm $45; (394-77090-0) with 2 cassettes 22:40, 18:42min $45. RH/M-B (I)

Realistic color illustrations based on descriptions given in the book. Characters are enthusiastically portrayed.

347R **The Noonday Friends** by Mory Stolz. Random House/Miller-Brody (394-77087-0) record $8.97; (394-77088-9) cassette $8.97. RH/M-B (I)

A dramatized version of the story for listening.

348 **Norman the Doorman**, by Don Freeman. Viking, 1959. 64p. lib. ed. $6.95 net; pap. $1.50 (P)

Norman, the mouse doorman at the rear mousehole of the Majestic Museum of Art, wins an award for his sculpture made from old mousetraps.

348F **Norman the Doorman**, Morton Schindel, 1971, 16mm color 15min $135, $6. WW (P-I)

Iconographic technique using illustrations adapted from the book. Narrated by Owen Jordan. Music by Joseph Ceremuga. The iconographic camera movements emphasize Don Freeman's delightful satire of the art world, giving the film as much humor as it has suspense.

348FS **Norman the Doorman**, Weston Woods, n.d. (FS 64) 56fr color $7.25; (SF 64) 10:45min with 7in 33rpm $9.20; (SF 64C) with cassette $12.75. WW (P)

Illustrations from the book, accompanied by picture-cued text booklet.

349 **Norwegian Folk Tales**, from the collection of Peter Christen Asbjornsen and Jorgen Moe; tr. by Pat Shaw Iverson and Carl Norman; illus. by Erik Werenskiold and Theodor Kittelsen. Vanous, 1961. 188p. $17.50 net (I)

A spirited new translation with drawings from the first illustrated edition of the tales.

349R **Norse Folk and Fairy Tales**, CMS Records, 1966 (CMS-X-4507) cassette $8.98. CMS (I)

Told by Anne Pellowski. Includes "The Squire's Bride," "The Giant Who Had No Heart," "The Princess No One Could Silence," "The Way of the World," and

"The Pancake." Miss Pellowski's understated style is particularly effective with these dramatic tales.

350 **The Nutcracker**, adapted and illustrated by Warren Chappell. Knopf, 1958. unp. lib. ed. $5.69 (I)

Main themes from the Tchaikovsky ballet are included in this airily illustrated version of the Nutcracker and the Mouse King.

350F **Nutcracker**, CBS-TV, 1965, 16mm color 60min $650 (life-of-print lease), $50. WB (P-U)

The performers featured are Melissa Hayden, Edward Villella, and Patricia McBride. Music by the Budapest Philharmonic Orchestra.

351 **The Nutshell Library**, by Maurice Sendak. Harper, 1962. Set, $7.95 (N-P)

Includes *Alligators All Around*, an alphabet book; *Chicken Soup with Rice*, activities to enjoy each month of the year; *One Was Johnny*, a counting song; and *Pierre*, a moralistic tale.

351F **Really Rosie**, Sheldon Riss, 1976, 16mm color 26min $365. WW (P-I)

The critically acclaimed television program starring the Nutshell kids from Maurice Sendak's *Nutshell Library* and *The Sign on Rosie's Door*. Animated, with songs by Carole King.

352 **Obadiah the Bold**, by Brinton Turkle. Viking, 1965. unp. $4.95; lib. ed. $3.77 net; pap. $1.50 (P)

A small Quaker boy who loves the sea longs to be a fearless pirate until he learns that something else is better.

352FS **Obadiah the Bold**, Viking, dist. by Live Oak Media, 1970 (0-670-905143) 29fr color cassette $19.95. LOM (P)

Illustrations from the book, accompanied by picture-cued text booklet. Narrated by John Thomas.

353 **Oh, Were They Ever Happy!**, by Peter Spier. Doubleday, 1978. $7.95 (P)

The children delight in a job well done when they decide to paint the house and surprise their parents upon their return.

353FS **Oh, Were They Ever Happy!**, Listening Library, 1978 (Look, Listen and Read JFS 176) color 1 filmstrip 1 cassette $21. LL (P)

Both the narration and accompanying music are clear and appealing.

354 **The Old Black Witch**, by Harry and Wende Devlin. Scholastic, 1980. Reprint of 1966 ed. 32p. lib. ed. $8.95 net (P-I)

A boy and his mother buy an old house in New England to use for a tearoom and have unusual trouble with a witch.

354F **Winter of the Witch**, Thomas Sand Enterprises, 1969, 16mm color 26min $245, $25. LCA (P-I)

Hermione Gingold stars. Narrated by Burgess Meredith (from *The Old Black Witch* by Devlin).

355 **Old Mother Hubbard and Her Dog**, illus. by Evalina Ness. Holt, 1972. 40p. lib. ed. $4.95 (N-P)

A splendid picture book of a huge, shaggy white sheep dog whose antics dominate the full-page color illustrations while the skinny, expressionless Mother Hubbard runs around trying to please him with all sorts of special treats.

355F **Old Mother Hubbard and Her Dog**, McGraw-Hill, 1963 (682533) 16mm color 4min $50, $10. CONT (N-P)

Animated version of this popular Mother Goose rhyme.

355FS **Old Mother Hubbard and Her Dog**, Weston Woods, n.d. (FS 37)

35fr color $7.25; (SF 37) with 7in 33rpm 4:05min $9.20; (SF 37C) with cassette $12.75. WW (N-P)
Accompanied by picture-cued text booklet.

355FS **Old Mother Hubbard and Her Dog**, Live Oak Media, 1977, 38fr color 4min 1 filmstrip 1 cassette 1 guide $19.95. LOM (N-P)
Evalina Ness's illustrations of Old Mother Hubbard's love and patience with unpredictable behavior of her dog.

356 **The Old Woman and Her Pig**; pictures by Paul Galdone. McGraw-Hill, 1961. 32p. lib. ed. $7.95 net (N-P)
The popular cumulative tale about the old woman's difficulties in getting her pig to market is enlivened with droll action pictures on every page.

356F **The Old Woman and Her Pig**, McGraw-Hill, 1963 (682532) 16mm color 7min $85, $10. CONT (N-P)
Animated artwork from the book.

356FS **The Old Woman and Her Pig**, Weston Woods, n.d. (FS 40) 52fr color $7.25; (SF 40) with 7in 33rpm 7:10min $9.20; (SF 40C) with cassette $12.75. WW (N-P)
Illustrations from the book, accompanied by picture-cued text booklet.

357 **Old Yeller**, by Fred Gipson; drawings by Carl Burger. Harper, 1956. 158p. $9.95; lib. ed. $9.89 net (I-U)
In the hard summer of 1860, fourteen-year-old Travis was the man of the family while his father drove his herd of cattle from Texas to Kansas. An ugly yellow dog fought by Travis's side to protect the family from many dangers.

357R **Old Yeller**, Random House/Miller-Brody (394-77127-3) record $8.97; (394-77128-1) cassette $8.97 (I-U)
An earthy, moving story of a boy who takes on a man's responsibilities and of the dog who helps him.

358 **Oliver Button Is a Sissy**, by Tomi dePaola. Harcourt, 1979. 48p. $6.95; pap. $2.45. IER (P)
Oliver is small, takes dancing lessons, and is called a sissy. He is able to erase that appellation when he proves what he can do at the local variety show.

358FS **Oliver Button Is a Sissy**, Imperial, 1980 (X4KG 18201) 45fr color 10min cassette $24. IER (P)
This story of a little boy who is thought a sissy because he takes dancing lessons has a most satisfactory ending. Tomi dePaola's fun in reading this adds to the pleasure of this production.

359 **Once a Mouse: A Fable Cut in Wood**, by Marcia Brown. Scribner, 1961. unp. $9.95 (P)
An ancient fable from India showing how a hermit uses his magic to save a mouse from its forest predators by changing it into a cat, then a dog, and finally, a tiger. But in the form of the tiger, the mouse becomes arrogant and ungrateful, and therefore must be humbled. Caldecott Medal winner, 1962.

359FS **Once a Mouse**, Random House/Miller-Brody, 1977 (394-76473-0) 42fr color 6 min with cassette $21. RH/M-B (P)
Based on Brown's Caldecott Medal book, this filmstrip adaptation skillfully constructs and frames the original woodcuts to focus on the action as it evolves. Arthur Custer's original score sets a magical mood that hints at the Indian origin of the fable.
ALA Notable Filmstrip.

359R **Once a Mouse**, by Marcia Brown. Random House/Miller-Brody (394-76655-5) cassette $8.97. RH/M-B (P)
Based on the Caldecott Medal-winning book.

360 **One Fine Day**, by Nonny

Hogrogian. Macmillan, 1971. $10.95; pap. $1.95 (N-P)

When the old woman cuts off the fox's tail, the fox must convince a series of animals, people, and things to give up something in order to please the old woman and get his tail sewn back on. Caldecott Medal winner, 1972.

360R **One Fine Day**, Weston Woods, 1973 (LTR 153C) cassette only 5min $6. WW (N-P)

Music with an Indian style by Tarik Bulut and an Anglo-Indian style of narration by Emergy Battis enhance the telling of this cumulative tale.

361 **One Monday Morning**, by Uri Shulevitz. Scribner, 1967. unp. lib. ed. $8.95; pap. $2.95 net (P)

Child's daydream of a royal family coming to visit him in his tenement home is inspired by a deck of playing cards.

361F **One Monday Morning**, Weston Woods, 1973. 16mm color 10min $120, $6. WW (P)

Low-keyed narration, background music of medieval brass and recorder plus city sounds.

362 **One Morning in Maine**, by Robert McCloskey. Viking, 1952. $8.95 (P)

In this Caldecott Honor Book, Sal's apprehension at losing a baby tooth is replaced by concern that her wish will not be granted when she loses the tooth in the mud of a clam bed. The morning comes to a happy conclusion when she accompanies her father across the harbor to the general store.

362FS **One Morning in Maine**, Viking, dist. by Live Oak Media, 1979 (0-670-90586-0) 65fr b/w 19:28min with cassette $19.95. LOM (P)

Filmstrip utilizes McCloskey's original book illustrations. Accompanied by picture-cued text booklet. Guide.

363 **One Was Johnny: A Counting Book**, by Maurice Sendak. Harper, 1962. unp. lib. ed. $7.89 net (P)

Johnny finds a surprising way to get rid of the queer creatures who overrun his house.

363FS **One Was Johnny**, Weston Woods, 1976 (FS 221) 23fr color 3min $7.25; (SF 221C) with cassette $12.75. WW (P)

Narrated by Maurice Sendak. Original music by H. D. Buch. Sound filmstrip adopted by C. B. Wismar; artwork adapted by Stephanie Adam.

364 **Onion John**, by Joseph Krumgold; illus. by Symeon Shimin. Harper, 1959. 248p. $10.95 (I)

The story of 12-year-old Andy Rusch and European-born Onion John, the town's odd-jobs man and vegetable peddler who lives in a stone hut and frequents the dump.

Newbery Medal winner, 1960.

364FS **Onion John**, Miller-Brody, 1978 (394-77070-6) 2 filmstrips 122, 114 fr color with 2 cassettes 14:12, 12:51min $45. RH/M-B (I)

Illustrations are drawn from the book's descriptions.

364R **Onion John**, by Joseph Krumgold. Random House/Miller-Brody (394-77067-6) record $8.97; (394-77068-4) cassette $8.97. RH/M-B (I)

Onion John is Serbo-Croatian, as is the actor who plays his role.

365 **Ote: A Puerto Rican Folk Tale**, by Pura Belpre; illus. by Paul Galdone. Pantheon, 1969. unp. lib. ed. $5.39 (P)

Ote, father of five children, goes to the forest to look for food. There he meets a near-sighted devil who forces Ote to take him home where he eats up everyone's food. It is Ote's youngest child who outwits the devil and saves the family from starvation.

Also available in Spanish.

365FS **Ote**, Weston Woods, 1976 (FS 197SP) 45fr color 12:50min $7.50; (SF 197SP) with cassette $12.75; (SF 197BL) bilingual cassette Spanish/English $15.75. WW (P-I)

Pura Belpre tells her own version of this Puerto Rican folktale.

366 **Otherwise Known as Sheila the Great**, by Judy Blume. Dutton, 1972. $8.95 (I)

Ten-year-old Sheila is secretly afraid of dogs, spiders, bees, ghosts and the dark. When she and her family leave New York for their summer home, she has to face her problems.

366FS **Otherwise Known as Sheila the Great**, Pied Piper (First Choice: Authors and Books), 1981, 108fr 16min 1 filmstrip 1 cassette $29. PP (I)

Color illustrations, strong characterizations, and realistic sound effects retain the flavor and sense of the original. Spirited vocal characterizations enhance the presentation.

367 **Over in the Meadow**, by John Langstaff; with pictures by Feador Rojankovsky. Harcourt, 1967. 32p. $5.95; pap. $1.50 (N-P)

A counting book based on the old song about the meadow animals and their babies. Includes music.

367F **Over in the Meadow**, Morton Schindel, 1968 (19355) 16mm color 9:30min $120, $5. WW (N-P)

Iconographic technique using illustrations from the book. Sung by John Langstaff.

367FS **Over in the Meadow**, Weston Woods, n.d. (FS 57) 46fr color $7.25; (SF 57) with 7in 33rpm 9:15min $9.20; (SF 57C) with cassette $12.75. WW (N-P)

Illustrations from the book, accompanied by picture-cued text booklet.

368 **The Owl and the Pussy-cat**, by Edward Lear; illus. by Barbara Cooney. Little, 1969. 26p. $6.95 (N-P)

A reissue of the picture-book version published in 1961 as *Le Hibou et la Poussiquette* by Francis Steegmuller. Delicate drawing in pea green and yellow.

368F **The Owl and the Pussy-Cat**, Morton Schindel, 1972 16mm color 3min $65, $5. WW (N-P)

Iconographic technique using illustrations from the book. Narrated by John Cunningham.

368FS **The Owl and the Pussy-Cat** and **Wynken, Blynken and Nod**, Weston Woods, n.d. (FS 76) 19, 20fr color $7.25; (SF 76) 2:45, 3min with 7in 33rpm $9.20; with cassette $12.75. WW (N-P)

Illustrations from the book, accompanied by picture-cued text booklet.

369 **The Ox-Cart Man**, by Donald Hall; illus. by Barbara Cooney. Viking, 1979. unp. $9.38 (P)

A poetic recounting of a year in the life of a New England family in the early nineteenth century. Dependent upon the land for all things, family life becomes an annual cycle of planting, growth, harvest, handcraft, trade, and conservation.

Caldecott Medal winner, 1980.

369FS **The Ox-Cart Man**, Viking, dist. by Live Oak Media, 1980 (0-670-90594-1) 34fr color 6:11min $19.95. LOM (P)

This award-winning book is faithfully reproduced in sound filmstrip format. A skilled male narrator reads Hall's words as Barbara Cooney's lovely illustrations are shown on the screen.

Accompanied by picture-cued text booklet.

370 **Paddle-to-the-Sea**, by Holling C.

Holling. Houghton, 1974. pap. $2.95; lib. ed. $9.95 (I)

A young boy carves the figure of an Indian in a canoe and launches him on a journey through the Great Lakes, down the St. Lawrence River, and finally to the Atlantic. Adventures are many along the way.

370F **Paddle-to-the-Sea**, Julian Biggs 1966 (0166061) 16mm color 28min $260, $11. NFBC (I-U). OP

Commentary by Stanley Jackson. Produced by Julian Biggs.

371 **Patrick**, by Quentin Blake. Walck, 1968. unp. (P). OP

With the music of an old fiddle, Patrick imbues every leaf and countryside creature with color and movement.

371F **Patrick**, Kratky Film, Prague, 1973. 16mm color 7min $135, $8. WW (P)

Colorfully animated. No narration. Background of lively Dvorak violin music.

371R **Patrick**, Weston Woods, 1973 (LTR 145C) cassette only 8min $6. WW (P)

Lou Bedford narrates this sprightly tale to the accompaniment of music by Anton Dvorak.

372 **Paul Bunyan**, by Esther Shephard; illus. by Rockwell Kent. Harcourt, 1952. 233p. $6.50 (U)

Stories collected from the loggers of the Northwest by the author and her husband.

372FS **The Adventures of Paul Bunyan: An American Folktale**, Guidance Associates, 1970 (300 507) 64fr color 12min with 12in 33rpm manual/automatic $16; (300 515) cassette $18. GA (P-I)

Text adapted from the version by Esther Shepard. Bold, color artwork by George Guzzi. Accompanied by a teacher's guide.

372R **Paul Bunyan in Story and Song**, Caedmon, 1970 (TC 1275) 2s 12in 33rpm $8.98; (CDL 51275) cassette $8.98. CAE (I-U)

Ed Begley reads seven Paul Bunyan stories selected from different collections including those by Esther Shephard, James Stevens, Dell J. McCormick, Wallace Wadsworth, Earl Clifton Beck, and from the Detroit *News*. Six original songs, written and performed by Oscar Brand, serve as an introduction for each side of the disc and as breaks between the stories.

373 **Paul Bunyan and His Great Blue Ox**; retold by Wallace Wadsworth; illus. by Enrico Arno. Doubleday, 1964. 205p. $3.50 (I-U). OP

A choice collection of stories about the mighty lumberjack of the North Woods.

373FS **Paul Bunyan and His Great Blue Ox**, Troll, 1970. 38fr color 1 filmstrip with cassette $18. ERS (P-I)

Gloria Fletcher's droll pictures portray the hale and hearty adventures of the famous logger and his oversized ox. One of the recommended filmstrips in Troll's American Folk Heroes and Tall Tales series.

373FS **Paul Bunyan**, Educational Enrichment Materials, 1969, 48fr color 10min with 12in 33rpm manual/automatic $22. EEM (P-I)

Godfrey Cambridge narrates Paul's childhood in Maine, his migration westward, and his amazing feats performed with the help of Babe the Blue Ox. Includes teacher's guide.

374 **Pecos Bill: The Greatest Cowboy of All Time**, by James Cloyd Bowman; pictures by Laura Bannon. Whitman, 1964. 296p. $7.50 (I-U)

Humorous tales of Pecos Bill's marvelous doings, from his childhood with the coyotes to his career as a famous cowpuncher.

374FS **The Adventures of Pecos Bill: An**

American Folktale, Guidance Associates, 1970 (301 901) 74fr color 13min with 12in 33rpm manual/automatic $16; (301 919) cassette $18. GA (P-I)

A series of episodes in the life of the tall tale hero based on several authoritative sources, including Botkin's *A Treasury of American Folklore*. Robust narration with various voices portraying the characters in Pecos Bill's life. Colorful, humorous illustrations by Arthur Chitouras. Accompanied by a teacher's guide.

374FS **Pecos Bill**, Educational Enrichment Materials, 1969, 48fr color 10:30min 12in 33rpm manual/automatic $22. EEM (P-I)

Godfrey Cambridge narrates the folktale of Pecos Bill. Includes teacher's guide.

375 **A Penny a Look: An Old Story**, retold by Harve Zemach; pictures by Margot Zemach. Farrar, 1971. unp. $6.95 (P)

Two rascals who decide to make money by exhibiting a one-eyed man get a rude awakening.

375FS **A Penny a Look**, Miller-Brody, 1976 (FA 109) 34fr color 5:22min 12in 33rpm $12.95; cassette $14.95. M-B (P-I)

Based on the book. Narrated by Tammy Grimes whose voice seems just right.

376 **Perez and Martina: A Puerto Rican Folk Tale**, by Pura Belpre; illus. by Carlos Sanchez. Warne, 1961. unp. $5.95 (P-I)

The romantic tale of the lovely Spanish cockroach who rejected all her suitors except the gallant mouse, Perez.

376R **Perez and Martina**, CMS Records, 1966 (CMS 505) $8.98; (CMS X4505) cassette $8.98 (P-I)

A traditional Puerto Rican folktale told by Pura Belpre in English and Spanish. A bilingual edition with English-Spanish text included.

377 **The Perilous Road**, by William O. Steele; illus. by Paul Galdone. Harcourt, 1958. 191p. $6.25 (I)

Ten-year-old Chris, enraged when the Yankees raid his father's farm and baffled when his older brother joins the Northern Army, tries to aid the Confederacy in every possible way.

377FS **The Perilous Road**, Miller-Brody, 1976 (394-77101-X) 2 filmstrips 106, 105fr color with 1 12in 33-1/3rpm $45; (394-77102-8) with 2 cassettes 17, 18min $48.75. RH/M-B (I)

Realistic illustrations, based on the book, are enhanced by appropriate sound effects.

377R **The Perilous Road**, Random House/Miller-Brody (394-77100-1) cassette only $10.95; (394-77099-4) record $10.95. RH/M-B (I)

Chris Brabson's family is divided by the Civil War; he is torn between love for his brothers and loyalty for what he believes. A dramatized version.

378 **Pet Show!**, by Ezra Jack Keats. Macmillan, 1972. unp. $4.95; pap. $2.25 (P)

On the day of the pet show Archie's cat is missing but Archie manages to win a blue ribbon when he enters his "invisible" pet germ.

378FS **Pet Show!**, Macmillan, 1974 (95176/77) 30fr color 4:35min 7in 33rpm $12.95; cassette $14.95. MAC (P)

Vibrant illustrations, straightforward narration, and jazzy music at beginning and end of story combine to make an outstanding filmstrip. Includes teacher's script.

379 **Peter and the Wolf**, by Sergei Prokofiev; tr. by Maria Carlson; illus. by Charles Mikolaycak. Viking, 1982. $12.95 (P-I)

Peter walks out into the big green

meadow, speaks to his friend the bird, high and safe in a tree. But soon the cat is after the bird, the wolf is after the duck, and it is up to Peter to save them all. You can almost hear the different instruments as you explore the vitally illustrated pages.

379F **Peter and the Wolf**, Shire Films, 1981, 16mm color 28min $425, $55. PYR (P-I)

Ray Bolger finds an orchestra playing in the forest and proceeds to narrate the musical story which is shown in live action with well-trained animals.

380 **Peter Pan**, by J. M. Barrie; illus. by Trina S. Hyman. Scribner, 1980. 183p. $14.95 (I)

An attractive edition of the classic story of the boy who never grew up.

380R **Peter Pan**, RCA Victor, n.d. (LSO-1019) 2s 12in 33rpm $5.79. RCA (P-U). OP

A musical version of the play by Sir James Barrie, starring Mary Martin as Peter Pan and Cyril Ritchard as Captain Hook. Music by Mark Charlop and lyrics by Carol Leigh.

381 **Peter Penny's Dance**, by Janet Quin-Harkin; illus. by Anita Lobel. Dial, 1976. $7.95; lib. ed. $7.47; pap. $2.50 (P)

Peter Penny loves to dance, so much so that he dances all the way around the world in time to claim the captain's daughter for his bride.

381R **Peter Penny's Dance**, Weston Woods, 1978 (LTR 231C) cassette only 17min $6. WW (P)

A sprightly hornpipe tune accompanies Peter Penny on his dancing adventures around the world. Narrated by Peter Thomas; music by Ernest V. Troost III.

382 **Peter's Chair**, by Ezra Jack Keats. Harper, 1967. unp. $8.95; lib. ed. $8.79 net (N-P)

Peter took his little blue chair and ran away because his parents were taking all his furniture for a baby sister; but when he found that the chair was too small for him, he realized that he was big enough to help his father get ready for the new baby.

382F **Peter's Chair**, Morton Schindel, 1971, 16mm color 5:30min $120, $6. WW (N-P)

Iconographic technique using illustrations from the book. Directed by Cynthia Freitag.

382FS **Peter's Chair**, Weston Woods, n.d. (FS 107) 28fr color $7.25;(SF 107) with 7in 33rpm 4:07min $9.20; with cassette $12.75. WW (N-P)

Illustrations from the book, accompanied by picture-cued text booklet.

383 **Petunia**, by Roger Duvoisin. Knopf, 1950. unp. lib. ed. $6.99 net (P)

Petunia, the silly goose, creates havoc in the barnyard by pretending that she can read.

383FS **Petunia**, Weston Woods, n.d. (FS 45) 51fr color $14; (SF 45C) with cassette 11:17min $20. WW (P)

Illustrations from the book, accompanied by picture-cued text booklet.

383R **Petunia**, Weston Woods, n.d. (LTR 45C) cassette only 11:17min $6. WW (P)

Story narrated by Ned Hoopes, with original background music by Phyllis Ohanian.

384 **Petunia Beware!**, by Roger Duvoisin. Knopf, 1958. unp. $6.99; pap. $.95 (P)

When Petunia, the goose, goes outside the fence for greener grass, Weasel, Fox, Raccoon, and Bobcat think that she will make a delicious meal.

384R **Let's Listen**, Caedmon, 1963 (CDL

51182) cassette only $8.98. CAE (P)

Four children's stories. Boris Karloff reads *Petunia, Beware!* by Roger Duvoisin and *The Pony Engine* by Doris Garn. Julie Harris reads *Six Foolish Fishermen* by Benjamin Elkin and *The Red Carpet* by Rex Parkin. Also includes *Maxie* and *Six Aesop's Fables* read by Gwen Verdon.

385 **The Phantom Tollbooth**, by Norton Juster; illus. by Jules Fieffer. Random House, 1961. pap. $2.95 (I-U)

The word play and strange happenings in The Lands Beyond keep Milo and the reader surprised and chuckling. Milo meets a ticking watchdog named Tock, a Mathemagician, and King Azoz, the Unabridged as he passes through the Foothills of Confusion, the Lands of Null, the Doldrums, the forbidden Mountains of Ignorance, and the Sea of Knowledge. Mature readers will enjoy the subtle puns and sharp wit.

385R **The Phantom Tollbooth**, Listening Library (ASWR 29) cassette with 4 paperbacks and teacher's guide $21.99. LL (I-U)

A professional reader begins narrating the first 30 to 40 pages and then allows the student to continue on his or her own. An attempt to use the cliff hanger technique to encourage reading.

386 **Philip Hall Likes Me, I Reckon Maybe**, by Bette Greene; illus. by Charles Lilly. Dial, 1974. 160p. $6.95; lib. ed. $6.46; pap. $1.25 (I)

Bright, eleven-year-old Beth has a crush on the smartest boy in her class. Warmth and humor characterize this story of growing up in rural Arkansas. Newbery Honor Book, 1975.

386FS **Philip Hall Likes Me, I Reckon Maybe**, Random House/Miller-Brody, 1979 (394-77098-6) 2 filmstrips 100, 95fr color 15:25, 13min with 2 cassettes $45. RH/M-B (I)

Two chapters of Bette Green's Newbery Honor Book are engagingly dramatized through Ruby Dee's interpretive reading that brings the characters to life. The filmstrip uses some music and flatly textured, colorful paintings to develop the country mood.

386R **Philip Hall Likes Me, I Reckon Maybe**, Random House/Miller-Brody (394-77083-8) record $8.97; (394-77084-8) cassette $8.97. RH/M-B (I-U)

Narrated by actress Ruby Dee. Musical background including original theme song, "Down with Sugar," written and sung by Lynn Ahrens. Excellent adaptation of the book.

387 **A Picture for Harold's Room**, by Crockett Johnson. Harper, 1960. 64p. $6.95; lib. ed. $7.89; pap. $.95 net (N-P)

A purple crayon and imagination carry Harold over land, air, and sea. He's a giant, he's Lilliputian. Finally, he's his own size in his own bed.

387F **A Picture for Harold's Room**, Morton Schindel, 1971, 16mm color 6:30min $175, $20; videocassette $175; Super 8 sound $175. WW (N-P)

Animated adaptation of the book.

387FS **A Picture for Harold's Room**, Weston Woods, 1971 (FS 133) 62fr color 6:02min $12; (SF 133C) with cassette $18. WW (N-P)

Illustrations from the book, accompanied by picture-cued text booklet.

387R **A Picture for Harold's Room**, Weston Woods, 1971 (LTR 133C) cassette $6. WW (N-P)

Narrated by Charles Cioffi.

388 **The Pied Piper of Hamelin**, by Robert Browning; illus. by Kate Greenaway. Warne, 1889. 48p. $9.95 (I-U)

This famous poem, illustrated by a distinguished nineteenth-century English artist, is a charming read-aloud period piece.

388FS **The Pied Piper of Hamelin**, Pied Piper (First Choice: Authors and Books), 1981, 1 filmstrip 112fr color 1 cassette 17min $29. PP (P-I)

Laced with flute melodies and robustly read by Orson Welles, this verbatim retelling of Browning's poem features intensely colored, interestingly detailed art.

388R **The Pied Piper**, Caedmon, 1957 (TC 1075) 1s 12in 33rpm $8.98; (CDL 51075) cassette $8.98. CAE (I)

Browning's poem read by Boris Karloff. Side 2: *The Hunting of the Snark* by Lewis Carroll.

389 **Pierre: A Cautionary Tale in Five Chapters and a Prologue**, by Maurice Sendak. Harper, 1962. unp. lib. ed. $9.89 (P)

Pierre gets his just deserts for always saying "I don't care."

389FS **Pierre**, Weston Woods, 1976 (FS 220) 30fr color 5:30min $12; (SF 220C) with cassette $18. WW (P)

About Pierre who learned to care. Read by Maurice Sendak. Original music by H. D. Buch. Sound filmstrip adapted by C. B. Wismar. Artwork adapted by Stephanie Adam.

389R **Pierre**, Weston Woods, 1976 (LTR 220C) cassette only 6min $6. WW (N-P)

Maurice Sendak's subtly humorous narration is accompanied perfectly by piano music by H. D. Buch.

390 **Pig Pig Grows Up**, by David McPhail. Dutton, 1980. 32p. $8.95 (P)

The story of a little pig who refuses to grow up until a near-disaster occurs.

390FS **Pig Pig Grows Up**, Weston Woods, 1981 (FS 266) 30fr color 7min $12; (SF 266C) with cassette $18. WW (P)

David McPhail's delightful story is brought to life with pig squeals, other appropriate background sounds, and music. Accompanied by picture-cued text booklet.

390R **Pig Pig Grows Up**, Weston Woods, 1981 (LTR 266C) cassette only 6min $6. WW (N-P)

Mary Lee Casson narrates this funny story; amusing sound effects and an upbeat musical accompaniment by H. D. Buch add humorous touches to the story.

391 **The Pinballs**, by Betsy Byars. Harper, 1977. $7.95; lib. ed. $8.79; Scholastic pap. $1.25 (U)

Three lonely foster children learn to care about themselves and each other.

391F **The Pinballs**, Martin Tahse, 1977, 16mm color 31min $445. DISN (U)

Kristy McNichols stars in this simplified adaptation which nevertheless captures the sense of the book.

392 **Pinkerton, Behave!**, by Steven Kellogg. Dial, 1979. $9.94; lib. ed. $9.90; pap. $3.95 (P)

Pinkerton simply can't seem to do anything right—he even fails obedience school. His family learns to suit their commands to Pinkerton's actions and he saves them from a burglar. A very funny picture book.

392R **Pinkerton Behave!**, Weston Woods, 1982 (LTR 278C) cassette only 5min $6. WW (P)

The funny sound effects and tongue-in-cheek narration by Dan Diggles bring out all of the humor of this extremely funny story. Background music by Ernest V. Troost.

393 **Pinky Pye**, by Eleanor Estes; illus. by Edward Ardizzone. Harcourt, 1958. $7.95 (I)

The Pye family, headed by Papa, a famous ornithologist, is spending the summer on Fire Island, because the government has urged Papa to study the puffins there. Then a new member of the family arrives on the scene—a puny, abandoned black kitten named Pinky, who proves to be a remarkable creature.

393FS **Pinky Pye**, Miller-Brody, 1979 (394-78427-8) 2 filmstrips 136, 143fr color with 2 cassettes 15:11, 15:40min $45. RH/M-B (I)

Color illustrations based on descriptions from the book and a catchy musical background enhance the filmstrip presentation.

393R **Pinky Pye**, by Eleanor Estes. Random House/Miller-Brody (394-77277-6) cassette $8.97; (394-77267-8) record $8.97. RH/M-B (I)

A little black kitten, Pinky, becomes a new member of the Pye family.

394 **Pippi Longstocking**, by Astrid Lindgren; tr. from the Swedish by Florence Lamborn; illus. by Louis Glanzman. Viking, 1950. 158p. lib. ed. $5.95; pap. $1.95 (I)

Pippi, though only nine, lives alone with her horse and her money and defies all efforts of her Swedish village to make her reform. Her wild escapades and wilder stories are a delight to children.

394R **Pippi Longstocking**, Viking, 1973 (9VK 107A/B) 2s 12in 33rpm side 1: 26:56min, side 2: 25:54min $8.95; cassette $8.95. LOM (I-U)

Dramatization of the book, performed by the High Tor Repertory Players. Narrated by Bill Phillips.

395 **The Planet of Junior Brown**, by Virginia Hamilton. Macmillan, 1971. 210p. $8.95; pap. $.95 (U)

Junior Brown and his friend, Buddy Clark, play truant from their eighth-grade class in a Manhattan public school. Their hangout is the basement of the school where the janitor, Mr. Pool, a former teacher, has built a model of the solar system with an extra planet—the planet of Junior Brown. When pressures become too great Junior begins to slip into the world of unreality and Buddy tries to help him by finding him a haven among street kids.

395FS **The Planet of Junior Brown**, Random House/Miller-Brody, 1977 (394-77085-4) 2 filmstrips 127, 123 fr color with 12in 33-1/3rpm $45; (394-77086-2) with 2 cassettes 19:58, 19:05min $45. RH/M-B (I)

A successful adaptation of a serious novel, this filmstrip features skillfully edited narration, dialogue, and illustration in an excellent presentation of Hamilton's haunting story.

395R **The Planet of Junior Brown**, Random House/Miller-Brody, 1975 (NAR 3078) side 1:19:48min, side 2:18:55min 12in 33rpm $8.97; (NAC 3078) cassette $8.97. RH/M-B (U)

A fine recorded dramatization of the book. Adapted by George Morin. Narrated by Nick Smith with Dennis Hines as Junior and James Weaver as Buddy. The background music enhances the storytelling.

396 **Play with Me**, by Marie Hall Ets. Viking, 1955. 31p. $3.50; lib. ed. $4.95 net; pap. $2.50 (N-P)

A little girl longs to play with the small creatures in the meadow, but they all run away until she sits quietly and waits for them to come near.

396FS **Play with Me**, Weston Woods, n.d. (FS 46) 31fr color $12; (SF 46C) $18. WW (N-P)

Illustrations from the book, accompanied by picture-cued text booklet.

396R **Play with Me**, Weston Woods, n.d. (LTR 46C) cassette $6. WW (N-P)

Story narrated by Owen Jordan, with original background music by Paul Csonka.

397 **A Pocket for Corduroy**, by Don Freeman. Viking, 1978. unp. $8.06 (P)

Relates an event-filled trip to the laundromat by Corduroy and Lisa, the girl who owns him. After learning that he does not have a pocket, Corduroy goes looking for one and gets left behind to spend the night in the strange surroundings of washers, dryers, and soap. It remains for Lisa to set things straight.

397FS **A Pocket for Corduroy**, Viking, dist. by Live Oak Media, 1979 (0-670-90590-9) 33fr color 6:30min with cassette $19.95. LOM (P)

Utilizes illustrations from Freeman's book. Accompanied by picture-cued text booklet.

398 **Poems for Youth**, by Emily Dickinson; ed. by Alfred Leete Hampson; foreword by May Lamberton Becker; illus. by George and Doris Hauman. Little, 1934. unp. $5.95 (I-U)

Seventy-eight poems written by Emily Dickinson for her young niece and nephews.

398R **A Gathering of Great Poetry for Children**, v. 1-4, Caedmon, 1968 (CDL 51235-8) each cassette $8.98. CAE (P-U)

Poems by Emily Dickinson, Robert Frost, Langston Hughes, Edna St. Vincent Millay, A. A. Milne, Carl Sandburg, and others are read by Julie Harris, Cyril Ritchard, David Wayne, and the poets themselves. Volume 1 is suggested for kindergarten and up; volume 2 for second grade and up; and volumes 3 and 4 for fourth grade and up. Richard Lewis selected the poems.

398R **Poems and Letters of Emily Dickinson**, Caedmon, 196? (TC 1119) 2s 12in 33rpm $8.98; (CDL 51119) cassette $8.98. CAE (U)

A fresh and sensitive reading by Julie Harris.

399 **Poems Selected for Young People**, by Edna St. Vincent Millay; illus. and decorations by J. Paget-Fredericks. Harper, 1951. 113p. $3.50; lib. ed. $3.79 net (I-U). OP

An attractively illustrated introduction to Millay, for the true poetry lover.

399R **Poetry of Edna St. Vincent Millay**, Caedmon, 195? (TC 1024) 2s 12in 33rpm $6.50. CAE (U)

Judith Anderson reads the poems which have appeal for older boys and girls, especially the latter.

400 **Poor Goose**, retold by Anne Rockwell. Harper, 1976. 32p. $7.95; lib. ed. $7.89 (N-P)

A French folktale of a goose who starts out to the castle to get something to relieve a headache. She gathers animal friends along the way who will all be needed before the tale is told. A short, easy-to-read, cumulative story which children love.

400FS **Poor Goose**, Listening Library, 1977 (AJFS 161) 41fr color 9min with cassette $21. LL (N-P)

Anne Rockwell's *Poor Goose* comes across well in the sound filmstrip medium.

401 **The Post Office Cat**, by Gail E. Haley. Scribner, 1976. 32p. $6.95 (P)

Clarence, the cat, felt a need for a place of his own. Leaving the farm, he made his way to London and set about finding food and shelter. Clarence experienced some difficult times until arriving at the post office just in time to scatter an assembly of mice. Clarence was given the job of Post Office Cat.

Winner of the Kate Greenaway Medal.

401FS **The Post Office Cat**, Weston Woods, 1978 (FS 234) 41fr color 11min $12; (SF 234C) with cassette $18. WW (P)

Illustrations for the filmstrip were adapted from Haley's Kate Greenaway Medal-winning book.

Accompanied by picture-cued text booklet.

402 **Private Zoo**, by Georgess McHargue; illus. by Michael Foreman. Viking, 1975. 32p. $7.95 (P)

Lewis Harvey's disappointment when he cannot find anyone to take him to the zoo to see live animals turns to amusement as he begins to detect resemblances between members of his family and some of his favorite animals. Lewis decides to go for a walk, and along his way, observes in the shadows cast by his neighbors and family the images of his own private zoo.

402FS **Private Zoo**, Viking, dist. by Live Oak Media, 1976 (0-670-90534-8) 38fr color 5:54min with cassette $19.95. LOM (P)

Filmstrip adaptation utilizes Michael Foreman's illustrations from the book. Accompanied by picture-cued text booklet.

403 **Puss in Boots**, by Charles Perrault; a free translation from the French; with pictures by Marcia Brown. Scribner, 1952. unp. lib. ed. $8.95 net (P)

All the wit, humor, and drama of the fairy tale are captured in the beautiful illustrations in this handsome picture book.

403FS **Puss in Boots**, Random House/Miller-Brody, 1979 (394-78396-4) 93fr color 12min with cassette $21. RH/M-B (P-I)

Uses the illustrations from the book which feature large patches of white contrasted by huge swatches of color finely detailed by ink outlines and features.

404 **Queenie Peavy**, by Robert Burch; illus. by Jerry Lazare. Viking, 1966. 159p. lib. ed. $7.95 net (I-U)

Unhappy because her adored father is in jail and resentful of being teased by other children, thirteen-year-old Queenie expresses her frustration in delinquent behavior. With the help of wise adults, she weathers her emotional crisis and faces her problems with courage and spirit. Set in Georgia during the depression.

404R **Queenie Peavy**, Viking, dist. by Live Oak Media, 1972, 2s 12in 33rpm 49:15min $8.95; cassette $8.95. LOM (I-U)

Dramatized version of the book performed by the High Tor Repertory Players.

405 **Rabbit Hill**, by Robert Lawson. Viking, 1944. 127p. lib. ed. $8.50 net; pap. $1.50 (I)

Georgie, a lively young rabbit, investigates the new family moving into the house on the hill and reports to the other animals that they live by the philosophy that "there is enough for all." Newbery Medal winner, 1945.

405R **Rabbit Hill**, Viking, dist. by Live Oak Media, 1972, 2s 12in 33rpm 50:05min $8.95; cassette $8.95. LOM (I)

Dramatized version of the book.

406 **Rachel and Obadiah**, by Brinton Turkle. Dutton, 1978. $8.95 (P)

A ship coming safely home to Nantucket Island was a great event. So great that the captain's wife might give a silver coin to the person who first brought her the news. Rachel Starbuck wanted more than anything to be the one who was sent with the news. But so did her brother, Obadiah, who was older and bigger and a faster runner.

406FS **Rachel and Obadiah**, Live Oak Media, 1982 (0-941078-04-3) 39fr color 9:53min with cassette $21.95. LOM (P)

The sound filmstrip utilizes the intricate illustrations from the book. Guide available.

407 **A Rainbow of My Own**, by Don Freeman. Viking, 1966. unp. lib. ed. $6.95 net; pap. $2.25 (P)

A little boy out walking fantasizes about a rainbow. When he returns home the sun shining through the water in his goldfish bowl has made a rainbow just for him.

407FS **A Rainbow of My Own**, Viking, dist. by Live Oak Media, 1975 (670-90530) 30fr color 4:20min with cassette $19.95. LOM (P)

Narrated by Larry Robinson. Illustrations from the book, accompanied by picture-cued text booklet. Appropriate sound effects and musical background. The recording is flawed by the narrator's imitative childlike delivery.

408 **Ramona and Her Father**, by Beverly Cleary; illus. by Alan Tiegreen. Morrow, 1977. $7.44 (P)

When Mr. Quimby suddenly loses his job, Ramona and Beezus find him becoming irritable. They also grow concerned about his smoking and launch a no-smoking campaign to save his life.

408FS **Ramona and Her Father**, Miller-Brody, 1980 (394-78390-5) 2 filmstrips 97, 107fr color 12, 11min with 2 cassettes $45. RH/M-B (P-I)

A sympathetic narrator is joined by performers who vigorously embody the various characters, while an expressive musical background strikes a lively note. Barbara Moore's watercolor illustrations for the strip vibrantly echo the style of those in the book.

408R **Ramona and Her Father**, by Beverly Cleary, Random House/ Miller-Brody (394-76892-0) record $8.97; (394-76893-0) cassette $8.97. RH/M-B (P).

Dramatized version.

409 **Ramona the Brave**, by Beverly Cleary; illus. by Alan Tiegreen. Morrow, 1975. 192p. $7.44 (P-I)

Six-year-old Ramona Quimby has troubles, beginning with her first day in first grade.

409FS **Ramona the Brave**, Random House/Miller-Brody, 1980 (394-64543-X) 151fr color 18:30min $21. RH/M-B (P-I)

Sympathetic narrator is joined by enthusiastic performers who vigorously act out the parts of the various characters. The twangy music strikes a lively note for Barbara Moore's watercolor illustrations which are patterned after those in the original.

409R **Ramona the Brave**, by Beverly Cleary. Random House/Miller-Brody (394-64517-0) cassette $8.97. RH/M-B (P-I)

Dramatized version.

410 **Ramona the Pest**, by Beverly Cleary; illus. by Louis Darling. Morrow, 1968. $7.44 (P-I)

Ramona, a spirited, loving, rambunctious, naive, funny little girl is just starting kindergarten. But she has a few problems and becomes a kindergarten drop-out.

410FS **Ramona the Pest**, Pied Piper (First Choice: Authors and Books), 1977, 1 filmstrip with 2 cassettes—interview cassette 11:11min, filmstrip cassette 11:12min $29. PP (P-I)

Capturing the spirit of Ramona's advent into kindergarten, brief episodes are dramatized with children's voices and with illustrations directly reflecting those in the book by Cleary.

411 **Ramona Quimby, Age 8**, by Beverly Cleary; illus. by Alan Tiegreen. Morrow, 1981. $7.63 (P-I)

Ramona is now in the third grade and has to help when her father returns to college to become a teacher. Ramona learns that everyone has ups and downs—even parents.

411FS **Ramona Quimby, Age 8**, Random House/Miller-Brody, 1981 (394-07749-0) 142fr color 22min with cassette $21. RH/M-B (P-I)

Barbara Moore's watercolor illustrations echo the style of those in the book. Enthusiastic portrayal by performers enhances the presentation.

411R **Ramona Quimby, Age 8**, by Beverly Cleary. Random House/Miller-Brody (394-07744-X) cassette $8.97. RH/M-B (P-I)

Dramatized version.

412 **Rapunzel**, by the Brothers Grimm; retold and illus. by Bernadette Watts. Harper, 1975. 32p. $8.95; lib. ed. $8.79 (P-I)

A young girl is imprisoned in a tower by a witch and the only way into the tower is by climbing up her long hair.

412F **Rapunzel**, Somersaulter-Moats and Somersaulter, 1980, 16mm color 10min $225. PER (P-I)

Lovely pastel animation bring this classic tale to life. Original music adds to the enjoyment.

412F **Rapunzel, Rapunzel**, Tom and Mimi Davenport, 1978, 16mm color 16min $240, $25. TD (I-U)

A live action retelling of the classic Grimms' fairy tale with an American setting. Psychological overtones make this a powerful and sometimes unsettling film.

413 **Rascal: A Memoir of a Better Era**, by Sterling North; illus. by John Schoenherr. Dutton, 1963. 189p. $9.95 (I-U)

The antics of Rascal, a roguish raccoon raised from wild infancy by Sterling, get his master into much trouble, but the two remain inseparable for a year of heartwarming adventure. The story takes place near the end of World War I.

413R **Rascal**, Miller-Brody, 1975 (NAR 3079) 12in 33rpm $8.97; (NAC 3079) cassette $8.97. M-B (I-U)

Recorded dramatization of the book. Narration by actor William Redfield.

414 **The Rat-Catcher's Daughter: A Collection of Stories**, by Laurence Housman; selected and with an afterword by Ellin Greene; illus. by Julia Noonan. Atheneum, 1974. 169p. $6.95 (I-U)

Twelve literary fairy tales, including such favorites as "Rocking-Horse Land" and "A Chinese Fairy Tale."

414R **Fairy Tale Favorites**, v.3, CMS Records, 1971 (CMS 632) 2s 12in 33rpm $7.98; cassette $7.98. CMS (P-I)

Mary Strang tells Laurence Housman's "Rocking-Horse Land" and three traditional tales, "Beauty and the Beast," "The Top and the Ball," and "The Frog Prince."

415 **Red Fairy Book**, ed. by Andrew Lang; illus. by H. J. Ford. Peter Smith, n.d. $6.50 (I)

Twenty-nine fairy tales collected from around the world and edited by an early folklorist.

415R **Snow-White and Rose-Red and Other Andrew Lang Fairy Tales**, Caedmon, 1973 (TC 1414) 2s 12in 33rpm $8.98; (CDL 51414) cassette $8.98. CAE (P-I)

Side 1: title story (16:31min) and "The True History of Little Goldenhood" (8:29 min). Side 2: "East of the Sun and West of the Moon" (27:32min). In her musical speaking voice Glynis Johns reads two favorites from Lang's *Blue Fairy Book* and Lang's version of "Little Red Riding-Hood" from his *Red Fairy Book*.

416 **The Reluctant Dragon**, by Kenneth Grahame; illus. by Ernest H. Shepard. Holiday, 1953. unp. $4.95 (P-I)

A little boy makes friends with a gentle dragon and arranges a match for him with Saint George.

416R **The Reluctant Dragon**, Caedmon, 1958 (TC 1074) 2s 12in 33rpm $8.98; (CDL 51074) cassette $8.98. CAE (P)

Boris Karloff's performance conveys the full quality of the extravagant tale by Kenneth Grahame.

417 **Ribsy**, by Beverly Cleary; illus. by Louis Darling. Morrow, 1964. $7.44 (I)

Ribsy, Henry Huggins' lost dog, has many misadventures including getting a bubble bath, wearing clothes, and even starring in a football game.

417FS **Ribsy**, Pied Piper (First Choice: Authors and Books), 1979, 1 filmstrip 107fr color 16:10min with cassette $29. PP (I)

The characters and scenes portrayed in this strip are based on the book's depictions, and the readers' voices sound authentic and lend spontaneity to the story.

418 **The Rich Man and the Shoemaker: A Fable**, by La Fontaine; illus. by Brian Wildsmith. Oxford Univ. Pr., 1980. pap. $3.95 (P)

A shoemaker decides it is better to be poor and happy than rich and miserable.

418FS **The Rich Man and the Shoemaker** and **Brian Wildsmith's Wild Animals**, Weston Woods, 1972 (FS 134) 37fr color 10:28min $12; (SF 134C) with cassette $18. WW (P-I)

Illustrations from the book, accompanied by picture-cued text booklet. Pleasant reading of the fable. *Wild Animals* consists of spoken captions and natural animal sounds.

418R **Rich Man and the Shoemaker** and **Brian Wildsmith's Wild Animals**, Weston Woods, 1972 (LTR 134C) cassette only 10:28min $6. (P)

Emery Battis narrates the first story; Charles Cioffi narrates the second, accompanied by natural animal sounds.

419 **The Rich Man and the Singer**, told by Mesfin Habte-Mariam; ed. and illus. by Christine Price. Dutton, 1971. 96p. $4.95 (I-U). OP

A collection of folktales from Ethiopia.

419R **Folk Tales and Legends of Ethiopia**, v.1, CMS Records, 1969 (CMS 572) 2s 12in 33rpm $7.98; cassette $7.98. CMS (I)

Includes "The Husband Who Wanted to Mind the House," "The Woman Who Wanted to Govern the Land," "The Adventurous Mouse," "The King and the Farmer," "The Three Thieves," "The Farmer and the Leopard," "The Clever Baboon," and "The Rich Man and the Singer." The wit and humor in these colorful tales are well shown in the skillful storytelling of Christine Price.

420 **Ride the Cold Wind**, by Anico Surany; illus. by Leonard Fisher. Putnam, 1964. $5.39 (P-I)

Surany tells the story of a young Andean boy seeking to fulfill his dream of catching the great fish of Lake Titicaca.

420FS **Ride the Cold Wind**, Westport Communications Group, rel. by Random House, 1977 (394-06343-0) 50fr color 10min with 12in 33-1/3rpm $24; (394-06342-2) with cassette $24. RH/M-B (P-I)

Utilizes Fisher's bold woodcuts from the book. Filmstrip version enhanced by pipe music background. Guide.

ALA Notable Filmstrip.

421 **Rifles for Watie**, by Harold Keith. Crowell, 1957. 332p. $8.95 (I-U)

This story of a young Union soldier fighting in Kansas during the Civil War reveals the futility of war and shows the courage displayed on both sides. 1958 Newbery Medal winner.

421R **Rifles for Watie**, Random House/Miller-Brody, 1971 (NAR 3019) 12in 33rpm 40-45min $8.97; (NAC 3019) cassette $8.97. RH/M-B (U)

A recorded dramatization. Narrated by Peter Thomas. Featured in the cast are Mark Kearney as Jeff, Lawson Zerbe as Watie, and Franklin Rohrbach as Clardy. Includes a teacher's guide.

422 **Rip Van Winkle and the Legend of Sleepy Hollow**, by Washington Irving; illus. by David Levine. Macmillan, 1963. 80p. $4.95 (U)

The legend of gawky schoolmaster Ichabod Crane and his rivalry with Brom Bones for the hand of Katrina Van Tassel, which was brought to an end by his encounter with the Headless Horseman.

422F **The Legend of Sleepy Hollow**, Bosustow, 1972, 16mm color 13min $225; videocassette $215. PYR (U)

Animated with humor (Ichabod's courting of plump Katrina) and mystery (the night ride) and special shivers afforded by John Carradine's narration.

422R **Rip Van Winkle**, Caedmon, 1968 (TC 1241) 2s 12in 33rpm 41:46min $8.98; (CDL 51241) cassette $8.98. CAE (I-U)

Ed Begley reads this favorite tale of a man who slept for twenty years.

423 **Robinson Crusoe**, by Daniel Defoe. Grosset (Classics Series), 1952. illus. deluxe ed. $8.95; 1981 Bantam pap. 288p. $1.75 (I)

Cast up on a deserted island, a young man has to survive with what is at hand.

423FS **Robinson Crusoe**, Educational Enrichment Materials, 1976, color 2 filmstrips 2 cassettes 1 paperback $48 (individual FS with sound $24). EEM (I)

An exceptionally well-illustrated and narrated adaptation.

424 **Roll of Thunder, Hear My Cry**, by Mildred Taylor; illus. by Jerry Pinkney. Dial, 1976. 276p. $8.95 (I)

Taylor tells the story of nine-year-old Cassie Logan and her family who live in Mississippi during the Great Depression. Cassie doesn't understand why her parents attach so much importance to owning their own land, nor does she understand the Night Riders—white men who terrorize her people. 1977 Newbery Medal winner.

424F **Roll of Thunder**, 1978, 16mm color 110min $800 (5-year lease). LCA (I)

Television feature film starring Claudia McNeil, Janet MacLachlan and Larry Scott. Directed by Jack Smight.

424FS **Roll of Thunder, Hear My Cry**, Random House/Miller-Brody, 1981 (394-66060-9) 2 filmstrips 152, 138 fr color with 2 cassettes 23, 22min $45. RH/M-B (I)

Tufts of pastel colors lushly texture the fine drawings that depict the upright Logan family and a Mississippi chafed by the Depression and segregation. Filmstrip captures the essence of the black family's trials. Includes generous excerpts from Taylor's dialogue. Mellow melodies of flute, piano, and harmonica enhance the presentation.

424R **Roll of Thunder, Hear My Cry**, Random House/Miller-Brody (394-76896-5) cassette only $10.95; (394-76895) record $10.95. RH/M-B (I-U)

The gripping story of a black family in the depression-era South. Narration is woven into the dialogue in a clear and distinct dramatized version. Abridged.

425 **Rootabaga Stories**, by Carl Sandburg; illus. and decorations by Maud and Miska Petersham. Harcourt, 1951. 218p. $10.95; pap. $1.95 (P-I)

The poet's whimsical humor is evident in these joyous tales.

425R **Frances Clarke Sayers, Storyteller**,

Weston Woods, 196? (WW 705, 706) 4s 12in 33rpm $14; also available on 2 cassettes (WW 705C, 706C) $14. WW (I)

Frances Clarke Sayers tells stories by Carl Sandburg and Hans Christian Andersen (WW 706).

WW 705 contains Sandburg stories. Side 1 (18:5min): "The Wedding Procession of the Rag Doll and the Broom Handle and Who Was in It" and "The Huckabuck Family and How They Raised Pop Corn in Nebraska and Quit and Came Back." Side 2 (19:48min): "Pip Wisps" and "The White Horse Girl and The Blue Wind Boy."

425R **Carl Sandburg: Rootabaga Stories**, Caedmon (TC 1159) "How to Tell Corn Fairies When You See 'Em" 1 12in LP $8.98; (CDL 51159) 1 cassette $8.98; (TC 1089) "The Finding of the Zig Zag Railroad" 1 12in LP $8.98; (CDL 51089) 1 cassette $8.98; (TC 1306) "The Haystack Cricket" 1 12in LP $8.98; (CDL 51306) 1 cassette $8.98. CAE (I)

Each recording contains several stories read by Carl Sandburg.

426 **Rosie's Walk**, by Pat Hutchins. Macmillan, 1968. unp. $6.95; pap. $2.25 (P)

In a series of bright pictures Rosie the hen takes a walk around the farm and unwittingly leads the fox stalking close behind her into one disaster after another.

426F **Rosie's Walk**, Morton Schindel, 1971, 16mm color 5min $125, $15; videocassette $125; Super 8 sound $125. WW (P)

Animated film adapted from the book. To the tune of "Turkey in the Straw" Rosie the hen struts about the farm, oblivious to the perils close at hand. Narrated by Gene Deitch.

Also available in Spanish.

426R **Rosie's Walk**, Weston Woods, 1971 (LTR 125C) cassette only 4:20min $6. WW (N-P)

Gene Deitch narrates this to the tune of "Turkey in the Straw" played by fiddles.

427 **Round the World Fairy Tales**, retold by Amabel Williams-Ellis; illus. by William Stobbs. Warne, 1963. 303p. $4.95 (I). OP

Lively retellings of familiar and less well-known tales from Asia, Europe, Africa, the Americas, Australia, Indonesia, and the Indies, with notes.

427R **Puss in Boots**, and **Other Fairy Tales from around the World**, Caedmon, 1968 (TC 1247) 2s 12in 33rpm $8.98; (CDL 51247) cassette $8.98. CAE (P)

Read by Cathleen Nesbitt. Includes: "Puss in Boots" (France); "Saturday, Sunday and Monday" (Italy); "The Hopi Turtle" (American Indian); "Cockle Lockle," "Henny Penny" (England); "Mr. Korbes the Fox" (Germany); "Biggoon and the Little Duck" (Australia); and "Baba Yaga" (Russia), all as retold by Amabel Williams-Ellis.

428 **Russian Folk Tales**, tr. by Natalie Duddington; illus. by Dick Hart. Funk, 1969. 144p. $4.95 (I). OP

Stories translated from the early folklore collection of Afanasyev.

428R **Russian Folk and Fairy Tales**, CMS Records, 1967 (CMS 515) 2s 12in 33rpm $7.98; cassette $7.98. CMS (I)

"Kuzma Quick-Rich," "The Twelve Months," and "Two out of the Knapsack" told by Christine Price.

429 **A Salmon for Simon**, by Betty Waterton; illus. by Ann Blades. Atheneum, 1980. 32p. $8.95 (P)

Simon, a young Canadian Indian boy, tries all summer to catch a shimmering, red salmon. When his luck suddenly changes, Simon is torn between sympathy for the fish and the desire to catch something of his own.

429FS **A Salmon for Simon**, Weston Woods, 1980 (FS 256) 38fr color 12min $12; (SF 256C) with cassette $18. WW (P)

Brightly colored illustrations taken directly from the book. Background music provided by a single English horn is supplemented by seagull sounds. Accompanied by picture-cued text booklet.

430 **Salt; a Russian Tale**, adapted by Harve Zemach from a literal translation, by Benjamin Zemach, of the Russian of Alexi Afanasyev; illus. by Margot Zemach. new ed. Farrar, 1977. 32p. $7.95 (P-I)

Ivan, the fool, is smart enough to win a fair princess for a wife, a giant for a friend, and a vessel full of gold and silver.

430FS **Salt**, Weston Woods, n.d.(FS 79) 40fr color $12; (SF 79C) with cassette $18. WW (P-I)

Illustrations from the book, accompanied by picture-cued text booklet.

430R **Salt**, Weston Woods, n.d. (LTR 79C) cassette only $6. WW (P-I)

Story narrated by Owen Jordan, with original background music by Howard Rovics.

431 **Sam, Bangs and Moonshine**, by Evaline Ness. Holt, 1966. 48p. $6.95 (P)

Sam, a fisherman's daughter, has a vivid imagination. Her father refers to her daydreams as "moonshine." Not until her "moonshine" talk sent her only friend with her beloved cat to near destruction did Sam realize the grown-up differences between true imagination and uncontrolled flights of fancy. Caldecott Medal winner, 1967.

431FS **Sam, Bangs and Moonshine**, Random House/Miller-Brody, 1976 (394-76472-2) 58fr color 13:36min with cassette $21. RH/M-B (P)

The music from the opening bars establishes the dreamy, mysterious, and sometimes melancholy mood of Sam's secret world. Illustrations, done in subtle colors, are taken directly from the book.

431R **Sam, Bangs and Moonshine**, by Evaline Ness. Random House/Miller-Brody (394-07622-2) read-along cassette with hardcover book $15. RH/M-B (P)

Narrated by Rosemary Harris.

432 **San Domingo: The Medicine Hat Stallion**, by Marguerite Henry; illus. by Robert Longheed. Rand, 1972. 244p. $8.95 (I-U)

Set in pre-Civil War Wyoming, this is the story of a boy and his horse, which his father wants to sell to the Pony Express.

432F **Story of a Book**, 2nd ed., Pied Piper, 1980, 16mm color 16min $270. PP (I-U)

The research, writing, and editing of Marguerite Henry's book, *San Domingo: The Medicine Hat Stallion*, is described from the original idea to the delivery of the book to the library shelf.

433 **The Sandburg Treasury**, by Carl Sandburg; introd. by Paula Sandburg; illus. by Paul Bacon. Harcourt, 1970. 480p. $8.95 (P-U)

Prose and poetry for young people including *Rootabaga Stories*, *Early Moon*, *Wind Song*, *Abe Lincoln Grows Up,* and *Prairie-Town Boy*.

433R **A Lincoln Album**, Caedmon, 195? (TC 2015) 4s 12in 33rpm $15.96; (CDL 52015) 2 cassettes $15.96. CAE (U)

Carl Sandburg reads from material and text which he used in his *Abe Lincoln: The Prairie Years* and *The War Years*.

434 **Scottish Folk-Tales and Legends**, retold by Barbara Ker Wilson; illus. by Joan Kiddell-Monroe. Walck, 1954. 270p. $6 (I). OP

Fine retellings of largely unfamiliar tales, including "The Faery Flag of Dunvegan."

434R **Folk Tales and Legends from Great Britain,** CMS Records, 1972 (CMS 633) $8.98; (X4633) cassette $8.98. CMS (I-U)

The four stories are told in versions especially written for the Jackanory storytelling program for children produced by BBC. Contents include "Cap of Rushes" (English) told by Lee Montague, "The Giant's Wife" (Irish) told by Maureen Potter, "The Faery Flag of Dunvegan" (Scottish) told by Magnus Magnusson, and "Where Arthur Sleeps" (Welsh) told by Ray Smith.

435 **Scrambled Eggs Super**, by Dr. Seuss. Random, 1953. unp. $5.99; pap. $2.95 (P-I)

Peter decides to give the world a great new recipe for scrambled eggs by collecting unusual and exciting eggs.

435R **Happy Birthday to You! and Other Stories**, Caedmon, 1969 (LP 1287) 2s 12in 33rpm $8.98; (CSS 51287) cassette $8.98. CAE (P)

Five Dr. Seuss stories read with verve by Hans Conreid. The electronic sounds of the Octopus, a sound machine with eight channels, are used to point up the action and give a suitably strange flavor to the nonsense. Includes: *Happy Birthday to You!*, *Scrambled Eggs Super*, *And to Think That I Saw It on Mulberry Street*, *Gertrude McFuzz*, and *The Big Brag*.

436 **The Secret Garden**, by Frances Hodgson Burnett; illus. by Tasha Tudor. Lippincott, 1962. 256p. deluxe ed. $10; pap. $1.75 (I)

Three children find a garden and make it bloom again. The garden, in turn, changes the children. An attractive edition of an old favorite illustrated with suitably sentimental pictures.

436R **The Secret Garden**, Caedmon, 1976 (TC 1463) 12in 33rpm side 1: 32:24min, side 2: 32:05min $8.98. CAE (I)

A skillfully abridged version of the children's classic. Superbly read by Claire Bloom.

437 **The Selfish Giant**, by Oscar Wilde; illus. by Gertraud and Walter Reiner. Harvey House, 1967. unp. $3.50; lib. ed. $3.36 net (P). OP

It was always winter in the Giant's garden until he learned to share it with the childen.

437F **The Selfish Giant**, Murray Shostak and Peter Sander, 1972, 16mm color 27min $395; videocassette $295; rental $35. PYR (P-I)

The selfish giant builds a high wall to keep the children out of his garden, but finds that spring will not come to his garden until the children are allowed back. Animated in naturalistic style. Directed by Peter Sander.

437FS **The Selfish Giant**, Weston Woods, 1972 (FS 132) 41fr b/w 12min $12; (SF 132C) with cassette $18. WW (P-I)

Illustrations from the book, accompanied by picture-cued text booklet.

437R **The Selfish Giant**, Weston Woods, 1972 (LTR 132C) cassette $6. WW (P-I)

Narrated by Charles Cioffi. Original background music by Karl von Feilitzsch.

438 **Seven Tales**, by Hans Christian Andersen; tr. from the Danish by Eva Le Gallienne; pictures by Maurice Sendak. Harper, 1959. 127p. lib. ed. $8.79 net (P-I)

Translator and artist show understanding and appreciation of Andersen's poignant stories. Includes "The Happy Family," "It's Absolutely True," "The Princess and the Pea," "The Steadfast Tin Soldier," and "The Ugly Duckling."

438R **The Happy Family** and **It's Absolutely True!**, Random

House/Miller-Brody, 1973 (L506-R/C) 12in 33rpm side 1: 8:50min, side 2: 7:24min $8.97; cassette $8.97. RH/M-B (I)
The Princess and the Pea, Random House/Miller-Brody, 1973 (L 504-R/C) 12in 33rpm side 1: 7:02min, side 2: 7:10min; cassette $8.97. RH/M-B (I)
The Steadfast Tin Soldier, Random House/Miller-Brody, 1973 (L 508-R/C) 12in 33rpm side 1: 6:10min, side 2: 6:09min $8.97; cassette $8.97. RH/M-B (I)
The Ugly Duckling, Random House/Miller-Brody, 1973 (1509-R/C) 12in 33rpm side 1: 12:50min, side 2: 12:26min $8.97; cassette $8.97. RH/M-B (P-I)

Actress Eva Le Gallienne brings sensitivity and zest to her reading of Andersen's fairy tales. Printed text included.

439 **Shadow of a Bull**, by Maria Wojciechowska; drawings by Alvin Smith. Atheneum, 1964. 165p. lib. ed. $6.95; pap. $1.95 (I-U)

Everyone in the little Spanish town thought that Manolo, son of a famous matador, should follow in his late father's footsteps. Because Manolo did not wish to kill, he thought himself a coward until he found a way to prove his courage. A fine story of a boy's inner struggle, set in the exciting world of the bull ring. 1965 Newbery Medal winner.

439FS **Shadow of A Bull**, Random House/Miller-Brody, 1978 (394-77112-5) 2 filmstrips 116, 139fr color 18, 21min with 2 cassettes $45. RH/M-B (I)

Based on the book. Lively Spanish music enhances the presentation.

439R **Shadow of a Bull**, Miller-Brody, 1970 (NAR 3013) 12in 33rpm side 1: 19:06min, side 2: 22:12min $8.97; (NAC 3013) cassette $8.97. RH/M-B (I-U)

Dramatized and directed by Peter Fernandez. Featured in this recording are Sam Gray as narrator, Jeff Somple as Manolo, William Griffis as Castillo, and Lawson Zerbe as Doctor. Background music by Herb Davidson includes a paso doble played at bullfights. Includes teacher's guide.

440 **She'll Be Comin' 'Round the Mountain**, by Robert Quackenbush. Lippincott, 1973. unp. $6.95 (P)

Inspired by the familiar railroad song the author introduces Little Annie, Handsome Larry, Colorado Jack, Sneaky Pete, Rattlesnake Hank, and Crumby Joe in a train robbery story with a happy ending.

440FS **She'll Be Comin' 'Round the Mountain**, Weston Woods, 1975 (FS 169) 40fr color $12; (SF 169C) with cassette only 7:24min $18. WW (P-I)

Illustrations from the book, accompanied by picture-cued text booklet. The singing, banjo playing, and sound effects are just right for this outlandish tale. Thoroughly enjoyable.

440R **She'll Be Comin' 'Round the Mountain**, Weston Woods, 1975 (LTR 169C) cassette only 7min $6. WW (P)

A lively cassette with singing, banjo music, and narration in an old-time movie style. Music arranged and narrated by H. D. Buch.

441 **The Shoemaker and the Elves**, by the Brothers Grimm; illus. by Adrienne Adams. Scribner, 1960. unp. $4.50; lib. ed. $5.95 net; pap. $.95 (P). OP

Two elves do a good deed for the shoemaker and his wife and are surprised when the deed is returned.

441F **The Shoemaker and the Elves**, Gakken Film, Tokyo, 1962 (1498) 16mm color 13:30min $260. COR (P)

Animated puppets. Unusual version of the story, but faithful to the spirit of the original.

441R **Fairy Tales for a Winter's Night**, CMS Records, 1968 (CMS 534) 2s 12in 33rpm $8.98; (X4534) cassette $8.98. CMS (P)

Mary Strang tells Andersen's "The Fir Tree" and "The Little Match Girl," Grimms' "The Elves and the Shoemaker," and "'Twas the Night Before Christmas" by Clement Moore.

442 **Shoeshine Girl**, by Clyde R. Bulla; illus. by Leigh Grant. Harper, 1975. 80p. $8.95; Scholastic pap. $1.25 (I)

A rebellious 10-year-old girl, sent to spend the summer at her aunt's, works for an old man running a shoeshine stand and, when he becomes ill, keeps the stand open alone.

442F **Shoeshine Girl**, Jane Startz, 1979, 16mm color 25min $425. LCA (I-U)

Live-action film faithful to the book. 1982 Notable Film for Children.

443 **The Shrinking of Treehorn**, by Florence Parry Heide. Holiday 1971 (P)

A droll story about a little boy who starts to shrink and cannot get the adults in his life to pay any attention to his problem.

443R **The Shrinking of Treehorn**. Listening Library, 1980, 1981 (#FTR) 22min 1 cassette 4 paperback books teacher's guide $15 (P)

A word-for-word reading of the story to stimulate reading along. Narrator is unidentified.

444 **The Silver Pony**, by Lynd Ward. Houghton, 1973. 175p. $10.95 (P-I)

In eighty pictures (and no dialogue) the artist tells the story of a lonely boy who escapes the limited world of his farm on a fantastic winged pony. The black-and-white illustrations have strength and beauty.

444FS **The Silver Pony**, Weston Woods, 1975 (FS 170) 92fr b/w $12. WW (P-I-U)

Illustrations from the book. Non-verbal.

445 **Sing Down the Moon**, by Scott O'Dell. Houghton, 1970. 137p. $7.95; pap. $.95 (I-U)

The poignant story of the forced migration of the Navahos from their homeland in Arizona to Fort Sumner, New Mexico, in the mid-1860s, is told from the viewpoint of Bright Morning, a young Navaho girl.

445R **Sing Down the Moon**, Random House/Miller-Brody, 1973 (NAR 3038) 2s 12in 33rpm side 1: 23min, side 2: 22min $8.97; (NAC 3038) cassette $8.97. RH/M-B (I-U)

Adapted and directed by Peter Fernandez. Narrated by Paulette Rubinstein supported by a cast, music, and sound effects.

446 **The Skating Rink**, by Mildred Lee. Houghton, 1969. 128p. $7.95 (U)

Ice skating lessons help give Tuck confidence to overcome his stammer and his emotional problems brought on when he saw his mother drown.

446F **The Skating Rink**, Martin Tahse, 1975, 16mm color 27min $450, $40. LCA (U)

Effective portrait of a shy teenager originally produced for the ABC Afterschool Special. 1977 Notable Film for Children.

447 **Sleeping Beauty**, adapted and illus. by Warren Chappell; music by Peter Ilyich Tchaikovsky. Knopf, 1961. unp. $2.95; lib. ed. $4.79 net (P-I). OP

This edition of the beloved fairy tale includes themes and music from Tchaikovsky's ballet.

447R **The Story of Sleeping Beauty**, by Charles Perrault. Caedmon (TC 1646) 12in LP $8.98; (CP 1646) cassette $8.98. CAE (P-I)

Claire Bloom tells the romantic tale to Tchaikovsky's score. Music performed by Orchestre de la Suisse Romande.

448 **A Smart Kid like You**, by Stella Pevsner. Houghton, 1975. 192p. $7.95; Scholastic pap. $1.50 (I-U)

Just beginning to accept her parents' divorce, Nina discovers to her chagrin that her father's new wife is to be her seventh-grade math teacher.

448F **Me and Dad's New Wife**, Daniel Wilson, 1975, 16mm color 33min $40. TLM (U)

Originally an ABC Afterschool Special starring Kristy McNichol. Well-acted.

449 **The Snow Queen**, by Hans Christian Andersen; tr. from the Danish by R. P. Keigwin; illus. by Marcia Brown. Scribner, 1972. 96p. pap. $1.79 (P-I)

A distinguished new edition of a classic. The pen-and-ink drawings have a delicacy and strength that perfectly complement Andersen's moving drama.

449R **The Snow Queen**, Random House/Miller-Brody, 1973 (1 510/511-R/C) 12in 33rpm part 1: side 1: 17:25min, side 2: 18:05min, part 2: side 1: 26:15min, side 2: 18:28min $17.94; cassette $17.94. RH/M-B (I)

Actress Eva Le Gallienne brings sensitivity and zest to her reading of Andersen's fairy tales. Printed text included.

450 **Snow White and the Seven Dwarfs**, by the Brothers Grimm; freely tr. and illus. by Wanda Gag. Coward, 1938. 43p. lib. ed. $5.49 (P)

Gaily illustrated edition of the traditional fairy tale of the lovely Snow White who lives with seven dwarfs until her prince comes to claim her.

450R **Snow White, and Other Fairy Tales by the Brothers Grimm**, Caedmon, 1970 (TC 1266) 2s 12in 33rpm $8.98; (CDL 51266) cassette $8.98. CAE (P-I)

Claire Bloom reads "Snow White," "Hare and the Hedgehog," and "Valiant Little Tailor," as retold by Amabel Williams-Ellis.

451 **Snowbound**, by Harry Mazer. Delacorte, 1973. 128p. $6.95; Dell pap. 1.25 (U)

Two teenagers, Tony and Cindy, are caught in a blizzard and must fight for survival in a desolate area.

451F **Snowbound**, Linda Gottlieb, 1978, 16mm color 50min $615, $50. LCA (U)

Very exciting film of the book. Also available in an edited 32-minute version ($450, $40).

452 **The Snowy Day**, by Ezra Jack Keats. Viking, 1962. 32p. lib. ed. $6.95; pap. $.95 (N-P)

In a simple story with striking collage illustrations the author perfectly captures a small boy's delight as he plays in the snow. Caldecott Medal winner, 1963.

452FS **The Snowy Day**, Weston Woods, n.d. (FS61) 28fr color $12; (SF61) with cassette 6min $18. WW (N-P)

Illustrations from the book, accompanied by picture-cued text booklet. Also available in Spanish.

453 **Some Merry Adventures of Robin Hood of Great Renown in Nottinghamshire**, by Howard Pyle. rev. ed. Scribner, 1954. 212p. $4.95 (I-U)

Twelve stories selected and adapted by Pyle from his longer account of Robin Hood's adventures and illustrated with the author's classic pictures.

453R **The Adventures of Robin Hood**, Caedmon, 1972 (TC 1369-72) 4 12in 33rpm $8.98 each; (CDL 51369-72) 4 cassettes $8.98 each. CAE (I-U)

Four volume set: v.1 "How Robin Became an Outlaw" (53:10min); v.2 "The Outlaw Band of Sherwood Forest" (38:25min); v.3 "Robin's Adventures with Little John" (45:13min); and v.4 "Robin and His Merry Men" (42:14min). Read by Anthony Quayle with musical bckground and sound effects.

454 **Something Queer at the Library**, by Elizabeth Levy; illus. by Mordecai Gerstein. Delacorte, 1977. $6.95; pap. $2.75 (I)

Gwen and Jill must discover who mutilated the library books that they borrowed so they won't be blamed. The clues lead them to a local dog show.

454F **Something Queer at the Library**, Jim Dennett, 1978, 16mm color 10min $175. BOS (I)

Live-action film with appealing children and dogs and a mild mystery story. Directed by Nell Cox.

455 **Sounder**, by William H. Armstrong; illus. by James Barkley. Harper, 1969. 116p. lib. ed. $6.95; pap. $1.50 net (I-U)

The story of a black family and their dog in the rural South as they face adversity with quiet stoicism and dignity. Movingly told. Newbery Medal winner, 1970.

455R **Sounder**, Random House/Miller-Brody, 1970 (NAR 3018) 12in 33rpm side 1: 19:43min, side 2: 24:46min $8.97; (NAC 3018) cassette $8.97. RH/M-B (U)

Dramatization by Aurora Jorgensen. Directed by Peter Fernandez. Featured in this recording are Al Fann as narrator, Barbara Fann as Mother, and Edward Luis Espinoza, Jr., as Boy. Negro spirituals provide themes for the background music composed by Herb Davidson. Includes teacher's guide.

456 **A Special Gift**, by Marcia L. Simon. Harcourt, 1978. 132p. $5.95 (U)

In the face of his father's opposition, 14-year-old Peter tries to cope with the difficulties of developing his skills as a ballet dancer while maintaining his identity as a basketball player.

456F **A Special Gift**, Martin Tahse, 1979, 16mm color 47min. $650. TLM (I-U)

Well-acted, thoughtful presentation with good dance sequences by the Los Angeles Ballet Company with John Clifford's choreography.

457 **A Special Trade**, by Sally Christensen Wittman; illus. by Karen Gundersheimer. Harper, 1978. unp. $7.95; lib. ed. $7.89 (N-P)

The special feeling of love and friendship is portrayed in this small volume. When Nelly was very young, old Bartholomew took her for walks, pushing her stroller. Now Nelly pushes her special friend in his wheelchair.

457FS **A Special Trade**, Encyclopaedia Britannica, 1980, 55fr color 6:51min 1 filmstrip 1 cassette $27. EB (N-P)

Simple line drawings and gentle narration underscored by sounds of a harmonica being played portray the feeling of concern as a small girl and an old man trade care and friendship with each other. Based on the book by Sally Christensen Wittman. 1982 Notable Filmstrip.

458 **Springtime for Jeanne-Marie**, by Francoise. Scribner, 1955. unp. lib. ed. $8.95 (N-P)

The little French girl, Jeanne-Marie, searches for her lost duck, Madelon, and makes a new friend. The softly colored pictures have a childlike simplicity and charm.

458FS **Springtime for Jeanne-Marie**, Random House/Miller-Brody, 1974 (SMB 104FR) 47fr color 6:35min with 12in 33rpm $21; (SMB 104FC) with cassette $21. RH/M-B (N-P)

Color has been added to the book illustrations giving them a livelier look. French folk songs played on an accordian provide pleasant background for the narration.

459 **Squawk to the Moon, Little Goose**, by Edna Mitchell Preston; illus. by Barbara Cooney. Viking, 1974. 31p. lib. ed. $6.95; pap. $1.50 (P)

On her way to the pond Little Goose fancies she sees a fox swallow the moon. Her efforts to convince the farmer of this disaster fail, as does a later attempt to convince him that the moon has fallen into the pond. When a real fox seizes the goose, the farmer pays no attention to her squawks and she is forced to use her wits to escape.

459FS **Squawk to the Moon, Little Goose**, Live Oak Media, 1975 (0-670-90532-1) 40fr color 7min cassette $19.95. LOM (N-P)

Using brief musical introduction and ending, the Barbara Cooney illustrations from the book, and a warm-voiced narrator, the filmstrip version is a most acceptable one.

460 **The Star-Spangled Banner**, illus. by Peter Spier. Doubleday, 1969. unp. $7.95 (P-U)

Peter Spier has illustrated the words of the national anthem with glowing color, each double-page drawing a bit of Americana. Music and historical notes are included as well as a reproduction of the original manuscript.

460R **The Star-Spangled Banner**, Weston Woods, 1975 (LTR 166C) 8min cassette only $6. WW (P-U)

A brief narration gives the historical background of our national anthem and the West Point Cadet Glee Club sings it in its entirety.

461 **The Steadfast Tin Soldier**, by Hans C. Andersen; illus. by Paul Galdone. Houghton, 1979. unp. lib.ed. $8.95 (N-P)

Large-page colored pictures of the adventures and sad fate of the little tin soldier and the dancing doll.

461FS **The Steadfast Tin Soldier**, Live Oak Media, 1979, 45fr color 1 filmstrip 1 cassette $19.95. LOM (N-P)

The power and movement of this tale are brought out by the noted Austrian illustrator, Monika Laimgruber, with her beautiful use of color, technical proficiency, and individual style.

461R **Fairy Tale Favorites**, v.2, CMS Records, 1970 (CMS 595) 2s 12in 33rpm $7.98; cassette $7.98. CMS (I)

"The Nightingale," "The Steadfast Tin Soldier," "The Princess on the Pea," and "The Fairies" ("Toads and Diamonds") beautifully told by Mary Strang.

461R **Frances Clarke Sayers, Storyteller**, Weston Woods, 196? (WW 705, 706) 4s 12in 33rpm $14; (WW705C, 706C) 2 cassettes $14. WW (I)

Frances Clarke Sayers tells stories by Carl Sandburg (WW 705) and Hans Christian Andersen.

WW706 contains Andersen stories. Side 1(20:35min): "The Tinder Box." Side 2 (22:50min): "The Swineherd" and "The Staunch Tin Soldier."

462 **Stone Soup**, by Marcia Brown. Scribner, 1947. unp. lib. ed. $7.95; pap. $2.95 (P)

Three French soldiers beguile the villagers into contributing their hidden vegetables to make "stone soup," thereby converting suspicion into friendliness.

462FS **Stone Soup**, Weston Woods, 1955

(SF7C) 42fr color 11min cassette $20. WW (P)

Illustrations from the book, accompanied by picture-cued text booklet.

462R **Stone Soup**, in **Folktales from the Picture Book Parade**, Weston Woods, 1981 (WW717) 12in 33rpm 32min $8. WW (P)

Five stories with music including *Arrow From the Sun* (told by Gerald McDermott), *Stone Soup*, (told by Marcia Brown), *The Great Big Enormous Turnip*, *Suho and the White Horse*, and *A Story-A Story*. Part of a series of collections of stories from Weston Woods' Picture Book Parade: *Christmas Stories from the Picture Book Parade*, *Bedtime Stories from the Picture Book Parade*, and *Musical Stories from the Picture Book Parade* (WW715, WW716, WW714). A 1981 Notable Recording for Children.

462R **Stone Soup**, Weston Woods, n.d. (LTR 007C) cassette only 11min $6. WW (P)

Marcia Brown reads her popular picture book with a musical accompaniment by Arthur Kleiner.

463 **The Stonecutter: A Japanese Folk Tale**, by Gerald McDermott. Viking, 1975. unp. lib. ed. $7.50; pap. $2.50 (P-I)

A poor stonecutter who envies a prince and is made a prince by the spirit of the mountain asks the spirit for more and more. Finally, when he becomes the mountain, he feels his base being quarried by a stonecutter. Illustrated with striking collage images.

463FS **The Stonecutter: A Japanese Folk Tale**, Weston Woods, 1976 (FS 178) 33fr color 7min $12; (SF 178C) with cassette $18. WW (P)

Japanese music accompanying the bright collages of oriental motifs enriches the visual experience of Gerald McDermott's book. McDermott reads his creation.

463R **The Stone Cutter**, Weston Woods, 1975 (LTR 178C) cassette only 6min $6. WW (P-I)

The moving narration by Gerald McDermott and the authentic Japanese music by Reiko Kamata add depth to this story of a stonecutter's ever increasing desire for power.

464 **Storm Boy**, by Colin Thiele; illus. by John Schoenherr. Harper, 1978. lib. ed. $9.89 (I-U)

An Australian boy lives with his widowed father in an isolated area where his friends are an old Aborigine and a pet pelican. When the pelican is killed by hunters, Storm Boy must eventually decide whether to stay in isolation or go to school.

464F **Storm Boy**, Matt Carroll, 1980, 16mm color 30min $450, $40. LCA (I-U)

A feature-length 90-minute version is also available ($1000, $100). Spectacular photography highlights this filmed version of the book. The edited version leaves out much character development, but the longer version is deliberately paced and doesn't seem as action-filled. A 1982 ALA Notable Film for Children.

465 **A Story-A Story**; An African Tale, retold and illus. by Gail E. Haley. Atheneum, 1970. lib. ed. $7.89; pap. $2.95 (P-I)

How stories came to belong to Anansi. Illustrated with striking woodcuts. Caldecott Medal winner, 1971.

465FS **A Story-A Story**, Weston Woods, 1955 (SF 123C) 35fr color 10min cassette $20. WW (P)

Adaptation and pictures by Gail E. Haley from her book, accompanied by picture-cued text booklet.

465R **A Story-A Story**, Weston Woods, n.d. (LTR 123C) cassette only 10min $6. WW (P)

An adaptation of Gail Haley's book.

466 **The Story about Ping**, by Marjorie Flack and Kurt Wiese. Viking, 1933. unp. lib. ed. $5.95; pap. $1.95 (P)

Ping, a little duck who lives on a houseboat on the Yangtze River, always gets a spanking to hurry him aboard. One night he stays ashore and almost comes to grief.

466FS **The Story about Ping**, Weston Woods, n.d.(FS8) 45fr color $14; (SF8C) with cassette 10min $20. WW (P)

Illustrations from the book accompanied by picture-cued text booklet.

466R **The Story about Ping**, Weston Woods, n.d. (LTR8C) cassette only 10min $6. WW (P)

Story narrated by Owen Jordan, with original background music by Arthur Kleiner.

467 **The Story of Ferdinand**, by Munro Leaf; illus. by Robert Lawson. Viking, 1936. unp. lib. ed. $6.95; pap. $1.95 (P)

Ferdinand, thought to be the most ferocious bull in Spain, was really a gentle soul who liked to sit and smell the flowers. His fiasco in the bull ring is told in a hilarious story and delightfully humorous pictures.

467R **The Story of Ferdinand**, Viking, n.d. (0-670-67431-1) cassette $10.95. LOM (P)

Famous story of the bull who would not fight. Price includes paperback edition of the book.

468 **The Story of King Arthur and His Knights**, by Howard Pyle. Scribner, 1903. 312p. lib.ed. $17.50 (I-U)

In story and pictures Pyle conveys the romantic aura of the Arthurian legend.

468R **Tales of King Arthur and His Knights: Excalibur**, Caedmon, 1975 (TC 1462) 12in 33rpm side A: 30:27min, side B: 32:31min $8.98; (CDL 51462) cassette $8.98. CAE (I-U)

This record is a carefully abridged version of part 2, "The Winning of a Sword," from Howard Pyle's book. Read by Ian Richardson.

469 **The Story of the Three Bears**, by Eleanor Mure. Walck, 1967. unp. $5 (P). OP

"The celebrated nursery tale of the Three Bears put into verse and embellished with drawings for a Birthday Present to Horace Broke Sept. 26, 1831." Photographic reproduction of the original manuscript. Endpiece by Judith St. John, Librarian of the Osborne Collection, gives history and background of Miss Mure's version.

469FS **Stories of Childhood**, Clearview, 1977, color 8 filmstrips 8 cassettes 1 guide $120 ($21 each). CL (N-P)

Exciting art, realistic sound effects, and compelling music combine to bring these famous tales to life.

"The Three Little Pigs" (CL 848-1) 50fr 10min

"The Gingerbread Boy" (CL 848-2) 72fr 6min

"The Magic Pot" (CL848-3) 47fr 5:45min

"Little Red Riding Hood" (CL848-4) 54fr 5:05min

"Three Billy Goats Gruff" (CL848-5) 30fr 3:01min

"The Boy Who Cried Wolf" (CL848-6) 30fr 4:58min

"The Princess and the Pea" (CL848-7) 31 fr 2:56min

"The Three Bears" (CL848-8)

469R **Three Little Pigs, and Other Fairy Tales**, Caedmon, 1962 (TC 1129) 2s 12in 33rpm $8.98; (CDL 51129) cassette $8.98. CAE (P)

Read by Boris Karloff. Includes an early version of "The Three Bears," in which the intruder is an old woman rather than a golden-haired little girl.

470 **The Strange but Wonderful Cosmic Awareness of Duffy Moon**, by Jean Robinson. Houghton, 1974. 144p. $6.95; Dell pap. $1.25 (I)

Because of his small size, Duffy Moon becomes a student of cosmic awareness through a mail order course, and develops powers beyond those he expected.

470F **The Amazing Cosmic Awareness of Duffy Moon**, Daniel Wilson, 1976, 16mm color 32min $450, $40. Time-Life (I)

Live-action film starring Lance Kerwin (as Duffy's friend Peter) and Jim Backus (as Dr. Flamel). Notable Film for Children, 1978.

471 **Strawberry Girl**, by Lois Lenski. Lippincott, 1945. 193p. $8.95 (I)

A strong sense of place pervades this story of Birdie Boyer, a little "Cracker" girl who helps her Florida family to raise strawberries and to cope with the shiftless Slaters next door. 1946 Newbery Medal winner.

471R **Strawberry Girl**, Random House/Miller-Brody, 1971 (NAR 3020) 12in 33rpm 40–45min $8.97; (NAC 3020) cassette $8.97. RH/M-B (I)

A recorded dramatization. Narrated by Pierre Cache. Featured in the cast are Amy Schectel as Birdie, Bryce Moss as Shoestring, Bryna Raeburn as Mrs. Boyer, Lawson Zerbe as Mr. Boyer, Jean Richards as Mrs. Slater, and Earl Hammond as Mr. Slater. Includes a teacher's guide.

472 **Strega Nona**, by Tomie de Paola. Prentice-Hall, 1975. unp. $8.95 (P-I)

When the good witch, Strega Nona, leaves him alone with her magic pasta pot, Big Anthony, the disobedient servant, is determined to show the townspeople how it works.

472F **Strega Nona**, Morton Schindel, 1978, 16mm color 9min $150, $10. WW (P)

Animated film by Gene Deitch with background music by Francesco Belfino using jew's harp, accordion, tambourine, and chorus.

472FS **Strega Nona**, Weston Woods, 1978 (FS 198) 55fr color 12min $12; (SF 198C) with cassette $18. WW (P-I)

The filmstrip version borrows the folksy, sometimes mystical, instrumental music and operatic arias from Gene Deitch's film production of the title. The music adds zest to de Paola's colorful illustrations.

Accompanied by picture-cued text booklet.

472R **Strega Nona**, Weston Woods, 1978 (LTR 198C) cassette only 12min $6. WW (P-I)

Peter Hawkins narrates this retelling of the old Italian tale.

473 **Stuart Little**, by E. B. White; pictures by Garth Williams. Harper, 1945. 131p. $6.95; lib. ed. $7.89; pap. $1.95 (I)

Into a normal American family there is born a second son, Stuart, whom everyone notices is not much bigger than a mouse. And since he is indeed a mouse, the story of Stuart Little and his adventures are humorous and unusual.

473FS **Stuart Little**, Bosustow, Barr 1978 (#53599E) 3 sets 12 cassettes 12 filmstrips and guides $199.50. BA (N-P). Set 1 (53300E) av 50fr color av 8min 4 cassettes 4 filmstrips 1 guide $78. Set 2 (53400E) av 75fr color av 10min 4 cassettes 4 filmstrips 1 guide $78. Set 3 (53500E) av 65fr color av 12min color 4 filmstrips 4 cassettes 1 guide $78. BA (I)

Stuart Little, a long-time children's favorite, becomes even more alive and real in this audiovisual format.

473R **Stuart Little**, Pathways of Sound,

n.d. (POS 1036/7) 4s 12in 33rpm $8.98 each. POS (I)

Julie Harris reads E. B. White's classic story.

474 **The Stupids Have a Ball**, by Harry Allard and James Marshall. Houghton, 1978. 30p. illus. lib.ed. $5.95 (P)

Buster and Petunia bring their report cards home showing they have flunked everything, even recess. Voila! A cause for a party the like of which has never been seen before. This book must be seen. It's really fun.

474FS **The Stupids Have a Ball**, Westport Communications, 1981, 33fr with cassette 5:20min $22. EEM (P)

Finding cause for celebration in their children's failure of every school subject, the Stupids throw a costume ball for the entire clan. Audio effects add delightful zest to the zany affair.

475 **Suho and the White Horse**, by Yuzo Otsuka; illus. by Suekichi Akaba. Viking, 1981. unp. $10.95 (I)

A beautiful retelling of a Mongolian legend of a boy, Suho, and his wonderful white horse and their tragic parting. Explains the origin of the horse-head fiddle of the Mongolian shepherds.

475F **Suho and the White Horse**, John Schindel, 1980, 16mm color 10min $140, $20. WW (P)

Iconographic treatment of this legend of Mongolia. Uses a male narrator and gentle music which is original horse-head fiddle music by Dr. Vaclav Kubica.

475R **Suho and the White Horse**, Weston Woods, 1978 (LTR 188C) cassette only 10min $6. WW (I)

Charles Cioffi narrates this poignant story. Mongolian music accompanies the telling.

476 **The Summer of the Swans**, by Betsy Byars; illus. by Ted CoConis. Viking, 1970. 142p. $7.95; pap. $1.75 (I-U)

Thirteen-year-old Sara gains insight into herself and others as she searches for her missing mentally retarded brother. 1971 Newbery Medal winner.

476F **Sara's Summer of the Swan**, Martin Tahse, 1974, 16mm color 33min $450, $40. TLM (U)

The plot is simplified to positive thinking and turned into a tender adolescent identity story with a touch of romance. Will appeal most to older girls.

476R **The Summer of the Swans**, Viking, 1972, 2s 12in 33rpm 51:04min $8.95; cassette $8.95. LOM (I-U)

Dramatized version of the book, performed by the High Tor Repertory Players.

477 **The Surprise Party**, by Pat Hutchins. Macmillan, 1969. unp. $6.95; pap. $.95 (P)

Rabbit's surprise party plans go awry when the animals misunderstand his whispered invitation.

477FS **Surprise Party**, Weston Woods, 1973 (FS139) 28fr color 5:33min $14; (SF193C) with cassette $20. WW (N-P)

Illustrations from the book, accompanied by picture-cued text booklet.

477R **Surprise Party**, Weston Woods, 1973 (LTR139C) cassette only 5:33min $6. WW (N-I)

Buffy Allen's narration conveys the humor of this story.

478 **Swan Lake**, adapted and illustrated by Donna Diamond, based on the Marius Petipa-Lev Ivanov version (1895). Holiday, 1980. $8.95 (I)

The graceful Swan Queen Odette must live her days as a bird, but at night the evil sorcerer allows her to become a beautiful and mysterious woman. The spell can only be broken if a man promises to love her, marry her, and never love another. A handsome prince accidentally meets her by a moonlit lake, and falls hopelessly in love with her. He begs her to attend the palace ball where he must choose his bride, but their love is doomed from the beginning.

478R **Swan Lake**, based on Petipa version; music by Tchaikovsky. Caedmon 61min (TC 1673) 1 12in LP $8.98; (CP or CDL 1673) cassette $8.98. CAE (I)

Adapted by Ward Botsford. Performed by Claire Bloom. Claire Bloom tells the romantic tale to Tchaikovsky's score. The enchantment of the balletic plot is captured in words and music.

479 **The Swineherd**, by Hans Christian Andersen; tr. and illus. by Erik Blegvad. Harcourt, 1958. 32p. $3.25 (P-I). OP

The humorous tale of the foolish princess who valued material things more than nature's gifts.

479R **The Swineherd**, Weston Woods, 1977 (LTR 186C) cassette only 12min $6. WW (P-I)

Pauline Brailsford narrates Gene Deitch's adaptation of this Andersen tale. The narration and sound effects add to the humor of the story.

479R **The Little Match Girl, and Other Tales**, Caedmon, 1960 (TC 1117) 2s 12in 33rpm $8.98; (CDL 51117) cassette $8.98. CAE (I)

Boris Karloff reads five Andersen tales as translated by Reginald Spink (Dutton, OP). Includes: "The Swineherd," "The Top and the Ball," "The Red Shoes," "Thumbelina," and "The Little Match Girl."

480 **The Tailor of Gloucester**, by Beatrix Potter. new ed. Warne, 1968. 59p. $6.95 (P-I)

When a poor tailor falls ill just at Christmas, little mice finish a beautiful embroidered coat for his richest customer the Mayor of Gloucester.

480FS **The Tailor of Gloucester**, Spoken Arts, 1976 (SA 2034-3 and SA 2034-4) Part 1: 31fr 11:55min, Part 2: 27fr 11:05min 12in 33rpm $28.95; (SAC 2034-3 and SAC 2034-4) cassette $28.95. SA (N-P)

Read by actress Frances Sternhagen. Artwork from the original book. Music by Florence and Rosine Klein. Includes teacher's guide and reader's script.

480R **Favorite Christmas Stories**, CMS Records, 1971 (CMS 629) LP $8.98; (CMS-x4629) cassette $8.98. CMS (P-I)

Mary Strang tells five favorite Christmas stories: "The Tailor of Gloucester," "The Poor Count's Christmas," "The Cat on the Dovrefell," "The Jar of Rosemary," and "Wee Robing's Yule Song."

481 **The Tale of Benjamin Bunny**, by Beatrix Potter. Warne, 1904. 58p. $3.50 net (N-P)

Benjamin and his cousin, Peter Rabbit, return to Mr. McGregor's garden to recover Peter's clothes.

481FS **The Tale of Benjamin Bunny**, Spoken Arts, 1974 (SA 2025-2) 35fr color 10:01min 12in 33rpm $28.95; record/cassette $28.95. SA (N-P)

Beautifully read by actress Frances Sternhagen. Artwork from the original book. Musical background by Jim Gold. Includes teacher's guide and reader's script.

481FS **The Tale of Benjamin Bunny**, Weston Woods, n.d.(FS 69) 31fr color $12; (SF 69) with 7in 33rpm 7:50min $18; with cassette $18. WW (N-P)

Illustrations from the book, accompanied by picture-cued text booklet.

481R **The Tale of Peter Rabbit**, Caedmon, 1970 (TC 1314)

record/cassette $8.98; (CDL 51314) cassette $8.98. CAE (N-P)

Claire Bloom reads Beatrix Potter's *Tales of Peter Rabbit*, *Benjamin Bunny*, *Mr. Jeremy Fisher*, *Mrs. Tiggy-Winkle*, and *Two Bad Mice*.

482 **The Tale of Little Pig Robinson**, by Beatrix Potter. Warne, 1930. 192p. $3.50 (P)

Little Pig Robinson leaves Piggery Porcombe to shop in a Devonshire town, is kidnapped and put out to sea. On board he discovers he is being fattened for the captain's birthday dinner. This is the tale of his capture and escape.

482R **The Tale of Little Pig Robinson**, Caedmon, 1975 (TC 1453) $8.98; (CDL 51453) cassette $8.98. CAE (N-P)

Delightfully read by Claire Bloom.

483 **The Tale of Mr. Jeremy Fisher**, by Beatrix Potter. Warne, 1906. 58p. $3.50 net (N-P)

The story of Mr. Fisher, the frog, who goes fishing—but almost gets caught himself!

483FS **The Tale of Mr. Jeremy Fisher**, Spoken Arts, 1974 (SA 2025-4) 26fr color 7:28min 12in 33rpm $28.95; with cassette $28.95. SA (N-P)

Beautifully read by Frances Sternhagen. Artwork from the original book. Musical background by Jim Gold. Includes teacher's guide and reader's script.

483FS **The Tale of Mr. Jeremy Fisher**, Weston Woods, n.d. (FS 70) 31fr color $12; (SF 70) with 7in 33rpm 5:40min $18; with cassette $18. WW (N-P)

Illustrations from the book, accompanied by picture-cued text booklet.

484 **The Tale of Mrs. Tiggy-Winkle**, by Beatrix Potter. Warne, 1905. 58p. $3.50 (N-P)

When Lucie loses her handkerchiefs she finds them at the home of a little hedgehog who is busy ironing the animals' clothes.

484FS **The Tale of Mrs. Tiggy-Winkle**, Spoken Arts, 1976 (SA 2034-2) 30fr color 11:35min 12in 33rpm $28.95; with cassette $28.95. SA (N-P)

Beautifully read by actress Frances Sternhagen. Artwork from the original book. Music by Florence and Rosine Klein. Includes teacher's guide and reader's script.

485 **The Tale of Peter Rabbit**, by Beatrix Potter. Warne, 1904. 58p. $2.50; lib. ed. $3 net (N-P)

Disobedient Peter learns why his mother told him not to go into Mr. McGregor's garden.

485FS **The Tale of Peter Rabbit**, Spoken Arts, 1974 (SA 2025-1) 31fr color 8:03min 12in 33rpm $28.95; with cassette $28.95. SA (N-P)

Beautifully read by actress Frances Sternhagen. Artwork from the original book. Musical background by Jim Gold. Includes teacher's guide and reader's script.

485FS **The Tale of Peter Rabbit**, Weston Woods, n.d. (FS 33) 34fr color $12; (SF 33) with 7in 33rpm 7min $18; with cassette $18. WW (N-P)

Illustrations from the book, accompanied by picture-cued text booklet. Also available in Spanish.

485FS **The Tale of Peter Rabbit**, Listening Library, 1976 (Look, Listen, & Read JFS 158) 41fr color 1 filmstrip 1 cassette $21. LL (N-P)

This all-time favorite becomes even more fascinating as we watch Peter's adventures in Mr. McGregor's garden through the original Potter illustrations.

486 **The Tale of Squirrel Nutkin**, by Beatrix Potter. Warne, 1903. unp. $3.50 (N-P)

In which Nutkin asks Old Mr. Brown, the owl, a series of riddles.

486FS The Tale of Squirrel Nutkin, Spoken Arts, 1974 (SA 2025-3) 40fr color 11:24min 12in 33rpm $28.95; with cassette $28.95. SA (N-P)

A spirited reading by actress Frances Sternhagen. Artwork from the original book. Musical background by Jim Gold. Includes teacher's guide and reader's script.

487 The Tale of the Shining Princess, adapted by Sally Fisher from a translation by Donald Keene. Metropolitan Museum of Art and Viking, 1980 (I)

A revival of the eighteenth-century edition of Taketori, the bamboo cutter.

487R The Tale of the Shining Princess, Caedmon (CDL or CP 1707) cassette $8.98; (TC 1707) 1 12in LP $8.98. CAE (I)

Using the Sally Fisher adaptation of the Donald Keene translation, Lillian Gish evokes the charm of the beautiful princess and the daring suitors with remarkable grace. Original music by Michael Karp based on traditional Japanese music. In Japan, the tale is known as "The Tale of the Bamboo Cutter" and is as familiar as *Cinderella* is to us.

488 The Tale of the Tales: The Beatrix Potter Ballet, by Rumer Godden. Warne, 1977. 208p. $21.95 (U)

The behind-scenes story of the ballet-film, *Tales of Beatrix Potter*. Includes stills taken from the film and some of Miss Potter's illustrations and letters.

488F Peter Rabbit and the Tales of Beatrix Potter, MGM, 1971, 16mm color 98min $75 (rental only). FI (P-U)

Scenes from the childhood of Beatrix Potter introduce this combination of several of Miss Potter's stories. Members of Britain's Royal Ballet, in animal costume, perform in this imaginative scenario. Musical background by the Covent Garden Opera House Orchestra.

488R Peter Rabbit and the Tales of Beatrix Potter, Angel, 1971 (S-36789) 2s 12in 33rpm $9.98. Cassette also available. ANG (P-I)

John Lanchbery's original score for the Royal Ballet film, *Tales of Beatrix Potter*. Performed by the Orchestra of the Royal Opera House.

489 The Tale of Tom Kitten, by Beatrix Potter. Warne, 1907. 59p. $2.50; lib. ed. $3.50 (N-P)

Mrs. Tabitha Twitchitt dresses up her three kittens for tea—but what a fright they become before tea is ever served.

489FS The Tale of Tom Kitten, Weston Woods, n.d. (FS 71) 31fr color $12; (SF 71) with 7in 33rpm 5:15min $18; with cassette $18. WW (N-P)

Illustrations from the book, accompanied by picture-cued text booklet.

490 The Tale of Two Bad Mice, by Beatrix Potter. Warne, 1904. 48p. $3.50; lib ed. $3 net (N-P)

Tom Thumb and his wife, Hunca Munca, create great havoc in the nursery.

490FS The Tale of Two Bad Mice, Spoken Arts, 1976 (SA 2034-1) 27fr color 7:03min 12in 33rpm $28.95; with cassette $28.95. SA (N-P)

Beautifully read by actress Frances Sternhagen. Artwork from the original book. Music by Florence and Rosine Klein. Includes teacher's guide and reader's script.

490FS The Tale of Two Bad Mice, Weston Woods, n.d. (FS 72) 31fr color $12; (SF 72) with 7in 33rpm 6:16min $18; with cassette $18. WW (N-P)

Illustrations from the book, accompanied by picture-cued text booklet.

491 Tales and Poems of Edgar Allan Poe, illus. by Russell Hoban; afterword by Clifton Fadiman.

Macmillan, 1967. 338p. $4.95 (I-U)

Seventeen stories and several of Poe's best-known poems in an attractive edition.

491R Poe, Edgar Allen – The Fall of the House of Usher and Other Works, Caedmon, 19?? (TC 1195) LP $8.98; (CDL5 1195) cassette $8.98. CAE (U)

Basil Rathbone reads "The Telltale Heart," "The Haunted Palace," "The Bells," and "The Fall of the House of Usher."

491R Poe, Edgar Allen–The Pit and the Pendulum and Other Works, Caedmon, 197? (TC 1115) record/cassette $8.98; (CLD 51115) cassette $8.98. CAE (U)

A fine reading by Basil Rathbone of "The Cask of Amontillado," "The Facts in the Case of M. Valdemar," and "The Pit and the Pendulum."

491R Poe, Edgar Allen–The Raven and Other Works, Caedmon, 197? (TC 1028) record/cassette $8.98; (CDL 51028) cassette $8.98. CAE (U)

Basil Rathbone reads two short stories, "The Masque of the Red Death" and "The Black Cat," and several poems including "The Raven."

492 Tales of a Fourth Grade Nothing, by Judy Blume; illus. by Roy Doty. Dutton, 1972. 128p. $8.95 (I)

The story describes the trials and tribulations of 9-year-old Peter Hatcher who is saddled with a pesky 2-year-old brother named Fudge who is constantly creating trouble, messing things up, and monopolizing their parents' attention.

492FS Tales of a Fourth Grade Nothing, Pied Piper (First Choice: Authors and Books), 1980 1 filmstrip 86fr with 2 cassettes (interview cassette 11min; filmstrip cassette 13min) $32. PP (I)

Retains the flavor and spirit of the original. Electronic music enhances the filmstrip presentation.

493 Tales Told Again, by Walter de la Mare; illus. by Alan Howard. Knopf, 1959. 208p. $3; 1980 Faber pap. $3.25 (I)

An imaginative retelling of nineteen favorite fairy tales.

493R Cinderella, and Other Fairy Tales, Caedmon, 1979 (TC 1330) record/cassette $8.98; (CDL 1330) cassette $8.98. CAE (I)

Claire Bloom reads "Cinderella and the Glass Slipper," "The Musicians of Bremen," and "Bluebeard" as retold by Walter de la Mare.

493R Little Red Riding Hood and The Dancing Princesses, Caedmon, 1970 (TC 1331) record/cassette $8.98; (CDL 1331) cassette $8.98. CAE (I)

Claire Bloom reads Walter de la Mare's versions of these two fairy tales.

494 Tall Tale America; A Legendary History of Our Humorous Heroes, by Walter Blair; illus. by Glen Rounds. Coward, 1944. 262p. lib. ed. $6.59 net (I-U)

American history as it was made by the heroes of the tall tales with which yarn-spinners have been delighting the world for years.

494F American Tall Tale Heroes, Coronet Instructional Media, 1974 (3671) 16mm color 15min $300. COR (P-I)

Animated adventures of four fictional heroes introduced by live actor as Old Timer: the sailor, Stormalong; the lumberjack, Paul Bunyan; the steel driver, John Henry; and the cowboy, Pecos Bill. Pleasant voice with folk song backgrounds.

495 Teach Us, Amelia Bedelia, by Peggy Parish; illus. by Lynn Sweat. Greenwillow, 1977. $5.95 (P-I)

School is terrific fun when Amelia Bedelia is substitute teacher for a day.

495FS Teach Us, Amelia Bedelia, Westport Communications Group, dist. by Educational Enrichment Materials, 1982 (#52590) 81fr color 13:10min with cassette $22. EEM (P-I)

Verbatim adaptation of Peggy Parish's book. Sweat's book illustrations are also used in the filmstrip adaptation.

496 Teeny-Tiny and the Witch Woman, by Barbara Walker; illus. by Michael Foreman. Pantheon, 1975. unp. $5.99 (P-I)

Despite their mother's warnings, three young brothers go into the forest to play, and while there encounter the witch-woman who eats little children.

496F Teeny-Tiny and the Witch Woman, Morton Schindel, 1980, 16mm color 14min $225, $25. WW P-I)

Animated film in which music and narration blend to create excitement and suspense. Sound effects such as bat wings, breathing and echoing voices are used to enhance the spookiness. 1982 ALA Notable Film for Children.

496FS Teeny-Tiny and the Witch Woman, Westport Communciations Group, released by Random House, 1978 (394-02984-4) 51fr color 14min with cassette $21. RH/M-B (P-I)

Filmstrip version utilizes Foreman's humorous-scary blend of illustrations and music to build suspense in this Turkish "Hansel and Gretel." Guide.

497 Thank You, Amelia Bedelia, by Peggy Parish; illus. by Fritz Siebel. Harper, 1964. 32p. lib. ed. $6.89 net (P)

Amelia Bedelia gets ready for great-aunt Myra's visit. She uses scissors to remove the spots from Mrs. Roger's dress, separates the eggs—"one is behind the clock, the other is over there"—but saves the day with her hot apple pie.

497FS Thank You, Amelia Bedelia, Teaching Resources Films, 1971 (72151) 54fr color 10min with 12in 33rpm $22; with cassette $22. TRF (P)

Original illustrations accompanied by word-for-word reading of the text.

498 Thank You, Jackie Robinson, by Barbara Cohen; illus. by Richard Cuffari. Lothrop, 1974. 128p. lib. ed. $8.59 (I-U)

In the 1940s, a fatherless white boy, Sammy, shares his love of the Brooklyn Dodgers with an elderly black chef, Davy. When Davy suffers a heart attack, Sammy travels alone to Ebbets Field to obtain an autographed baseball from Jackie Robinson as a gift for his ailing friend.

498F A Home Run for Love, Martin Tahse, 1979, 16mm color or b/w 47min $650, $60. TLM (I-U)

This 1981 ALA Notable Film was originally aired on television in black and white with vintage footage of the Dodgers. A powerful film dealing with loneliness and friendship and the pain of loss.

499 They Were Strong and Good, by Robert Lawson. Viking, 1940. lib. ed. $8.95 net (I)

The author relates the stories of his parents and his four grandparents with pride, not because they were great and famous, but because they were strong and good. Caldecott Medal winner, 1941.

499FS They Were Strong and Good, Weston Woods, n.d.(FS 81) 39fr color $12; (SF 81) with 7in 33rpm 12:30min $18; with cassette $18. WW (P-I)

Illustrations from the book, accompanied by picture-cued text booklet.

500 Thimble Summer, by Elizabeth Enright. Holt, 1938. 124p. $5.95; lib. ed. $5.95 net (I)

Garnet Linden thinks that her summer of fun and adventure on a Wisconsin farm all came because she had found a magic thimble. 1939 Newbery Medal winner.

500FS **Thimble Summer**, Random House/Miller-Brody, 1978 (394-77125-7) 2 filmstrips 131, 125fr color 18, 15min with 12in 33-1/3rpm disc $45; (394-77126-5) with two cassettes $45. RH/M-B (I)

Filmstrip based on book. Realistic illustrations are accentuated by an instrumental background (harmonica) which conveys the rural atmosphere of the setting of the story.

500R **Thimble Summer**, Random House/Miller-Brody, 1969 (394-77123-0) record $8.97; (394-77124-9) cassette $8.97. RH/M-B (I)

A recorded dramatization narrated by Lloyd Moss. Cast: Corinne Orr as Garnet, Eddie Gaynes as Jay. Original background harmonica music by Herb Davidson. Includes teacher's guide.

501 **The Three Bears and Fifteen Other Stories**, by Anne Rockwell. Crowell, 1975. 117p. $9.95 (N)

Treasury of stories from traditional sources that are an important part of every child's heritage, exquisitely illustrated with clear, bright, watercolor paintings on each page. Only changes in wording necessary for clear comprehension by modern children have been made.

501F **Goldilocks and the Three Bears**, Coronet Instructional Media, 1953 (816) 16mm color 10min $215. COR (N)

Three real bears in the retelling of this story.

501R **Goldilocks and the Three Bears and Other Stories**, Caedmon, 1972 (TC 1392) 1 12in record $8.98; (CDL 51392) cassette $8.98. CAE (P-I)

Claire Bloom reads "Goldilocks and the Three Bears," "Little One Eye, Little Two Eyes and Little Three Eyes," "The Brave Little Tailor," and "The Babes in the Wood."

502 **The Three Billy Goats Gruff**, by Peter Christen Asbjornsen and Jorgen E. Moe; pictures by Marcia Brown. Harcourt, 1957. unp. $6.50; pap. $2.25 (N-P)

Three brave billy goats outwit a wicked troll.

502FS **The Three Billy Goats Gruff**, Weston Woods, n.d. (FS 48) 29fr color $12; (SF 48) with 7in 33rpm $18; with cassette $18. WW (P)

Illustrations from the book, accompanied by picture-cued text booklet.

503 **The Three Little Pigs**, illus. by Erik Blegvad. Atheneum, 1980. 32p. $8.95 (P)

A retelling of the classic folktale about two lazy little pigs whose poorly built houses fail to protect them from the hungry wolf and their hard-working brother whose sturdily built brick house enables him to survive and eventually triumph over the wolf.

503FS **The Three Little Pigs**, Weston Woods, 1981 (FS 267) 41fr color 8:35min $12; (SF 267C) with cassette $18. WW (P)

Filmstrip version uses Blegvad's delightful illustrations. Accompanied by picture-cued text booklet.

504 **The Three Robbers**, by Tomi Ungerer. Atheneum, 1962. unp. lib. ed. $6.93 net (P)

Three fierce robbers terrify the countryside until they meet a little girl named Tiffany. Under Tiffany's golden charm the robbers turn their gold to good use, and all ends happily in this droll tale heightened by bold, colorful illustrations.

504F **The Three Robbers**, Kratky Films, Prague, 1972, 16mm color 5min

$175, $20. Also available in videocassette. WW (P)
Animated by Tomi Ungerer, faithfully following the story.

504FS **The Three Robbers**, Weston Woods, n.d. (FS 63) 25, 22fr color $12; (SF 63) 3:42, 4:05min with 7in 33rpm $18; with cassette $18. WW (P)
Illustrations from the original book, accompanied by picture-cued text booklet.

505 **Through the Looking Glass and What Alice Found There**, by Lewis Carroll; illus. by John Tenniel. St. Martins, 1977. $7.95; pap. $4.95 (P-I)
Contains "The Walrus and the Carpenter" and Jabberwocky poems.

505FS **The Walrus and the Carpenter and Jabberwocky**, Listening Library, n.d. color 1 filmstrip 1 cassette $18. LL (N-P)
Colorful, new illustrations and sprightly music and narration make for great fun.

506 **Thumbelina**, by Hans Christian Andersen; tr. by R. P. Keigwin; illus. by Adrienne Adams. Scribner, 1961. unp. lib. ed. $5.95 net (P)
The miniature world of Thumbelina and her friends is portrayed in delicate watercolors rich in detail.

506R **Thumbelina**, Random House/Miller-Brody (394-07807-1) cassette and paperback $10.98; (394-07905-1N) filmstrip cassette $22.95. RH/M-B (P-I)
Based on the version illustrated by Kaj Beckman. A word-for-word reading of Hans Christian Andersen's lovely story.

507 **Thy Friend, Obadiah**, by Brinton Turkle. Viking, 1969. unp. $6.95; lib. ed. $6.95 net; pap. $.95 (P)
Obadiah Starbuck, a young Quaker boy in nineteenth-century Nantucket, is faced with the problem of being constantly followed by a sea gull. A Caldecott Honor Book.

507FS **Thy Friend, Obadiah**, Viking, 1971 (670-90520-8) 28fr color 6:11min with cassette $19.95. LOM (P)
Narrated by the author. Illustrations from the book, accompanied by picture-cued text booklet.

508 **The Tiger Skin Rug**, by Gerald Rose. Prentice-Hall, 1979. unp. lib. ed. $6.95 (N-P)
The story of a tiger who pretends to be a rug in the Rajah's palace. Colorful illustrations and humorous incidents make this a favorite.

508FS **The Tiger Skin Rug**, Encyclopaedia Britannica, 1980, 41fr color 6:25min 1 filmstrip 1 cassette $27. EB (N-P)
Authentic East Indian music and effective narration enhance the illustrations from Gerald Rose's humorous and fast-paced story of a tiger who lives temporarily undetected as a rug in the rajah's palace.
1982 Notable Filmstrip.

509 **Tikki Tikki Tembo**, retold by Arlene Mosel; illus. by Blair Lent. Holt, 1968. unp. $7.95; Scholastic pap. $1.95 (P)
When Tikki Tikki Tembo-No Sa Rembo-Chari Bari Ruchi-Pip Peri Pembo fell into the well, it took his little brother so long to say his name and get help that Tikki almost drowned. An amusingly retold Chinese folktale handsomely illustrated in gay, rich colors.

509F **Tikki Tikki Tembo**, Morton Schindel, 1974, 16mm color 9min $140, $20. Also available in videocassette, $140. WW (P)
Iconographic technique using illustrations from the book.

509FS **Tikki Tikki Tembo**, Weston Woods, 1970 (FS 115) 33fr color $14; (SF

115) 8:12min with 7in 33rpm $20; with cassette $20. WW (P)

Illustrations from the book, accompanied by picture-cued text booklet.

510 **Tilly's House**, by Faith Jaques. Atheneum, 1979. unp. $9.95 (P)

Tilly, the dollhouse's kitchen maid, endures endless drudgery and constant nagging from Cook. Fed up, she walks out, determined to find a place of her own. When she reaches the lower floor, she meets Edward, the teddy bear, who locates the perfect place for Tilly to set up housekeeping.

510FS **Tilly's House**, Weston Woods, 1981 (FS 265) 55fr color 16:30min $12; (SF 265C) with cassette $18. WW (P)

Faith Jaques' illustrations, which carefully capture the details of the miniature dollhouse and those of the bigger world into which Tilly journeys, are effectively maximized through related close-ups taken from larger scenes. A delicate piano melody quietly underlines the narrator's words. Picture-cued text included.

510R **Tilly's House**, Weston Woods, 1981 (LTR 265C) cassette only 17min $6. WW (N-P)

Buffy Allen's narration gives a nice British touch to this charming story. Original background music by H. D. Buch.

511 **Tim All Alone**, by Edward Ardizzone. Walck, 1956 (P). OP

Tim comes home to find a sign on the door: "Gone Away." And we follow him through a series of adventures to find his parents.

511FS **Tim All Alone**, Weston Woods, (#SF252C) 65fr 15min with cassette reading script $8; (#FS252) silent $12 (P)

A faithful adaptation of the original book.

512 **Time of Wonder**, by Robert McCloskey. Viking, 1957. 63p. $8.95; lib. ed. $8.95 net (P-I)

Summer on a Maine island is sensitively evoked in poetic text and the author's beautiful pictures portraying the beauty of sea and shore, the moods of the weather, and the fury of a hurricane. Caldecott Medal winner, 1958.

512F **Time of Wonder**, Morton Schindel, 1951 (10917) 16mm color 12:45min $175, $25; videocassette $175. WW (P-I)

Iconographic technique using illustrations from the book. Narrated by Ted Hoskins. Music by Arthur Kleiner.

512FS **Time of Wonder**, Weston Woods, n.d. (FS 31) 59fr color $14; (SF 31) 13min with 7in 33rpm $20; with cassette $20. WW (P-I)

Illustrations from the book, accompanied by picture-cued text booklet.

513 **Timothy Goes to School**, by Rosemary Wells. Dial, 1981. $7.50; lib. ed. $7.28 (N-P)

Timothy is happy and proud as he starts school—until he meets Claude who tells him he doesn't wear the "right" clothes and who does everything better than he does. Timothy finally finds a friend more to his liking.

513R **Timothy Goes to School**, Weston Woods, 1982 (LTR 271C) cassette only 6min $6. WW (N-P)

Dan Diggles gives a nicely done, straight narration of this amusing little story. The orchestral music accompanies the moods of Timothy's trials at school.

514 **A Toad for Tuesday**, by Russell Erickson. Lothrop, 1974. 64p. $8.16 (P-I)

Warton and Morton, two toad brothers, enjoy some delicious soup. Warton decides to take some to an elderly aunt but he is captured by a dangerous owl who says he will save the delicious morsel toad until Tuesday, his birthday. By that time,

Warton has so endeared himself to the owl that the plans change—but Warton doesn't know it. He escapes but returns to rescue the owl from a fox. Good fun.

514R **A Toad for Tuesday**, Listening Library, 1980, 1981 (FTR 55) 1 cassette 61min with 4 paperback books teacher's guide $15. (P-I)

A melodious pleasant female voice narrates the exact text of the book.

515 **The Tomten**, by Astrid Lindgren; adapted from a poem by Viktor Rydberg; illus. by Harald Wiberg. Coward, 1961. unp. $6.50; lib. ed. $5.99 net; pap. $2.50 (P)

The author and the artist have captured a silent, snow-covered night on a Swedish farm as they tell the story of the tomten, a little troll who talks to all the animals.

515F **The Tomten**, Morton Schindel, 1982, 16mm color 8min $140, $20. WW (P)

Iconographic treatment using the lovely Harald Wiberg illustrations. Quiet and serene film useful for winter programs.

515FS **The Tomten** and **Christmas in the Stable**, Weston Woods, n.d. (FS 66) 19, 21fr color $12; (SF 66) 6:42, 5:45min with 7in 33rpm $18; with cassette $18. WW (P)

Illustrations from the book, accompanied by picture-cued text booklet.

516 **The Tomten and the Fox**, adapted by Astrid Lindgren from a poem by Karl-Erik Forsslund; illus. by Harald Wiberg. Coward, 1965. unp. lib. ed. $5.89; pap. $2.50 net (P)

When the sly fox comes on Christmas Eve to raid the hen house, the tomten shares food left for him by the children and sends the fox away content to spare the hens.

516FS **The Tomten and the Fox**, Weston Woods, 1973 (FS 131) 18fr color 4:30min $12; (SF 131) with 7in 33rpm $18; (SF 131C) with cassette $18. WW (P)

Illustrations from the book, accompanied by picture-cued text booklet.

517 **The Treasure**, by Uri Shulevitz. Farrar, 1978. unp. $8.95 (P)

Tale of an old man who dreams three times that a treasure is buried under a bridge in a far-off city. He makes the long journey, but is directed back to the treasure in his own home.

517FS **The Treasure**, Weston Woods, 1980 (FS 250) 26fr color 6min $12; (SF 250 C) with cassette $18. WW (P)

Visuals taken from Shulevitz's picture book are accompanied by doleful violin strains which intensify the description of Isaac's life burden of poverty.

ALA Notable Filmstrip.

517R **The Treasure**, Weston Woods, 1981 (LTR 250C) cassette only 6min $6. WW (P-I)

The quiet narration and full orchestral accompaniment are especially appropriate for this thoughtful tale.

518 **A Tree Is Nice**, by Janice May Udry; pictures by Marc Simont. Harper, 1956. unp. $6.95; lib. ed. $7.89 net (N-P)

The delights to be found under, near, or because of trees. Caldecott Medal winner, 1957.

518FS **A Tree Is Nice**, Weston Woods, n.d. (FS 32) 31fr color $12; (SF 32) with 7in 33rpm 4min $18; with cassette $18. WW (N-P)

Illustrations from the book, accompanied by picture-cued text booklet.

519 **A Treeful of Pigs**, by Arnold Lobel. Greenwillow, 1979. $7.95 (P)

Promising to help his wife when pigs grow from the trees like apples, the lazy husband finally jumps into action when his precious fat pigs simply disappear.

519FS **A Treeful of Pigs**, Westport Communications Group, dist. by Educational Enrichment Materials, 1980 (#52376) 45fr color 5:55min with cassette $22. EEM (P)

The luminous illustrations from Lobel's book positively shine in the filmstrip adaptation of this delightful story. Roly-poly pink pigs cavort across the screen.

520 **The Trip**, by Ezra Jack Keats; illus. by the author. Greenwillow, 1978. $8.95; lib. ed. $8.59; Scholastic pap. $1.95 (P)

Lonely in a new neighborhood, Louie converts a shoebox into a diorama of the city and finds himself flying in an airplane high above it.

520F **The Trip**, Morton Schindel, 1980, 16mm color 5min $115, $15. WW (P)

Iconographic style with animated airplane sequences. Electric piano provides the background music. Narrator: Charles Turner.

521 **Truck**, by Donald Crews. Greenwillow, 1980. unp. $9.83 (P)

Without the use of a single word, the cross-country travels of a bright red tractor-trailer truck are brought to life as it winds its way through city streets, tunnels, freeways, coffee shops and bridges to deliver a load of tricycles.

521FS **Truck**, Live Oak Media, 1981 (0-941078-00-0) 32fr color 6:30min with cassette $21.95. LOM (P)

The colorful and graphic illustrations of the book are augmented in the filmstrip by the actual sounds of diesel engines, highway traffic, gas pumps, windshield wipers and other sounds of the road and make the viewer a passenger as the truck rolls from east coast to west.

Guide available.

522 **The Trumpeter of Krakow,** by Eric P. Kelley; decorations by Janina Domanska. Macmillan, 1966. 208p. $7.95; pap. $1.95 (U)

A new and beautifully illustrated edition of a tale of adventure and heroism in medieval Poland. 1929 Newbery Medal winner.

522R **Folk Tales and Legends of Eastern Europe**, CMS Records, 1968 (CMS 519) 1 12in record $8.98; (CMS-X4519) cassette $8.98. CMS (I)

Five traditional tales and legends, including "The Sword of Yanosik" (Polish), "Little Carved One" (Czech), "Nine Crying Dolls" (various countries), "Grandfather Matthew" (Czech) and "The Trumpeter of Krakow" (Poland). Told by Anne Pellowski.

522R **The Trumpeter of Krakow**, Random House/Miller-Brody, 1969 (394-77133-8) record $8.97; (394-77134-6) cassette $8.97. RH/M-B (I-U)

A recorded dramatization narrated by Bob Lloyd. Original background music by Herb Davidson is based on the earliest known Polish religious song, "Bogurodzica." Includes teacher's guide.

523 **The Twelve Days of Christmas**, in pictures by Ilonka Karasz. Harper, 1949. unp. $7.95; lib. ed. $8.79 net (P-I)

The exuberance of the old folk song is caught in lovely illustrations with a medieval setting. The melody is given at the end.

523FS **The Twelve Days of Christmas**, Weston Woods, 1971 (FS 121) 16fr color $14; (SF 121) with 7in 33rpm 5:30min $20; with cassette $20. WW (P-I)

Illustrations from the book, accompanied by picture-cued text booklet.

524 **The Twenty-One Balloons**, by

William Pene du Bois. Viking, 1947. 179p. $8.95; pap. $1.25 (I-U)

Dr. William Waterman Sherman decides to take a balloon trip to get a rest from teaching arithmetic. After three weeks of adventure he is picked up in the Atlantic amid the wreckage of twenty balloons. A fabulous tale with a background of scientific facts. 1948 Newbery Medal winner.

524R **The Twenty-One Balloons**, Live Oak Media, 1972, 12in record $8.98; tape cassette $8.95; hardcover book $8.95; pap. $1.25. LOM (I-U)

Excellent characterizations of Professor William Waterman Sherman and Mr. F. plus lively narration carry the story along.

525 **A Twister of Twists, a Tangler of Tongues**, by Alvin Schwartz; illus. by Glen Rounds. Lippincott, 1972. 127p. $6.95; pap. $1.95 (I-U)

Tongue twisters and tongue-twisting tales arranged by topics: "Love and Marriage," "Overwear and Underwear," "Food and Drink," etc. Includes a section, "Twists in Other Tongues." An enjoyable book which has its serious uses.

525R **Tongue Twisters**, Caedmon, 1974 (TC 1432) record/cassette $8.98; (CDL 51432) cassette $8.98. CAE (P-U)

Actor George S. Irving has a hilarious time with word games from Alvin Schwartz's collection. Side 2 has the twisters arranged alphabetically by initial sound to help the beginning reader and the student in speech therapy.

526 **Tuck Everlasting**, by Natalie Babbitt. Farrar, 1975. 160p. $8.95 (I-U)

Many years before, the Tuck family had drunk from a spring whose water prevents one from ever growing old. Now, the secret is in the hands of a 10-year-old girl and a malevolent stranger.

526F **Tuck Everlasting**, Howard Kling, 1980, 16mm color 100min $1500. CV (I-U)

Good acting, photography and settings all combine to bring this haunting story to life.

527 **The Two of Them**, by Aliki. Greenwillow, 1979. unp. $9.75; lib.ed. $9.36 (P)

The tender story about the love between a little girl and her grandfather and the inevitability of death.

527FS **The Two of Them**, Weston Woods, 1981 (FS 264) 28fr color 7min $12; (SF 264C) with cassette $18. WW (P)

Utilizes the eloquent illustrations from the book. The mood is set by a soft musical background while the story is narrated in a caring tone. Accompanied by picture-cued text.

527R **The Two of Them**, Weston Woods, (LTR 264C) cassette only 6min $6. WW (P)

Gentle narration of this sensitive story. Musical accompaniment has an Italian flavor.

528 **Two Roman Mice**, by Marilynne K. Roach. Crowell, 1975 (P-I). OP

The two mice emulate the customs and lifestyle of the wealthy ancient Romans in well-illustrated washover line drawings. Based on a fable by Horace, "The Country Mouse and the City Mouse."

528FS **Two Roman Mice**, Westport Communications, 1980 (#52287) 30fr color 4:40min 1 strip with 1 cassette $22. EEM (P-I)

A version of the town mouse and country mouse who decide that the grass on the other side of the fence is not always greener—or best. The narration is simple, expressive but unobtrusive.

529 **The Ugly Duckling**, by Hans Christian Andersen; tr. by R. P.

Keigwin; illus. by Johannes Larsen. Macmillan, 1955. 54p. $3.95 (P-I). OP

Watercolor drawings by the Danish painter illustrate this edition of the story of the ugly duckling who became a beautiful swan.

529F **The Ugly Duckling**, Coronet, 1953 (616) 16mm color 11min $215; b/w $65. COR (N-P)

Filmed in Europe with live animals.

529FS **The Ugly Duckling**, Spoken Arts, 197? (SA 2009-A) Part 1: 38fr 9:15min, Part 2: 47fr 12min color with 2 12in 33rpm $59.95; 2 cassettes $59.95. SA (P-I)

Elinor Basescu's warm rich voice seems just right for Andersen's poignant tale. Harp music and sound effects by Christopher Casson and soft, rather somber watercolor drawings by Julia Noonan complement the reading. Includes teacher's guide, activity sheets, and reading script.

529R **The Ugly Duckling**, Weston Woods, 1977 (LTR 187C) cassette only 17min $6. WW (P-I)

Pauline Brailsford narrates this beloved Andersen story. Taken from the version by Svend Otto S.

529R **The Ugly Duckling, and Other Tales**, Caedmon, 1959 (TC 1109) record/cassette $8.98; (CDL 51109) cassette $8.98. CAE (P-I)

Boris Karloff follows the Andersen fairy tales as translated by Reginald Spink (Dutton, OP). Includes: "The Ugly Duckling," "The Shepherdess and the Chimney Sweep," "The Princess on the Pea," "The Collar," "Clod-Poll," and "The Fir Tree."

530 **Umbrella**, by Taro Yashima. Viking, 1958. 30p. lib. ed. $7.95 net; pap. $2.75 (N-P)

Momo, given an umbrella and a pair of red boots on her third birthday, is overjoyed when at last it rains and she can wear her new rain togs.

530FS **Umbrella**, Weston Woods, n.d. (FS 105) 23fr color $12; (SF 105) with 7in 33rpm 5:20min $18; with cassette $18. WW (N-P)

Illustrations from the book, accompanied by picture-cued text booklet.

531 **Up a Road Slowly**, by Irene Hunt. Follett, 1966. 192p. $4.95; lib. ed. $4.98 net; pap. $.95 (I-U)

After her mother's death Julie Trelling was sent to live with her severe but fair schoolteacher aunt. Julie's growing up is followed in a perceptive story peopled with interesting characters. Newbery Medal winner, 1967.

531FS **Up a Road Slowly**, Random House/Miller-Brody, 1980 (394-65795-4) 2 filmstrips 130, 119fr color with 2 cassettes 21, 19min $45. RH/M-B (I)

Filmstrip based on Hunt's book. Illustrations drawn from descriptions in book. Musical background enhances presentation.

531R **Up a Road Slowly**, Random House/Miller-Brody, 1973 (394-77137-0) record $8.97; (394-77138-9) cassette $8.97. RH/M-B (I-U)

The recording captures the warmth of this fine story of a girl growing up.

532 **The Velveteen Rabbit**, by Margery Williams; illus. by William Nicholson. Doubleday, 1958 (c1922). 44p. $3.95; deluxe ed. $5.95; pap. $1.95 (P-I)

A toy rabbit becomes real through a boy's love and the help of a fairy godmother.

532FS **The Velveteen Rabbit**, Miller-Brody, 1976, 120fr color 24:15min 2 filmstrips Part 1: 77fr 14:05min, Part 2: 51fr 10:55min 1 12in 33rpm $45; cassette $45. RH/M-B (P-I)

The original artwork by Diane Dawson complements the old-fashioned charm of the book. Beautifully read by actress Eva Le Gallienne.

532R **The Velveteen Rabbit**, Random House/Miller-Brody, 1975 (394-76381-5) read-along record with 8 paperback books $26.97; (394-76382-3) read-along cassette with 8 paperback books $26.97. RH/M-B (P-I)

Actress Eva Le Gallienne's dramatic reading has warmth and charm.

533 **A Visit to William Blake's Inn**, by Nancy Willard; illus. by Alice and Martin Provensen. Harcourt, 1981. 45p. $10.95 (P-U)

1982 winner of the Newbery Medal and a Caldecott Honor book. This book is rich in poetry, nonsense verse, fantasy, and tantalizing illustrations.

533FS **A Visit to William Blake's Inn**, Random House/Miller-Brody, 1982, 151fr color 17:10min with cassette $28. RH (P-U)

The dimension of music has been added to the original art and eloquent reading of the text. A most successful combination.

533R **A Visit to William Blake's Inn: Poems for Innocent and Experienced Travelers**. Random House/Miller-Brody, 1982 (676-30170-3) listening cassette: side 1: 23:27min; read-along version: side 2: 22min $8.97; (676-30368-4) read-along cassette with hardcover book $21.90. RH/M-B (P-I)

Two Broadway and television actors, Vilma Vaccaro and Roy Alan Wilson, both narrate and sing the poems Nancy Willard wrote about William Blake's poetry.

534 **Warton and Morton**, by Russell Erickson; illus. by Lawrence DiFiorio. Lothrop, 1976 (P-I)

The brother toads, Warton and Morton, start out on a well-deserved camping holiday. They pitch their tent on the bank of a small stream but during the night it rains. They are swept away in different directions. Before they are reunited, each ends up with a colony of creatures they have never seen; they learn much about tolerance and understanding.

534R **Warton and Morton**, Listening Library (ASWR 28) cassette 28min with 4 paperbacks teacher's guide $21.95. LL (P-I)

A verbatim reading of the text which ends at the climax of the story. The listener must read the book to find out what happens.

535 **What Mary Jo Shared**, by Janice M. Udry; illus. by Eleanor Mill. Whitman, 1966. 40p. $7.50; Scholastic pap. $1.50 (P-I)

Mary Jo, a little black girl, never has anything for show and tell at school until she thinks of sharing her father.

535F **What Mary Jo Shared**, Bernard Wilets, 1980, 16mm color 13min $265, $40. PHX (P-I)

Nicely done live action presentation of the picture book with likeable and attractive children.

536 **The Wheel on the School**, by Meindert De Jong; pictures by Maurice Sendak. Harper, 1954. 298p. $10; lib. ed. $9.89 net; pap. $2.95 (I)

Because storks are said to bring good luck, the children of a Dutch village set out to attract a pair to their school. With the help of the schoolmaster, they persist in their efforts until the whole town becomes involved. Vivid characterization, exciting incidents, and fine background details. 1955 Newbery Medal winner.

536FS **The Wheel on the School**, Miller-Brody, 1971, 3 filmstrips 172fr color 45min with 12in 33rpm manual/automatic $45; with cassette $45. RH (I)

Robert Ulm's artwork depicting an old-fashioned fishing village in Holland is accompanied by the full sound track of the original recording. Includes teacher's guide.

536R **The Wheel on the School**, Random House/Miller-Brody, 1955 (394-77148-6) record $8.97; (394-77149-4) cassette $8.97; (394-65820-5) 10 student activity booklets $12.30. RH/M-B (I)

A recorded dramatization. Background music by leading Netherlands composers is played by the Amsterdam Concertgebouw Orchestra. Includes teacher's guide.

537 **When Shlemiel Went to Warsaw and Other Stories**, by Isaac Bashevis Singer; illus. by Margot Zemach. Farrar, 1968. 115p. $8.95; pap. $1.25 (I)

A collection of eight Jewish folktales, full of humor and insight into human nature.

537FS **When Shlemiel Went to Warsaw**, Miller-Brody, 1974, 200fr color 45min with 2 12in 33rpm or cassettes $45. RH/M-B (I-U)

Includes "Shrewd Todi and Lyzer the Miser," and "Rabbi Lieb and the Witch Cunegunde." Illustrated in watercolor with black ink.

538 **When Will I Read?**, by Miriam Cohen; illus. by Lillian Hoban. Greenwillow, 1977. $8.25; lib.ed. $7.92 (N-P)

An impatient first grade boy wonders when he will learn to read. Although his teacher tries to show him that he already can, he remains unconvinced until he discovers a torn sign on the gerbil cage. The sign announced "Do let the gerbil out," and his discovery not only saves the gerbil's life but convinces him he *can* read. His joy, reflected in his statement, "It's something I've been waiting for all my life," echoes children's feelings about learning the magical process of reading.

538FS **When Will I Read?**, Educational Enrichment Materials, n.d. color 1 filmstrip 1 cassette $22. EEM (N-P)

One of the 1977 *SLJ's* Best Books of 1977, by Miriam Cohen and illustrated by Lillian Hoban, adapts well to this medium.

539 **Where the Buffaloes Begin**, by Olaf Baker; illus. by Stephen Gammell. Warne, 1981. 47p. $8.95 (P-I)

Little Wolf's journey to the legendary lake where buffalo are born is created in the beautiful, misty illustrations which give the feeling of the lonely, wide-open prairie.

539FS **Where the Buffaloes Begin**, Random House/Miller-Brody, 1982, 110fr color 14min with cassette $28. RH/M-B (P-I)

The musical background with the use of the original black-and-white illustrations gives the illusion and atmosphere of the origins of the prairie and the buffalo.

539R **Where the Buffaloes Begin**, Random House/Miller-Brody (676-30194-0) read-along cassette $8.97; (676-30367-6) read-along cassette with hardcover book $17.85. RH/M-B (P-I)

Narration by Jamake Highwater combined with authentic Native American music. Ethnic musicologist Charlotte Heth recorded the music of the Great Plains Indians on site.

540 **Where Do You Think You're Going, Christopher Columbus?**, by Jean Fritz; illus. by Margot Tomes. Putnam, 1980. 80p. $8.95; pap. $3.95 (P-I)

Christopher Columbus determines to be the first to reach the Indies. A clever and readable biography of Christopher Columbus with humorous illustrations to accompany the text.

540R **Where Do You Think You're Going, Christopher Columbus?**,

Weston Woods, 1982 (WW 483C) cassette only 77min $6. WW (P-I)

Jean Fritz gives an even and low-key reading to her work.

541 **Where Does the Butterfly Go When It Rains?**, by Mary Garlick; illus. by Leonard Weisgard. Addison-Wesley, 1961. unp. lib. ed. $6.95; pap. $1.25 (N-P)

How animals protect themselves from rainstorms. Poetic text and beautiful illustrations.

541FS **Where Does the Butterfly Go When It Rains?** and **The Happy Day**, Weston Woods, n.d. (FS 96) 20, 19fr color $12; (SF 96) 3:08, 2:22min with 7in 33rpm $18; with cassette $18. WW (N-P)

Illustrations from the book, accompanied by picture-cued text booklet.

542 **Where the Red Fern Grows**, by Wilson Rawls. Doubleday, 1961. 256p. $7.95; 1974 Bantam pap. $2.50 (U)

The story of two dogs and a boy and growing up in the Depression in the Ozark Mountains.

542FS **Where the Red Fern Grows**, Media Basics, 1979 (MB5510) 3 filmstrips av 185fr 3 cassettes av 17min $109.95. MED (U)

Growing up on a poor farm in the Depression, Billy struggles to own and train the two best coon hounds in the valley. In a story of beauty and power he tastes both triumph and tragedy.

543 **Where the Wild Things Are**, by Maurice Sendak. Harper, 1963. unp. $7.95; lib. ed. $7.89 net (P)

Max, sent supperless to bed, escapes in imagination to the land where he is king of the "wild things." Imaginative illustrations show playfully horrendous creatures cavorting in a never-never land of great beauty. Caldecott Medal winner, 1964.

543F **Where the Wild Things Are**, Kratky Films, 1974, 16mm color 8min $175, $20; videocassette $175; Super 8 sound $175. WW (P)

Gene Deitch uses unconventional techniques (the wild things move in and out of focus, the sound track sounds warped) to create a delightfully scary effect. Also available in Spanish (16mm). ALA Notable Children's Film, 1974.

543FS **Where the Wild Things Are**, Weston Woods, n.d. (FS 84) 39fr color $12; (SF 84) with 7in 33rpm 4:30min $18; with cassette $18. WW (P)

Illustrations from the book, accompanied by picture-cued text booklet.

544 **Whistle for Willie**, by Ezra Jack Keats. Viking, 1964. 33p. lib. ed. $5.95; pap. $1.95 (N-P)

Peter longs to whistle for his dog Willie, but finds that whistling is not as easy as it looks.

544F **Whistle for Willie**, Morton Schindel, 1965 (17026) 16mm color 5:30min $175, $20; videocassette $175; Super 8 sound $175. WW (N-P)

Animated and directed by Mal Whittman. Narrated by Jane Harvey. Music by Barry Galbraith. Also available in Spanish (16mm).

544FS **Whistle for Willie**, Weston Woods, n.d. (FS 65) 29fr color $12; (SF 65) 5:13min with 7in 33rpm $18; with cassette $18. WW (N-P)

Illustrations from the book, accompanied by picture-cued text booklet.

Also available in Spanish.

545 **White Snow, Bright Snow**, by Alvin Tresselt; illus. by Roger Duvoisin. Lothrop, 1947. 32p. $8.25; lib. ed. $7.92 net (P)

Arresting pictures effectively convey the frosty beauty of a heavy snowfall and depict the fun and work that come with it. Brief, poetic text. Caldecott Medal winner, 1948.

545FS **White Snow, Bright Snow**, Weston Woods, n.d. (FS 24) 37fr color $12; (SF 24) with 33rpm 7min $18; with cassette $18. WW (P)

Illustrations from the book, accompanied by picture-cued text booklet.

546 **Who's in Rabbit's House?**, by Verna Aardema; illus. by Leo and Diane Dillon. Dial, 1969, 1977. $11.95; lib. ed. $11.89; pap. $2.50 (P)

Rabbit comes home to find that a creature who can trample elephants has taken up residence in his house. All of the larger animals are afraid to face this terrible creature, but frog gets him out. A Masai tale.

546R **Who's in Rabbit's House?**, Weston Woods, 1982 (LTR 279C) cassette only 9min $6. WW (P)

This story is told by Jackie Torrence in an unaccompanied and even storytelling style.

547 **Whose Mouse Are You?**, by Robert Kraus; illus. by Jose Aruego. Macmillan, 1970. unp. $9.95; pap. $2.25 (N)

A sad little mouse belongs to no one until he takes matters into his own hands. A simple question-and-answer text is complemented by large, bright illustrations.

547R **Whose Mouse Are You?**, Weston Woods, 1972 (LTR 148C) cassette only 4min $6. WW (N)

Frances Kelly's narration distinguishes between the questioner and the sad little mouse. Music by Douglas Wood captures the change in the mouse's mood.

548 **Why Mosquitoes Buzz in People's Ears**, by Verna Aardema; illus. by Leo and Diane Dillon. Dial, 1975. 30p. $7.95; lib. ed. $7.45; net pap. $2.50 (N-P)

A West African folktale. Caldecott Medal winner, 1976.

548FS **Why Mosquitoes Buzz in People's Ears**, Weston Woods, 1976 (FS 199) 43fr color 10:35min $12; (SF 199C) with cassette $18. WW (P-I)

Filmstrip adaptation by Kristine Holm and C. B. Wismar. Artwork captures the striking beauty of the original illustrations. Fine narrations by James Earl Jones.

549 **Why the Sun and the Moon Live in the Sky**, by Elphinstone Dayrell; illus. by Blair Lent. Houghton, 1977. 26p. $3.75; lib. ed. $3.40 net; pap. $1.95 (P)

An African myth strikingly illustrated with puppet figures wearing ceremonial masks to represent the sun, moon, water, and sea creatures.

549F **Why the Sun and the Moon Live in the Sky**, ACI Films, 1971 (4099) 16mm color 11min $220. ACI (P-I)

Cardboard puppets by Blair Lent. Narration by Spencer Shaw. Produced by Emily Jones. Animation and an especially composed score, based on African rhythms, bring to life an authentic legend of eastern Nigeria.

550 **Wild Robin**, by Susan Jeffers. Dutton, 1976. unp. $9.95 (P)

A sly, disobedient, mischievous boy — Robin — runs away from home when even his loving sister Janet loses patience with his wild ways. He is captured by the fairies, and although he leads a care-free life, Robin becomes lonely and homesick. Finally, from an elf, Janet learns the spell which will free her young brother from the fairies. An illustrated version of the Scottish ballad "Tamlane."

550FS **Wild Robin**, Weston Woods, 1978 (FS 232) 34fr color 7min $12; (SF 232C) with cassette $18. WW (P)

A low-key narration and unobtrusive

musical background complement Jeffers' misty illustrations. Fairyland is shown in eerie patches of blues and lavenders defined by ink accents.

Accompanied by picture-cued text booklet.

550R **Wild Robin**, Weston Woods, 1978 (LTR 232C) cassette only 7min $6. WW (I)

Pauline Brailsford narrates this Scottish tale.

551 **Wiley and the Hairy Man**, adapted by Molly Bang. Macmillan, 1976. 64p. $6.95 (P)

An easy-to-read version of the traditional story of how Wiley and his mother outwit the hairy man of the swamp.

551R **The Hairy Man and Other Wild Tales**, Weston Woods, 1982 (WW722) 43min $8; (WW722C) cassette $8. WW (P-I)

David Holt tells the story of Wiley and the Hairy Man and some other folk stories. An ALA Notable Recording in 1982.

552 **Will I Have a Friend**?, by Miriam Cohen; illus. by Lillian Hoban. Macmillan, 1967. unp. $7.95; 1971 pap. $2.50 (N-P)

Jim is very apprehensive about his first day at school and the children he will meet.

552FS **Will I Have a Friend**?, Educational Reading Service (Library 4) color 1 filmstrip 1 cassette $14.95. ERS (N-P)

Clear male voice for the narration; illustrations taken from the book; appropriate music and background sounds; appealing.

553 **Will's Quill**, by Don Freeman. Viking, 1975. 32p. $7.95 (P-I)

A kind-hearted country goose serves as the vehicle for introducing the young reader to William Shakespeare and the clamorous, colorful London of Elizabethan times. Unaccustomed to the fast pace of city life, the goose is befriended by the budding playwright and repays his kindness by supplying him with the quills necessary to his writing.

553FS **Will's Quill**, Viking, dist. by Live Oak Media, 1976 (0-670-90536-4) 44fr color 9:48min with cassette $19.95. LOM (P-I)

Adaptation of Don Freeman's book using the same delicately composed watercolors.

Accompanied by picture-cued text booklet.

554 **The Wind in the Willows**, by Kenneth Grahame; illus. by Michael Hagne. Holt, 1980. 216p. $16.95 (I)

The adventures of Toad, Ratty, Mole, and Badger in a beautifully illustrated edition.

554FS **The Wind in the Willows**, Educational Enrichment Materials, n.d. color 8 filmstrips av 70fr 8 cassettes av 8min 1 guide 1 paperback $172; set of 4 filmstrips with sound $87 (individual FS with sound $24). EEM (P)

A colorful fun-filled adaptation of the novel by Kenneth Grahame. A welcome introduction to a great classic.

554R **The Wind in the Willows**, v. 1, Pathways of Sound, 1953 (POS 1022) 1 12in record $8.98. POS (I)

The Christmas chapter, "Dulce Domum," and "The Piper at the Gates of Dawn" are read by Robert Brooks.

554R **The Wind in the Willows**, v.2, Pathways of Sound, 1953 (POS 1026) 1 12in record $8.98. POS (I)

"The Open Road" and "Mr. Toad" are read with humor and delight by Jessica Tandy and Hume Cronyn.

554R **The Wind in the Willows**, v.3, Pathways of Sound, 1953 (POS

1029) 1 12in record $8.98. POS (I)

"Wayfarers All" is read by Robert Brooks.

554R **The Wind in the Willows**, v.4, Pathways of Sound, 1953 (POS 1039) 1 12in record $8.98. POS (I)

"Toad's Adventures," read by Hume Cronyn and "The Further Adventures of Toad," read by Jessica Tandy.

554R **The Wind in the Willows**, Caedmon, 1972 (TC 1416) $8.98; (CDL 514165) cassette $8.98. CAE (I-U)

David McCallum reads this skillfully abridged version of Grahame's book.

555 **Wingman**, by Manus Pinkwater. Dodd, 1975 (I)

Donald Chen, the only Chinese boy in his class, takes refuge from his unhappy school life to read comics while sitting on a girder of the George Washington Bridge in New York City. There he meets Wingman, a Chinese Superman, who helps him resolve his problems. The psychology employed by Donald's new teacher is noteworthy.

555R **Wingman**, Listening Library, 1981 (FTR 51) 1 cassette 81min 4 paperbacks teacher's guide $15. LL (I)

Narrated by a woman with a clear expressive voice who provides a model for oral reading.

556 **The Witch of Blackbird Pond**, by Elizabeth George Speare. Houghton, 1958. 249p. $6.95; pap. $1.50 (I-U)

Kit Tyler comes from her luxurious Barbados home to live with relatives in colonial Connecticut. Rebelling against the bigotry of the times, Kit becomes friendly with an old woman thought to be a witch and sets off a terrifying witch-hunt. Three romances within the story add appeal for older girls. 1959 Newbery Medal winner.

556R **The Witch of Blackbird Pond**, Random House/Miller-Brody, 1970 (394-77140-0) record $8.97; (394-77141-9) cassette $8.97. RH/M-B (I-U)

Dramatization by Len Safir. Directed by Peter Fernandez. Featured in this recording are Elizabeth Hale as Kit, Lawson Zerbe as Nat, Fay Sappington as Hannah, and Lisa Bellaran as Prudence. Music by Herb Davidson is based on melodic motifs from the Bay Psalm Book. Includes teacher's guide.

557 **The Witches of Worm**, by Zilpha K. Snyder; illus. by Alton Raible. Atheneum, 1972. 183p. $8.95 (I)

Jessica, the neglected child of a swinging divorcee, finds a deserted, blind kitten which she calls "Worm." Jessica feels she is in the grip of a hellish force—Worm—that makes her play harmful tricks on her mother and on her neighbors.

557FS **The Witches of Worm**, Miller-Brody, 1979 (394-78392-1) 2 filmstrips 145, 168fr color with 2 cassettes 19min each $45. RH/M-B (I)

Realistic illustrations based on the descriptions in the book. Filmstrip makes use of appropriate sound effects to enhance the presentation.

557R **The Witches of Worm**, by Zilpha K. Snyder. Random House/Miller-Brody (394-76915-5) record $8.97; (394-76916-3) cassette $8.97. RH/M-B (I)

The mood established matches the witchcraft theme of the story.

558 **The Wizard of Oz**, by L. Frank Baum; illus. by W. W. Denslow. Macmillan, 1970. 244p. $5.95 (I)

As swiftly as the heroine is whirled away by a Kansas cyclone, the reader is transported, through picture and word, into the magical land of Oz. Afterword by Clifton Fadiman.

558F **The Wizard of Oz**, M-G-M, 1939, 16mm color 101min $200 (rental only). FI(P-I)

A cyclone transports Dorothy and her dog from a Kansas farm into a world of intriguing characters and magical adventure. The fabulous sets and songs, and the cast, headed by Judy Garland, Ray Bolger, and Bert Lahr, have combined to create a film classic.

559 **The Woodcutter's Duck**, by Krystyna Turska. Macmillan, 1973. 32p. $5.95 (P). OP

Bartek, a poor woodcutter, lived in the mountains of Poland. His only companion was his little duck. One day the kind Bartek saved the life of a frog who bestowed upon him magical power that was to help Bartek save his companion's life.

559FS **The Woodcutter's Duck**, Weston Woods, 1977 (FS 226) 44fr color 11min $12; (SF 226C) with cassette $18. WW (P)

Expressive musical background adds zest and meaning to Turska's lustrous illustrations. Accompanied by picture-cued text booklet.

560 **The World of Christopher Robin**, by A. A. Milne; illus. by E. H. Shepard. Dutton, 1958. 235p. $9.95 (P)

An attractive volume which includes the complete *When We Were Very Young* and *Now We Are Six*.

560R **A Gathering of Great Poetry for Children**, v. 1 and 2, Caedmon, 196? (CDL 51235 and 51236) each cassette $8.98. CAE (P-U)

Poems by Robert Frost, Langston Hughes, Edna St. Vincent Millay, A. A. Milne, Carl Sandburg, and others are read by Julie Harris, Cyril Ritchard, David Wayne, and the poets themselves. Volume 1 is suggested for kindergarten and up; volume 2 for second grade and up.

561 **Wynken, Blynken and Nod**, by Eugene Field; illus. by Barbara Cooney. Hastings, 1964. unp. $4.95 (N-P). OP

Soft, dreamlike illustrations illuminate the haunting beauty of Field's lullaby.

561F **Wynken, Blyken and Nod**, Morton Schindel, 1972, 16mm color 3:30min $115, $15; videocassette $115. WW (N-P)

Iconographic technique using illustrations from the book. Narrated by John Cunningham.

561R **Wynken, Blynken and Nod, and Other Poems**, by Eugene Field. Caedmon, 1970 (TC 1298) $8.98; (CDL 51298) cassette $8.98. CAE (P-I)

Julie Harris conveys the full charm of Eugene Field's poetry.

562 **Yankee Doodle**, by Edward Bangs; illus. by Steven Kellogg. Reprint ed. Scholastic, 1980. $9.95 (P)

A little boy meets General Washington and dreams of martial glory until he is captured by the British.

562F **Yankee Doodle**, Morton Schindel, 1976 16mm color 10min $140, $20; videocassette $140; Super 8 sound $140. WW (P-I)

A visually colorful and imaginative interpretation of the patriotic song written by a Harvard sophomore who served as a minuteman at Lexington in 1775. Music by the Colonial Williamsburg Fife and Drum Corps.

562R **Yankee Doodle**, Weston Woods, 1976 (LTR 173C) cassette only 10min $6. WW (N-P)

A short history of the song precedes the song itself played by the Colonial Williamsburg Fife and Drum Corps and sung by children.

563 **The Yearling**, by Marjorie Kinnan Rawlings; illus. by N. C. Wyeth.

Scribner, 1961. 428p. pap. $4.94 (I-U)

Jody Baxter and his pet fawn, Flag, roam the scrub pine forests of Florida until Flag's destruction of crops forces the boy to make a man's decision. Descriptions of the place, the people, and, most of all, the pangs of a boy's maturing make this a memorable story.

563F **The Yearling**, M-G-M, 1946, 16mm color 135min $75 (rental only). FI (I)

Gregory Peck, Jane Wyman, and Claude Jarman, Jr., star. Directed by Clarence Brown. Screenplay by Paul Osborn.

564 **Yertle the Turtle and Other Stories**, by Dr. Seuss. Random House, 1958. $4.99 (P)

"Yertle the Turtle" is the tale of a turtle King whose greed for power eventually strips him of everything.

"Gertrude McFuzz" tells of a bird dissatisfied with her one-feathered tail until she is burdened with a many-feathered one.

In "The Big Brag," a rabbit and a bear foolishly argue about who's better than who until an old worm exposes the emptiness of their boasts.

564FS **Yertle the Turtle and Other Stories**, Paratore Pictures, rel. by Random House, 1977 (394-04645-5) 4 filmstrips 45, 31, 62, 71fr color with 4 records 12in 33-1/3 rpm 6:33, 4:55, 7:45, 9:57min $103.50; (394-04644-7) with 4 cassettes $103. RH/M-B (P)

Enhanced by bright color illustrations which are faithful to the original drawings, the filmstrip has a lively pace, retaining the marvelous Seuss rhymes while adding suspense. The catchy music is beautifully integrated with the narrative.

564R **Yertle the Turtle and Other Stories**, Random House/Miller-Brody. (394-06930-7) cassette only $8.97; (394-69366-3) cassette with hardcover book $15.96. RH/M-B (P)

A read-along version of the book.

565 **You Come Too: Favorite Poems for Young Readers**, by Robert Frost; with wood engravings by Thomas W. Nason. Holt, 1959. 94p. $5.95 (I-U)

A perceptive foreword introduces Frost's own selection of his poems to be read to and by young people.

565R **A Gathering of Great Poetry for Children**, v. 3 and 4, Caedmon 196? (51237 and 51238) each cassette $8.98. CAE (P-U)

Poems by Emily Dickinson, Robert Frost, Edna St. Vincent Millay, Carl Sandburg, and others are read by Julie Harris, Cyril Ritchard, David Wayne, and the poets themselves. Volumes 3 and 4 are suggested for fourth grade and up. Richard Lewis selected the poems.

565R **Robert Frost Reads "The Road Not Taken and Other Poems,"** Caedmon, 1956 (TC 1060) record $8.98; (CDL 51060) cassette $8.98. CAE (U)

The poet reads "The Road Not Taken," "Birches," "Death of a Hired Man," "Choose Something Like a Star," and other favorites.

566 **You Read to Me, I'll Read to You**, by John Ciardi; illus. by Edward Gorey. Lippincott, 1962. 64p. $8.95 net (P-I)

"All the poems printed in black, you read to me. All the poems written in blue, I'll read to you." Poems for sharing out loud.

566R **You Read to Me, I'll Read to You**, Spoken Arts, 1966 (SA 835) LP $8.98; (6037) individual cassette $8.98 (P-I)

Read by the author, John Ciardi, and his children, Myra, Benn and John.

567 **Zeely**, by Virginia Hamilton; illus.

by Symeon Shimin. Macmillan, 1967. 122p. $7.95; pap. $1.25 (I-U)

A farm woman who looks like a Watusi princess helps a young girl understand her racial identity.

567R **Zeely**, Caedmon, 1974 (CDL 51443) cassette $8.98. CAE (I-U)

Virginia Hamilton reads, and in one place sings, her own edited version of her story of Geeder and her imagined encounter with the Watusi Queen Zeely.

568 **Zlateh the Goat and Other Stories**, by Isaac Bashevis Singer; illus. by Maurice Sendak. Harper, 1966. 90p. $10; lib. ed. $9.89 (I)

Seven tales drawn from European-Jewish village life.

568F **Zlateh the Goat**, Morton Schindel, 1973, 16mm color 20min $275; videocassette, $25 (rental). WW (P-I-U)

The film begins with a storyteller reading a short passage from "Zlateh the Goat." Then, without words, poetic imagery, music, and a slow pace are used to evoke Singer's tale. An unusually beautiful film, adapted and directed by Gene Deitch, with Maurice Sendak as consultant.

568FS **Zlateh the Goat/The First Shlemiel**, Miller-Brody, 1974 (NSF 3063) 200fr color 43min with 2 12in 33rpm or 2 cassettes $45. RH/M-B (I-U)

Includes "The Snow in Chelm" and "Fool's Paradise." Illustrated in watercolor with black ink.

AUTHORS AND ILLUSTRATORS

Lloyd Alexander

FS **Lloyd Alexander**, Miller-Brody, 1974 (394-77227-X) 94fr color 12:15min with 12in 33rpm $34.50 (394-77244-X) with cassette $34.50; RH/M-B (I-U)

The author is shown creating his fantasy stories in predawn hours in his Philadelphia home. He talks about his writing, his love of music, and cats. Special emphasis placed on the Chronicles of Prydain, including the Newbery Medal book, *The High King*.

Edward Ardizzone

F **Edward Ardizzone**, Weston Woods, 1978, 16mm color 13min $225, $15. WW (I-U)

The creator of the *Little Tim* books talks about his love of drawing and the background of his stories. The film is set in Kent, England where the artist has his studio. Illustrations from his books complement the narration.

William H. Armstrong

FS **William H. Armstrong**, Random House/Miller-Brody, 1977 (394-77236-9) 87fr color 9min with 12in 33rpm $31.98; (394-77253-9) with cassette $31.98. RH/M-B (I-U)

The quietly busy life of author William H. Armstrong is depicted in this filmstrip that catches the man in his many roles as teacher, writer, shepherd, gardener, cabinet maker, and real estate agent. The narrator tells how history has been a part of the author's life and books. Photos, family snapshots, and book illustrations add another dimension to the few remarks on Armstrong's childhood, education, and Connecticut home built with his own hands.

Natalie Babbitt

FS **Natalie Babbitt**, Miller-Brody, 1978 (394-77239-3) 104fr color 15min with 12in 33rpm $31.98; (394-77256-3) with cassette $31.98. RH/M-B (P-I)

The filmstrip utilizes interplay between the voices of the informal narrator and the vivacious author/artist. Warm anecdotes, examples of her earliest artwork and writing and family photos help depict Babbitt's multifaceted, talented personality. Throughout the filmstrip, the music captures the changing moods.

Arna Bontemps

R **An Anthology of Negro Poetry for Young People**, Folkways/Scholastic Records, 1958 (7114) 2s 10in 33rpm $8.98. FSR (I-U)

Arna Bontemps reads from his anthology, *Golden Slippers*.

Carol Ryrie Brink

FS **Carol Ryrie Brink**, Miller-Brody, 1976 (394-77235-0) 83fr color 15min with 12in 33rpm $31.98; (394-77252-0) with cassette $31.98. RH/M-B (I-U)

Carol Ryrie Brink shares her old family album with the listener. Some photographs of the Wisconsin countryside provide a feeling for the settings of her stories. This filmstrip provides an account of the author's life and how it is related to her books.

Betsy Byars

FS **Betsy Byars**, Miller-Brody, 1978 (394-77257-1) 95fr color 12min with cassette $31.98. RH/M-B (I-U)

Betsy Byars talks of the things she loved as a child and her ideas about writers. Filmstrip utilizes photos from the family album. While she discusses her work, some pictures from the television shootings of "Troubled River" and "The Pinballs" are shown, in addition to illustrations from her books.

Richard Chase

R **Richard Chase Tells Three "Jack Tales" from the Southern Appalachians**, Folk Legacy Records, 196? (FTA-6) 2s 12in 33rpm $7.98. FL (P-I)

Richard Chase tells "Jack and the Robbers," "Jack and the King's Girl," and "Jack and the Three Sillies" to a group of mountain children in northeastern Tennessee.

Beverly Cleary

FS **Beverly Cleary**, Random House/Miller-Brody, 1979 (394-78374-3) 112fr color 13min with cassette $31.98. RH/M-B (P-U)

The photographs of young Beverly engaging in various childhood antics and more recent photos of Ms. Cleary with her twins and their cats provide glimpses of what have inspired her stories. Ms. Cleary also explains how she writes.

James Lincoln Collier/ Christopher Collier

FS **James Lincoln Collier and Christopher Collier**, Random House/Miller-Brody, 1981 (394-66206-7) 113fr color 11min with cassette $31.98. RH/M-B (I-U)

These two award-winning brothers provide the narration and the musical background for this filmstrip. The Collier brothers—one the writer, the other the historian—are pictured working independently and together. Shows how the authors use authentic historical documents as sources of details essential to their stories. Family photos show a typical sibling relationship that has evolved into a genuine mutual respect.

Barbara Cooney

F **The Lively Art of Picture Books**, Morton Schindel, 1964, 16mm color 57min $500, $40. WW (U)

An introduction to the who, what, and why of the modern picture book, including interviews with Barbara Cooney, Robert McCloskey, and Maurice Sendak in their homes. Narrated by John Langstaff. Written and directed by Joanna Foster Dougherty. Produced under the auspices of the Children's Services Division of ALA.

Susan Cooper

FS **Susan Cooper**, Miller-Brody, 1977 (394-77237-7) 97fr color with 12in

33rpm $31.98; (394-77254-7) with cassette $31.98. RH/M-B (I)

Photographs of the Thames River Valley and Buckinghamshire, where Susan spent her childhood, are used to introduce this author. Scrapbook pictures of the author throughout her early life create a vivid picture of Susan Cooper.

Appropriate, lively background music enhances presentation.

Eleanor Estes

FS **Eleanor Estes**, Miller-Brody, 1974 (394-77226-1) 95fr color 13:50min with 12in 33rpm $34.50; (394-77243-1) cassette $34.50. RH/M-B (I)

Captures moments in the author's childhood, early and later influences on her writings (such as the dog that inspired *Ginger Pye* and the events that triggered the Moffats series). This filmstrip has greater appeal to older children who are studying Newbery authors and who are familiar with Mrs. Estes's books than to younger children for whom the books were written.

Theodor S. Geisel (Dr. Seuss)

FS **Who's Dr. Seuss? Meet Ted Geisel**, by Theodor Seuss Geisel. Random House/Miller-Brody, 1980 (394-66070-6) 122fr color 13min with cassette $31.98. RH/M-B (P-U)

The catchy musical background of this upbeat filmstrip includes clarinet, piano, drums, voice and spoons. A jovial narrator enthusiastically traces Geisel's career, while excerpts and photos from an interview with the subject supplement the account. Many early samples of the artist's work are shown.

Jean Craighead George

FS **Jean Craighead George**, Miller-Brody, 1974 (394-77228-8) 99fr color 15:50min with 12in 33rpm $34.50; (394-77245-8) cassette $34.50. RH/M-B (I-U)

Viewers accompany Ms. George on a walk through autumn woods, learn about her childhood, her career as a writer, and how she came to write the Newbery Medal winner, *Julie of the Wolves*.

Nikki Giovanni

FS **First Choice: Poets and Poetry**, Pied Piper, 1979, 5 filmstrips 107-140fr color 11-14min with cassettes $87.50 for series; $22 each. Includes Eve Merriam, Myra Cohn Livingstone, Karla Kuskin, Nikki Giovanni, David McCord. PP (I)

Five famous children's poets read their work and talk about how and why they write poetry. Useful for poetry study or creative writing.

Bette Greene

FS **Bette Greene**, Miller-Brody, 1978 (394-77242-3) 104fr color 12:40min with 12in 33rpm $31.98; (394-77259-8) with cassette $31.98. RH/M-B (I-U)

Bette Greene invites viewers into her home and shares with them her interests and the feelings and experiences of her youth that so richly flavor her books. Newspaper clippings and family photos lend immediacy to the reminiscences of Greene's childhood, while shots of the author in her everyday pursuits add dimension to Greene's personality. In her clipboard-covered studio, Bette Greene explains how she works, writing and rewriting passages.

Gail E. Haley

FS **Gail E. Haley: Wood and Linoleum Illustration**, Weston Woods, 1978 (SF 456C) 72fr color 17min with cassette guide $30. WW (I-U)

Author-illustrator Gail Haley discusses her method of using wood and linoleum blocks to create a story's mood through illustration. She begins by tracing the historical development of printmaking and she then demonstrates her own printmaking technique.

FS **Tracing a Legend: The Story of the Green Man**, Weston Woods, 1980 (SF 463C) 66fr color 15min with cassette guide $30. WW (I-U)

Gail E. Haley discusses how her accidental "encounter" with the figure of the Green Man on a London pub sign launched a voyage of discovery through history to learn more about him, eventually inspiring her to create her book, *The Green Man*. In museums, libraries, cathedrals and pubs, Haley learns how this universal character had been portrayed in history, myth, and European and American folklore and how he appears in modern life.

Virginia Hamilton

FS **Virginia Hamilton**, Miller-Brody, 1976 (394-77232-6) 101fr color 15min with 12in 33rpm $34.50; (394-77249-0) cassette $34.50. RH/M-B (I-U)

From her home situated on a two-acre field—part of the farm where she grew up in Yellow Springs, Ohio—Ms. Hamilton reveals the influences on her books. Songs composed and sung by the author, as well as excerpts from *M. C. Higgins, the Great*, are included in the filmstrip.

Marguerite Henry

F **The Story of a Book**, 2nd ed., by Marguerite Henry. Pied Piper, 1982, 1 filmstrip 124fr color 16min with cassette $30. PP (P-I)

The true story of how a real-life author conceives and writes a book: where ideas come from, research in the library and on location, writing and rewriting, creating the illustrations, planning the dummy, and printing.

Jamake Highwater

FS **Jamake Highwater**, Random House/Miller-Brody, 1980 (394-78454-5) 118fr color 18:07min with cassette $31.98. RH/M-B (I-U)

Traditional melodies wafting from a native American flute surround the narrator's informative comments and the mellow, dramatically trained voice of the author, art and music critic, and anthropologist Jamake Highwater. Historic photos of Highwater's Blackfoot ancestors, documentary snapshots, and candid views of Highwater's predawn writing hours offer visual variety almost as rich as the subject's diversified experiences.

Ezra Jack Keats

F **Ezra Jack Keats**, Morton Schindel, 1971, 16mm color 17min $275, $20. WW (U)

Directed by Cynthia Freitag. In his New York studio Ezra Jack Keats discusses the experiences which have influenced his work as a children's book illustrator and demonstrates his collage work. The film concludes with the motion picture adaptation of *A Letter to Amy*.

Steven Kellogg

FS **How a Picture Book Is Made**, Weston Woods, 1976 (SF 451C) 66fr color 10min with cassette and guide $30. WW (P-U)

Steven Kellogg describes the many steps involved in creating his picture book, *The Island of Skog*. He discusses his childhood interests which led him to become a storyteller and artist. Kellogg also explains the creation of the illustrations, the characters and the dummy for the book. The second half of the filmstrip deals with the steps involved in printing and binding the book.

Karla Kuskin

FS **Poetry Explained by Karla Kuskin**,

Weston Woods, 1980 (SF 465C) 43fr color 16min with cassette and guide $30. WW (I-U)

Kuskin first focuses the audience's attention on how things look: the things in her workroom, the view from the windows. These provide images for her poems and drawings. She discusses how the poem is held together by rhythm and word sounds, and how rhyme can serve a poem. Kuskin gives examples of all the elements that go into a poem.

ALA Notable Filmstrip.

FS **First Choice: Poets and Poetry**, Pied Piper, 1979, 5 filmstrips 107-140fr color 11-14min with cassettes $87.50 for series; $22 each. Includes Eve Merriam, Myra Cohn Livingstone, Karla Kuskin, Nikki Giovanni, David McCord. PP (I)

Five famous children's poets read their work and talk about how and why they write poetry. Useful for poetry study or creative writing.

Madeleine L'Engle

FS **Madeleine L'Engle**, Miller-Brody, 1974 (394-77230-X) 102fr color 15:50min with 12in record $34.50; (394-77247-4) with cassette $34.50. RH/M-B (I-U)

Connecticut countryside, a Manhattan apartment, and St. John's Cathedral are the backgrounds for this interview with the author of the Newbery Medal book, *A Wrinkle in Time*. Narration by Ms. L'Engle's husband, actor Hugh Franklin.

Myra Cohn Livingstone

FS **First Choice: Poets and Poetry**, Pied Piper, 1979, 5 filmstrips 107-140fr color 11-14min with cassettes $87.50 for series; $22 each. Includes Eve Merriam, Myra Cohn Livingstone, Karla Kuskin, Nikki Giovanni, David McCord. PP (I)

Five famous children's poets read their work and talk about how and why they write poetry. Useful for poetry study or creative writing.

Arnold Lobel

FS **Arnold Lobel**, Random House/Miller-Brody, 1978 (394-77238-5) 95fr with 12in 33rpm $31.98; (394-77255-5) with cassette 11min $31.98. RH/M-B (P-U)

Informal photos, family stills, and many samples from Lobel's books complement information about the author/illustrator's working methods and occasional collaboration with illustrator wife, Anita. Information is presented to a background of lively music.

Robert McCloskey

F **Robert McCloskey**, Morton Schindel, 1965, 16mm color 18min $275, $20. WW (I-U)

An interview with the author-illustrator in his studio in Maine, where he describes the making of his books from the initial idea to finished product.

David McCord

FS **First Choice: Poets and Poetry**, Pied Piper, 1979, 5 filmstrips 107-140fr color 11-14min with cassettes $87.50 for series; $22 each. Includes Eve Merriam, Myra Cohn Livingstone, Karla Kuskin, Nikki Giovanni, David McCord. PP (I)

Five famous children's poets read their work and talk about how and why they write poetry. Useful for poetry study or creative writing.

Gerald McDermott

FS **Evolution of a Graphic Concept: The Stonecutter**, Weston Woods, 1977 (SF 454C) 71fr color 15min with cassette guide $30. WW (I-U)

Artist-filmmaker Gerald McDermott begins this sound filmstrip by introducing his childhood interests in art and story books. He explains how his desire to bring the story of *The Stonecutter* to life led him to make first an animated film and then a book. McDermott shows how the graphic symbols in his book help to unify the story and how the artistic elements blend to shape his personalized, stylized expression of traditional forms of Japanese art.

Eve Merriam

FS **First Choice: Poets and Poetry**, Pied Piper, 1979, 5 filmstrips 107-140fr color 11-14min with cassettes $87.50 for series; $22 each. Includes Eve Merriam, Myra Cohn Livingstone, Karla Kuskin, Nikki Giovanni, David McCord. PP (I)

Five famous children's poets read their work and talk about how and why they write poetry. Useful for poetry study or creative writing.

A. A. Milne

F **Mr. Shepard and Mr. Milne**, Andrew Holmes, 1973, 16mm color 29min $375, $30. WW (U)

Live-action film tells the story of the collaboration between A. A. Milne and Ernest Shepard. Shepard reminisces about his experiences with Milne as the camera visits some of the places depicted in the books about Christopher Robin and Pooh. C. R. Milne reads from his father's stories and poems.

The Enchanted Places, by Christopher Milne (Dutton, 1974) is "a memoir of the real Christopher Robin and Winnie-the-Pooh." It is illustrated with photographs and E. H. Shepard's line drawings.

Scott O'Dell

FS **Scott O'Dell**, Miller-Brody, 1974 (394-77229-6) 85fr color 13:15min with 12in 33rpm $34.50; (394-77246-6) with cassette $34.50. RH/M-B (I-U)

Scott O'Dell recalls his childhood and his days in Hollywood as a cameraman before he turned to writing. Includes scenes from the filmstrip based on his Newbery Medal book, *Island of the Blue Dolphins*.

Katherine Paterson

R **Katherine Paterson**, Random House, 1983 (394-63114-5) cassette 45min $12.96. RH/M-B (I-U)

Newbery Medal winner Paterson discusses her life, her family, and her writing in an interview conducted by Charles Seldon. Careful questioning reveals the depth and sensitivity of the writer and her works.

Carl Sandburg

R **A Lincoln Album**, Caedmon, 195? (TC 2015) 4s 12in 33rpm $17.96; (CDL 52015) 2 cassettes $17.96. CAE (U)

Carl Sandburg reads from material and text which he used in his *Abe Lincoln: The Prairie Years* and *The War Years*.

R **Rootabaga Stories**, v. 1-3, Caedmon, 1958 (TC 1089, TC 1159, TC 1306) 2s 12in 33rpm $8.98 each; (CDL 51089, CDL 51159, CDL 51306) each cassette $8.98. CAE (P-I)

Carl Sandburg, with his slow-moving rhythmic voice, tells his own stories about the Rootabaga country.

Maurice Sendak

F **Maurice Sendak**, Morton Schindel, 1965, 16mm color 14:15min $225, $15. WW (U)

Interview with author in his Manhattan apartment where he explains his philosophy and methods of production.

Ernest Shepard

F **Mr. Shepard and Mr. Milne**, Andrew Holmes, 1973, 16mm color 29min $375, $30. WW (U)

Live-action film tells the story of the collaboration between A. A. Milne and Ernest Shepard. Shepard reminisces about his experiences with Milne as the camera visits some of the places depicted in the books about Christopher Robin and Pooh. C. R. Milne reads from his father's stories and poems.

The Enchanted Places, by Christopher Milne (Dutton, 1974) is "a memoir of the real Christopher Robin and Winnie-the-Pooh." It is illustrated with photographs and E. H. Shepard's line drawings.

Isaac Bashevis Singer

FS **Isaac Bashevis Singer**, Miller-Brody Productions, 1976 (394-77233-4) 88fr color 18:33min with 12in 33rpm record $34.50; with cassette $34.50. RH (I-U)

The author's childhood in the Polish ghettoes during the 1900s is documented by Roman Vishniak's photographs. Includes filmstrip clip from *Zlateh the Goat*.

J. R. R. Tolkien

R **Poems and Songs of Middle Earth**, Caedmon, 1967 (TC 1231) 2s 12in 33rpm $8.98; (CP 12311) cassette $8.98. CAE (I-U)

Poems of Middle Earth read by the author, and songs from "The Road Goes Ever On" sung by William Elvin, with the composer, Donald Swann, at the piano. Critical notes by W. H. Auden on slipcase.

R **J. R. R. Tolkien Reads and Sings His *The Hobbit* and *The Fellowship of the Ring***, Caedmon, 197? (TC 1477) 12in 33rpm $8.98; (CDL 51477) cassette $8.98. CAE (U)

Made by the author on a home tape recorder in August, 1952, and now available to the public. On Side A Tolkien reads the riddle scene from *The Hobbit*. On Side B he reads selections of prose and poetry from *The Fellowship of the Ring*. *J. R. R. Tolkien Reads and Sings His The Lord of the Ring* (TC 1478/CDL 51478) is a companion volume.

Pamela Travers

R **Mary Poppins from A to Z**, Caedmon, 196? (CDL 51254) cassette only $8.98. CAE (P-I)

This is Robert Stephen's word-for-word reading of the book, with an introduction and conclusion read by the author, Pamela Travers.

Tomi Ungerer

F **Tomi Ungerer: Storyteller**, Weston Woods, 1982, 16mm color 21min $325, $25. WW (U)

Gene Deitch, animation director for the filmed adaptations of Ungerer's books, interviews the popular but controversial artist. Scenes from the animated versions of the three children's books, *The Three Robbers*, *The Beast of Monsieur Racine*, and *Moon Man*, are shown, but the appeal of the film is to an older audience.

Laura Ingalls Wilder

FS **Laura Ingalls Wilder**, Random House/Miller-Brody, 1980 (394-78456-1) 122fr color 17min with cassette $31.98. RH/M-B (P-U)

The filmstrip traces the life of Laura Ingalls Wilder, just as she tells it in the Little House books and with explanatory narration. Her story is made visual by maps showing the Ingalls family's travels; historic, regional and family photos; photos of Laura's homes as they are restored today; and artists' interpretations of her life from the illustrations of her books.

E. B. White

R **Charlotte's Web**, Pathways of Sound, 1970 (POS 1043) 8s 12in

33rpm 25min each side $42.50; also available on 10 cassettes $79.50. POS (P-I)

In the accents of a born storyteller, E. B. White reads aloud his beloved classic.

Laurence Yep

FS **Laurence Yep**, Random House/ Miller-Brody, 1981 (394-78375-1) 86fr color 12min with cassette $31.98. RH/M-B (I)

The filmstrip utilizes period prints and archival photos of San Francisco's Chinatown plus aged family snapshots to introduce Laurence Yep. The narrator gives biographical facts which trace the themes of Yep's novels to his childhood experiences, and the author adds some of his own personal reminiscences.

DIRECTORY OF DISTRIBUTORS

ABC	ABC Media, 1330 Avenue of the Americas, New York, New York 10019
ACI	ACI Productions, 35 West 45th Street, New York, New York 10036
ANG	Angel Records, Division of Capitol Records, Inc., 1370 Avenue of the Americas, New York, New York 10019
ARI	Arista Records, Arista Corporation, P.O. Box 6146, Concorde, California 94524
BA	Barr Films, P.O. Box 5667, Pasadena, California 91107
BFA	BFA Educational Media (a division of Columbia Broadcasting System), 2211 Michigan Avenue, Santa Monica, California 90404
BFI	Brandon Films, Inc., 34 MacQuesten Parkway South, Mt. Vernon, New York 10550
BOS	Bosustow Productions, 1649 Eleventh Street, Santa Monica, California 90404
BUD	Billy Budd Films, 235 East 57th Street, New York, New York 10022
CAE	Caedmon Records, 505 Eighth Avenue, New York, New York 10018
CAR	Carousel Films, Inc., 1501 Broadway, New York, New York 10018
CBC	Children's Book Council, Inc., 67 Irving Place, New York, New York 10003
CCM	Macmillan Films, Inc. (CCM Films), 35 MacQuesten Parkway South, Mt. Vernon, New York 10550
CHU	Churchill Films, 662 North Robertson Boulevard, Los Angeles, California 90069

CL Clearvue, Inc., 6666 N. Oliphant Avenue, Chicago, Illinois 60631
CMS CMS Records, Inc., 12 Warren Street, New York, New York 10007
CONT Contemporary Films, McGraw-Hill, Inc., 1221 Avenue of the Americas, New York, New York 10036
COR Coronet Instructional Media, 65 East South Water Street, Chicago, Illinois 60601
CV Cinema Ventures, 1569 Spruce Street, Berkeley, California 94709
DISN Walt Disney Educational Media Company, 800 Sonora Avenue, Glendale, California 91201
EB Encyclopaedia Britannica Educational Corporation, 425 North Michigan Avenue, Chicago, Illinois 60611
EEM Educational Enrichment Materials, A Company of the New York Times, Catalog Department BL, Bedford Hills, New York 10507
ERS Education Reading Services, Audio Visual Division, 320 Route #17, Mahwah, New Jersey 07430
FI Films, Inc., Division of Public Media, Inc., 1144 Wilmette Avenue, Wilmette, Illinois 60091
FL Folk Legacy Records, Inc., Sharon, Connecticut 06069
FSR Folkways/Scholastic Records, 906 Sylvan Avenue, Englewood Cliffs, New Jersey 07632
GA Guidance Associates, Pleasantville, New York 10570
HRW Holt, Rinehart & Winston, Inc., 383 Madison Avenue, New York, New York 10017
IER Imperial Educational Resources, Inc., 19 Marble Avenue, Pleasantville, New York 10570
IFB International Film Bureau, Inc., 332 South Michigan Avenue, Chicago, Illinois 60604
LCA Learning Corporation of America, 1350 Avenue of the Americas, New York, New York 10019
LEM Landmark Educational Media, Inc., 1600 Broadway, New York, New York 10019
LL Listening Library, One Park Avenue, Old Greenwich, Connecticut 06870
LOM Live Oak Media, Box 116, Somers, New York 10589
LON London/Polygram Classics, Inc., 137 West 55th Street, New York, New York 10019
LUC Lucerne Films, Inc., 37 Ground Pike Road, Morris Plains, New Jersey 07950
MAC Macmillan Library Services, 866 Third Avenue, New York, New York 10022
MED Media Basics, Larchmont Plaza, Larchmont, New York 10538

MH	McGraw Hill, Inc., 1221 Avenue of the Americas, New York, New York 10020
NFBC	National Film Board of Canada, 1251 Avenue of the Americas, 16th Floor, New York, New York 10020
ORL	Orlando Public Library, 10 North Rosalind, Orlando, Florida 32801
PER	Perspective Films and Video, 65 East South Water Street, Chicago, Illinois 60681
PFD	Pictura Films Distribution Corporation, Suite 4B, 48 East 13th Street, New York, New York 10003
PHX	Phoenix Films and Video, Inc., 468 Park Avenue South, New York, New York 10016
PP	Pied Piper Productions Instructional Media, P.O. Box 320, Verdugo City, California 91046
POS	Pathways of Sound, Inc., 102 Mt. Auburn Street, Cambridge, Massachusetts 02138
PYR	Pyramid Films, Box 1048, Santa Monica, California 90406
RCA	RCA Records-Educational Department, P.O. Box RCA 1000, Indianapolis, Indiana 46291
REMB	Rembrandt Films, 59 East 54th Street, New York, New York 10022
RH/M-B	Random House/Miller Brody, 201 East 50th Street, New York, New York 10022
SA	Spoken Arts, Inc., 310 North Avenue, New Rochelle, New York 10801
STE	Sterling Educational Films, Division of the Walter Reade Organization, Inc., 241 East 34th Street, New York, New York 10016
SVE	Society for Visual Education, Inc., 1345 Diversey Parkway, Chicago, Illinois 60614
TD	Tom Davenport Films, Pearlstone, Delaplane, Virginia 22025
TEX	Texture Films, Inc., 1600 Broadway, New York, New York 10019
TLM	Time-Life Multimedia, 1271 Avenue of the Americas, New York, New York 10020
TRF	Teaching Resources Films, 2 Kisco Plaza, Mount Kisco, New York 10549
UEVA	Universal Education and Visual Arts, 445 Park Avenue, New York, New York 10022
WB	Warner Brothers, Inc., Non-Theatrical Division, 4000 Warner Boulevard, Burbank, California 91522
WDS	William D. Stoneback Film Production, 6 Cobble Hill Road, Westport, Connecticut 06880
WLS	Westchester Library System, 280 Central Avenue, Hartsdale, New York 10530
WW	Weston Woods, Weston, Connecticut 06880

INDEX TO AUTHORS

The author, film, filmstrip, and record indexes were prepared by Kristina Masiulis.

Includes authors, editors, compilers, translators, and illustrators when the last are responsible for editing or selecting the material illustrated. The number given is the item number, not the page number.

INDEX TO FILM TITLES

INDEX TO FILMSTRIP TITLES

INDEX TO RECORD TITLES

INDEX TO SUBJECTS

Caldecott Medal Books

Christmas

Dance see **Music and Dance**

Ethnic Groups

Fables, Fairy Tales, and Folklore

Fantasy

Foreign Lands (see also **Fables, Fairy Tales, and Folklore**)

Africa

Australia

China

England

Music and Dance (see also **Poetry and Song**)

Mystery and Horror

Mythology see **Religion and Mythology**

Nature (see also **Animals**)

Newbery Medal Books

Picture Books

Concepts

Alligators All Around, 11, FS
Bruno Munari's ABC, 73, FS
Changes, Changes, 85, F
Charlie Needs a Cloak, 87, FS, R
Chicken Soup with Rice, 89, FS, R
Curious George Learns the Alphabet, 114, FS, R
Freight Train, 157, FS
Ida Fanfanny and the Four Seasons, 223, F
Little Blue and Little Yellow, 255, F
Mothers Can Do Anything, 327, FS
Nutshell Library, 351, F
One Was Johnny, 363, S
Truck, 521, FS
Where Does the Butterfly Go When It Rains?, 541, FS

Mood

A Father like That, 142, FS
Gilberto and the Wind, 171, F, FS, R
The Giving Tree, 174, F, FS
The Happy Day, 192, FS, R
The Happy Owls, 193, F, FS, R
The Hating Book, 200, FS
A Hole Is to Dig, 211, FS
Houses from the Sea, 216, FS
Johnny Crow's Garden, 236, FS
Just Me, 243, FS
The Lace Snail, 247, FS
The Little Island, 259, FS
My Grandson Lew, 332, F
The Ox-Cart Man, 369, FS
Pierre, 389, FS, R
Play with Me, 396, FS, R
The Silver Pony, 444, FS
A Special Trade, 457, FS
Time of Wonder, 512, F, FS
A Tree Is Nice, 518, FS
The Two of Them, 527, FS, R
White Snow, Bright Snow, 545, FS
Wynken, Blynken and Nod, 561, F, R

Participation

All in the Morning Early, 10, F
Brian Wildsmith's Circus, 68, FS, R
Brian Wildsmith's Mother Goose, 324, F
Bruno Munari's Zoo, 74, FS
Complete Version of Ye Three Blind Mice, 104, FS, R
Fox Went Out on a Chilly Night, 154, F, FS, R
Hey Diddle Diddle Picture Book, 208, FS, R
Hush Little Baby, 221, F, FS
I Know an Old Lady, 222, F, FS
London Bridge Is Falling Down, 271, FS
May I Bring a Friend? 301, FS
Mother Goose Treasury, 325, FS
Old Mother Hubbard and Her Dog, 355, F, FS (2)
The Old Woman and Her Pig, 356, F, FS
Over in the Meadow, 367, F, FS
She'll Be Comin' 'Round the Mountain, 440, FS, R
The Twelve Days of Christmas, 523, FS

Plot

Alexander and the Wind-Up Mouse, 7, FS, R (2)
The Amazing Bone, 13, FS, R
Amelia Bedelia, 14, FS
Anatole and the Piano, 18, F
And I Mean it, Stanley, 19, R
And to Think That I Saw It on Mulberry Street, 21, R
Androcles and the Lion, 22, FS
Andy and the Lion, 23, F, FS, R
Angus and the Cat, 24, FS, R
Angus and the Ducks, 25, FS, R
Annie and the Old One, 27, FS, R
Apt. 3, 29, FS
As I Was Crossing Boston Common, 33, FS
Awful Mess, 35, FS
Babar the King, 36, FS, R
Bartholomew and the Oobleck, 37, FS, R
Bear Hunt, 38, FS
The Bear's Bicycle, 39, FS
The Beast of Monsiur Racine, 40, F, FS, R
Benjamin and Tulip, 47, FS
Ben's Trumpet, 48, FS
The Berenstain Bears and the Spooky Old Tree, 49, FS, R
The Big Snow, 51, FS, R
The Biggest Bear, 42, FS, R

Religion and Mythology

Song see **Poetry and Song**

United States–Family Life